THE STRUGGLE FOR THE CONSTITUTION
1603–1689

BLANDFORD HISTORY SERIES

[General Editor—R. W. Harris]

THE HISTORY OF ENGLAND

REFORMATION AND RESURGENCE · 1485–1603 England in the Sixteenth Century	G. W. O. Woodward
THE STRUGGLE FOR THE CONSTITUTION · 1603–1689 England in the Seventeenth Century	G. E. Aylmer
ENGLAND IN THE EIGHTEENTH CENTURY · 1689–1793 A Balanced Constitution and New Horizons	R. W. Harris
REACTION AND REFORM · 1793–1868 England in the Early Nineteenth Century	John W. Derry
DEMOCRACY AND WORLD CONFLICT · 1868–1970 A History of Modern Britain	T. L. Jarman

THE HISTORY OF EUROPE

RENAISSANCE, REFORMATION AND THE OUTER WORLD 1450–1660	M. L. Bush
ABSOLUTISM AND ENLIGHTENMENT · 1660–1789	R. W. Harris
THE AGE OF TRANSFORMATION · 1789–1871	R. F. Leslie
THE END OF EUROPEAN PRIMACY · 1871–1945	J. R. Western
RUIN AND RESURGENCE · 1939–1965	R. C. Mowat

PROBLEMS OF HISTORY

THE DISSOLUTION OF THE MONASTERIES	G. W. O. Woodward
THE EXPANSION OF EUROPE IN THE EIGHTEENTH CENTURY	Glyndwr Williams
FRANCE AND THE DREYFUS AFFAIR	Douglas Johnson
COLONIES INTO COMMONWEALTH	W. D. McIntyre
PAPISTS AND PURITANS UNDER ELIZABETH I	Patrick McGrath
THE REIGN OF HENRY VII	R. L. Storey

HISTORY AND LITERATURE

REASON AND NATURE IN EIGHTEENTH-CENTURY THOUGHT · 1714–1780	R. W. Harris
ROMANTICISM AND THE SOCIAL ORDER · 1780–1830	R. W. Harris
THE TRIUMPH OF ENGLISH · 1350–1400	B. Cottle
DOCUMENTARY AND IMAGINATIVE LITERATURE 1880–1920	J. A. V. Chapple
THE CHORUS OF HISTORY · 1485–1558	A. M. Kinghorn
SHAKESPEARE'S EDEN · 1558–1629	B. Joseph

1603–1689

THE STRUGGLE
FOR THE CONSTITUTION

England in the Seventeenth Century

G. E. AYLMER

M.A., D.Phil.(Oxon.)
Professor of History, University of York

LONDON

BLANDFORD PRESS

First published in 1963
Revised edition 1965
Third edition 1968
Reprinted 1971

© 1963, 1965 Blandford Press Ltd
167 High Holborn London WC1V 6PH

ISBN 0 7137 03091 (Trade edition)
ISBN 0 7137 03083 (School edition)

Printed in Great Britain by Richard Clay (The Chaucer Press), Ltd.,
Bungay, Suffolk

CONTENTS

v

LIST OF ILLUSTRATIONS

TABLES

MAPS

ACKNOWLEDGEMENTS

Photograph number 11 has been reproduced by gracious permission of Her Majesty the Queen.

The remaining photographs have been reproduced by permission of the following:

1 National Buildings Record
2 and 4 Manchester City Art Gallery
3 Sir William Worsley, Bt
5 The Trustees of the National Portrait Gallery
6, 9, 10, 12, 14, 15, 19, 20 and 21 The Trustees of the British Museum
7 and 8 Country Life
13 The Duke of Buccleuch
16 The Trustees of the London Museum
17 The Trustees of the National Maritime Museum
18 The Syndics of the Fitzwilliam Museum, Cambridge

Introduction

Importance of the Period

THE first question to ask about any period of history is what matters most in it and why. The span of English history that is covered in this book, the eighty-six years from the accession of King James I to that of William III and Mary II, both of whom were his great-grandchildren, can simply be thought of as the part that follows the story of England under the Tudors, and comes before that of England in the eighteenth century. This is a perfectly proper and sensible way of looking at any period of history, but it does not follow that all centuries or epochs are equally important. English seventeenth-century history has a special claim to be studied more thoroughly than most other periods.

What happened in England under the Stuarts was important not only for the people living at that time and for those who have lived in this country since then, but also for a great many other people living in other countries. For instance, if we consider the differences in the forms of government, in the relations between the state and its subjects, indeed in the whole political pattern, between the modern United States and Soviet Russia, between India on the one hand and China on the other, we shall find that these differences still owe something to those apparently remote events in England about three hundred years ago. This is certainly true if we study the spread of parliamentary government during the nineteenth century in Europe, and during the nineteenth and twentieth centuries in some of the countries of America, Asia, Africa and Australasia which were once the colonial possessions of European powers. Perhaps most striking of all, the American War of Independence which resulted in the birth of the United States, and the great French Revolution of 1789, which marks the rise of political democracy in continental Europe, followed the general pattern and example set by the English Revolution in the previous century.

This revolution was the outcome of the constitutional conflict. Before discussing that, we ought to decide what we mean by the word 'constitutional'. This is not something remote or theoretical. It concerns the system of government, the way the country is run, and above all—the most important question—who has the decisive power. In the more abstract language used by political theorists, this means asking where sovereignty resides, which really comes to much the same as asking, who has the final say. In seventeenth-century England, this entails a study of the victory of parliamentary government (and thus of the classes represented in Parliament) over absolute monarchy—the unfettered rule of a royal despot. It is very important to understand that in the seventeenth century and for quite a long time afterwards, indeed until the last hundred years or so, the establishment of parliamentary government did not mean the victory of democracy, in the sense of a government elected by and answerable to the majority of the population. Full democracy was only achieved much later, and most of those who won these early victories for parliamentary government were in fact strongly opposed to it. None the less, the system of parliamentary government did eventually lead, through the various Reform Acts of the nineteenth and early twentieth centuries, to the modern system of political democracy under which Britain is governed today.

These changes in seventeenth-century England were all the more significant by contrast with the rest of Europe. At that time most of the countries on the Continent, with the exception of the Netherlands and one or two German states, were moving towards a more centralised, autocratic system and increased royal power; representative assemblies and other parliamentary institutions were in decline. This is related to a question which foreigners quite often ask, and people in this country sometimes ask too. That is, why has England not had a revolution in modern times? We must be almost the only country in the world that has not. Is this because of some peculiarity in the British character; is it because of our

social system, or our political system, or because we are better—
or duller—than other people, or why? Part of the answer to this
is that we did have a revolution; we had ours in the seventeenth
century.

This way of looking at the subject means that a good deal of
this book is going to be about the development, outcome and
significance of the constitutional conflict. On the other hand, we
cannot understand this conflict unless we relate it to other aspects
of life: that is, to social and economic history—the way people
lived, and how they earned their livings, as well as to politics (outside strictly constitutional history) and the development of the law
and the main branches of government. There is also another vitally
important aspect of the history of any civilised community: what
people believed and thought, that is religious, and intellectual or
cultural history. All these different topics are interesting in their
own right, but in order to concentrate on the story of the constitutional struggle in this book we shall consider them as they relate
to that central subject.

Facts and Explanations

One way to understand any period of history is to see how
different historians have written about it. It is not so much that
the facts are in dispute, though they quite often are. But if we study
history at all closely, it soon appears that what is meant by a fact
is itself frequently disputed, and things which look like facts turn
out to be subjects for argument. If we simply say that James I
succeeded Elizabeth I in 1603, or that Charles I lost the Civil War,
almost everybody would agree that these are both factual statements, and that both are correct. On the other hand, suppose we
extend our notion of facts, to such obviously important questions
about the seventeenth century as to ask, 'How many Members of
Parliament formed a really determined opposition to the early
Stuart kings, what percentage of the total number were they?' or
'In what proportions were the landed gentry divided between the
two sides in the Civil War?' If we put that kind of question to
people who have studied the subject for many years, we shall be
given some widely differing answers. This is even more marked if

we consider what different historians offer in the way of 'interpretations' of history. In these they seek to explain why certain things happened, such as why there was a conflict between Crown and Parliament, and why Parliament was victorious. This means that once we get beyond the barest outline of facts, the history of almost any period is a subject of argument. Historians do not all agree; and if a historian sticks to 'facts' and nothing else, he writes very little and what he does write is extremely dull. Historians must interpret their facts, and in doing so they inevitably come to disagree with each other. But that does not mean that all historians are on a level, just squabbling away. Some of them interpret their facts more purposefully and convincingly for the rest of us than others do. Only we have to remember that even the greatest historians, even people who have spent a whole lifetime studying the period that this book is concerned with, have not always agreed in what they thought about it and what their interpretations were. History is not a subject where we can just find a certain body of knowledge and learn it, and then that is the answer. We have to know a certain amount of facts or else the story does not make sense; but once we get beyond this, it is a matter of judgment and interpretation, and we should not expect everybody to agree with everybody else.

Different Interpretations

Let us consider a few of the wide variety of interpretations that can be found among the most important historians who have written about this period. To take first of all the greatest contemporary historian, who lived through the events he was writing about—Edward Hyde, Earl of Clarendon. Hyde was on the King's side in the Civil War, he was basically a Royalist. On the other hand he believed in constitutional, not absolute monarchy. His *History* has a very definite interpretation of what happened and why, and you have to be careful if you read Clarendon, even if you only read extracts (some of the character sketches and other descriptions have been published in the Oxford World's Classics series), to watch his prejudices, especially when he is talking about the people who were on the opposite side to him in the Civil War—

the Parliamentarians. Still, because of his determination to interpret his story and not just to recount facts, for all his faults Hyde has many of the qualities of a great historian. Through most of the nineteenth century, what have come to be known as the 'Whig', that is basically pro-parliamentarian historians dominated the way in which English seventeenth-century history was written and taught. T. B. Macaulay is the most famous of these; several of his *Essays* (for instance the one on Hampden) and his *History of England* deal with the seventeenth century. Down to the later nineteenth century, that way of looking at seventeenth-century England was dominant.

About that time, history itself was in the process of becoming a different kind of subject. It ceased to be merely a branch of literature, as it had been until that date, and it became in addition what it is now—a social science. The rise of 'scientific' history has itself been a major influence on the mental outlook of the modern world, and it can be dated to the middle and later part of the nineteenth century. It is important to understand what was involved in this change. In several different countries, many more historical records became available; the archives were opened, and at the same time historians developed better methods for testing the value of different kinds of evidence. In the study of seventeenth-century England, the rise of scientific history can largely be spelt out in the name of one man, S. R. Gardiner. He edited a very large number of original texts—letters and memoirs, etc. of the period—and wrote a full-scale *History of England* which put the whole subject on a new basis. He covered the years from 1603 to 1656; and his work was continued on the same scale by two other historians (C. H. Firth and G. Davies) down to 1660. Gardiner follows a chronological narrative method, but every now and then he digresses to discuss particular aspects of history. Perhaps the most impressive thing about him is the immense amount of material of which he is the master, and for this reason he has been called 'a historian's historian'. But although Gardiner put our knowledge of the seventeenth century on an altogether sounder footing, his own political, and even more his religious sympathies caused him to have very strong preferences in the conflict that he was writing about. He was himself a minister of a small Nonconformist church, and sacrificed his prospects of academic promotion in nineteenth-century England on this account. Gardiner was basically pro-parliamentarian in outlook, and even more strongly pro-Puritan. This does not mean that he was partial, still less dishonest, in his handling of evidence. But he was partisan and tended to make assumptions about the history of the period some of which are rather misleading, if we think of it either as contemporaries found it at the time or in the way we should see it now.

Recent Influences

The most important changes since Gardiner have been the development of more new methods and approaches to history, in this century. These stem from three main sources. The first is from the study of economics and economic history. This is particularly associated with the founder of modern communism, Karl Marx, who was a great economic historian quite apart from the political movement that has stemmed from him. Marx's contribution to our understanding of history is to insist that in studying any period we must first look for the material, the economic basis of life in that period. He insisted that it is only possible to understand the political, constitutional, religious, cultural and suchlike developments by first looking at society's economic foundations. This means studying how people lived, what their position was in relation to the means of production, and examining the conflicts between different classes within that society. Even if, like most people in this country and the rest of the non-Communist world, we reject Marx's doctrines about class war and his prophecies about the future course of history, his emphasis on the role of economic factors is still important. It has been accepted in some degree by almost all historians, including the large majority who reject Marx's political teachings. This does not mean that all those who have been influenced by Marx and who think that economic factors are important, have all arrived at the same interpretation of the way in which they were, still less in applying such an interpretation to a particular historical situation, like that in seventeenth-century England. But there is fairly general agreement that these things mattered much more than would be supposed from reading earlier historians including even Gardiner. A great deal of work has been done on seventeenth-century economic history, especially in the last thirty years or so. However most of it is only to be found in rather specialised books and articles; there is no good full-scale general history written since Gardiner's which puts these results together in a way that is reliable, readable and not too complicated, for the person who is not going on to specialise in studying this period. The best starting point here is probably G. N. Clark's *The Wealth of England, 1496–1760* (Home University Library series). The volume by C. Wilson, on the seventeenth century, in Longman's *Economic and Social History of England*, is at present the most useful at a slightly more advanced level.

The second influence which has altered the way in which we look at history is a greater interest in the institutions of government, in what has come to be called 'administrative history'. This influence owes a good deal to the rise of sociology (that is the study of man in society) as one of the social sciences and a related subject to history. Curiously enough the first large-scale application of this study of institutions, in order to understand the political history of a period better, was made not by somebody working on very recent history (that is the nearest to sociology) but by the early twentieth-century Manchester historian, T. F. Tout, in his work on medieval English history. This is another aspect which was hardly touched on by Gardiner.

The third new influence is a greater interest on the part of historians, as of other educated people, in the unconscious motives of human beings, as a help to understanding how and why they behave as they do. There is much less readiness than there was fifty years ago to accept people's beliefs and motives and their own statements of their intentions, at their face value. This is not because all or even most human beings are deliberately dishonest, but because we know—through the study of modern psychology—that people are very often unaware of their own feelings on many important subjects. It is the discovery of the unconscious mind, through the school of psychologists of whom Sigmund Freud was the greatest, that a whole new way of looking at man has developed in the last fifty years. This influence has not yet had so much effect on the writing of history; very few historians are qualified to make use of these psychological discoveries in their writings. Most historians have, however, been influenced indirectly. They do not pronounce so confidently about people's motives and intentions; they are inclined to pay more attention to emotions, collective impulses and the way people are carried along mentally without always knowing quite where they are going or why.

All these influences have led to a general questioning of human motives. This means a greater reluctance to accept what people said their reasons were for acting as they did, and a greater awareness of the need to look for other explanations of their behaviour. Some modern historians have thought that the real underlying forces in any particular historical situation were primarily economic, others primarily psychological, while some have thought that they arose from institutional pressures on individuals. These influences on the writing of history can be seen clearly in the period which follows the one that we are concerned with, in the great studies of eighteenth-century politics made by L. B. Namier, the historian who was born in what is now southern Poland but was formerly part of the Austrian Empire and who settled in England at the beginning of this century. But they are also present in writings by historians on the seventeenth century, notably in the recent debates about the nature and causes of the English Civil War. There is, of course, a danger in reading only the latest books and articles, and neglecting the older works. Whatever his limitations, for the years he covered Gardiner remains the standard authority.

Narrative and Analysis

There is one obvious difference between most books produced in the last thirty or forty years and earlier historical writings. For instance comparing Gardiner with some of the works written under these more recent influences, the modern ones spend much less time, and do not concentrate as much on telling the story. They tend to be studies of a particular aspect of a period, or to be what is called analytical rather than chronological in their arrangement. Even the most large-scale recent works on the period are not chronological histories in the old sense. For example, David Ogg's books, which cover the years 1660 to 1702, use a combination of narrative and analysis. Among historians of serious repute only C. V. Wedgwood, whose two volumes so far published, *The King's Peace* and *The King's War*, cover the years 1637–47, has gone back to strictly narrative treatment. In a sense she has gone back beyond Gardiner; Miss Wedgwood has made use of the work of historians who have been influenced by the ideas just mentioned, but she herself has deliberately tried to look at events from the viewpoint of contemporaries. There are pitfalls in all these approaches, and there is no single answer about the best way to write history. As long as people go on writing it at all, there will be some who mainly want to tell a story, for whom a narrative form is most suitable. There will be others who want to describe some particular aspect of the period, to look at it from a particular point of view, or to take a single branch of the subject and concentrate on that, for whom an arrangement by topics or an analytical treatment will be the right answer.

Considering how much has been written about seventeenth-century England in the last fifteen years or so, there is a surprising shortage of first-class general histories (on a smaller scale than those of Gardiner or Ogg). For instance there is nothing as good, in the way of a text-book, as G. R. Elton's *England under the Tudors*. The best general history is the volume in the Oxford History of England, G. N. Clark's *The Later Stuarts 1660–1714*, but it covers less than half the period we are concerned with here. In the same series there is also G. Davies, *The Early Stuarts 1603–60*. The recent book by Christopher Hill, *The Century of Revolution 1603–1714* (Nelson's *History of England*, volume 5) is much the most interesting interpretative study, but it is not a comprehensive general history. Perhaps the very fact of the many conflicting viewpoints, the many unsolved and disputed historical problems has made it more difficult for historians to produce good introductory works. In general, with the exception of Hill's *Century of Revolution* and

B

Clark's *Later Stuarts*, for further reading and certainly for specialist work in a senior form at school or for a college course, it is better to go straight to books on particular epochs or topics, or to biographies of individual statesmen and other important figures. This will be more rewarding than spending too long on general works, some of which are not very good and are less likely to satisfy an intelligent interest in the subject than slightly more specialised books. These may look more difficult but often are not, and they are generally more worthwhile.

Main Chronological Divisions

The chapters of this book are arranged on a broadly chronological plan. A much fuller comparative date-list will be found at the end, before the Index. The most important dates, indeed the absolute minimum to remember, are as follows:

1603—the accession of James I.

1629—the dissolution of the third Parliament of Charles I.

1640—the meeting of the Long Parliament.

1649—the execution of Charles I and establishment of the Republic.

1660—the restoration of Charles II.

1678–9—the Popish Plot-Exclusion Bill crisis.

1688–9—the 'Glorious Revolution'.

1 : Government and Society (1603–29)

The Succession (see Table 1)

THE most important fact about the succession of King James I on the death of Queen Elizabeth in the spring of 1603 is that it was peaceful. To appreciate this, we have only to look at the confusion which disputed successions had plunged this country into earlier, in the Middle Ages, or at the crisis provoked by Northumberland in 1553, as well as at similar situations in other countries. The history of the early seventeenth century in England was greatly influenced not only by James' peaceful succession, but also by the fact that he succeeded as a mature grown-up man and not as a child. The situation need only be compared with that in France in 1610 on the death of Henry IV, or in 1643 on the death of Louis XIII. The fact that James' succession went so smoothly is in itself a major tribute to the success of Tudor rule and—no less—of Tudor propaganda.

James VI of Scotland was the son of Mary Stuart, better known to history as Mary Queen of Scots, and her second husband and first cousin, Lord Darnley. So that James was descended on both his mother's and his father's side from the elder daughter of the founder of the house of Tudor, King Henry VII. He was first cousin once removed to Queen Elizabeth, and even on a purely hereditary argument he was certainly one of the strongest claimants to succeed her. On the other hand, James had never been publicly recognised by Elizabeth as the person who was to succeed, although she may have named him on her deathbed. But his succession had come to be tacitly accepted by the later 1590s. This can be seen from the correspondence which Elizabeth herself conducted with James, instructing him in the art of kingship, and from the contacts which leading members of Elizabeth's government in her last years were careful to build up with James, particularly from his correspondence with the Queen's chief minister Robert Cecil in the years 1601–3.

James owed a great deal to the fact that there were no serious rivals. There was his own cousin the Lady Arabella Stuart, who was also descended from the elder daughter of Henry VII. But Arabella neither had the personal strength and importance, nor the backing of a sufficiently powerful following—perhaps, too, men were tired of being ruled by women—and she is a slightly pathetic figure who suffered from her nearness to the throne but was politically unimportant. Another possible claimant was an English nobleman Lord Beauchamp, the eldest son of the house of Seymour who was a great-grandson of Henry VII's younger daughter and the Duke of Suffolk (a man who had taken a prominent part in his brother-in-law, Henry VIII's reign). The Beauchamp claim had to be taken seriously, because the succession to the throne had been fixed by Act of Parliament to go according to the will of King Henry VIII, and this had given the Suffolk priority over the Stuart line. As against this, Beauchamp's own legitimacy was doubtful; secondly, powerful and indeed terrifying a king as Henry VIII had been in his lifetime, his will was not felt any longer to be binding fifty years after his death; thirdly there were felt to be very strong arguments against a king succeeding from an English noble house. This feeling was itself a product of Tudor propaganda and the fear of going back to the bad old days of the fifteenth century—the Wars of the Roses and baronial anarchy. Finally, militating against either Arabella or Beauchamp, there was Elizabeth's known preference—powerful even on her deathbed, but expressed before that—first for a man and second for a king—both of which pointed to James. One other claimant should be mentioned, the candidate of the extreme Roman Catholic party in the country, that is mainly of the Jesuits, for by no means all the catholic laity favoured her—Isabella, Princess of Spain, daughter of the great King Philip II, whose country had been at war with England since the time of the Armada. Isabella could not be taken seriously as a claimant by most people in England. The fact of the Spanish war meant that she was the 'enemy' candidate who could only be imposed as a

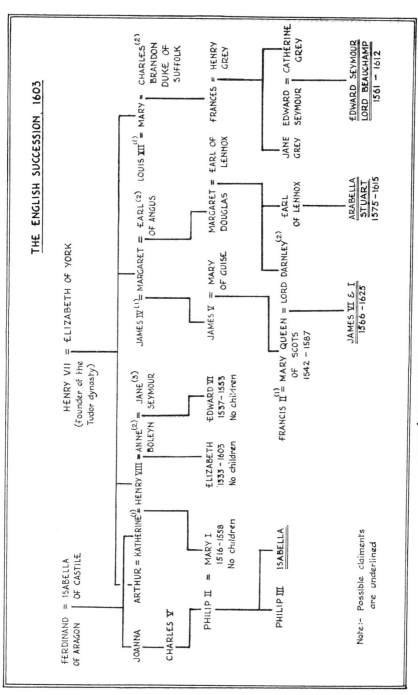

TABLE 1. THE ENGLISH SUCCESSION, 1603

result of Spanish military victory and the complete destruction of English protestantism. Next to the Bible, and indeed until the publication of the 'Authorised Version' perhaps even better known than the Bible itself, the book which was most widely found in English households at the end of the sixteenth and beginning of the seventeenth century was Foxe's *Book of Martyrs*. This did all that could be done in print to keep alive the memories of the burnings of protestants under Mary Tudor in the 1550s.

So for practical purposes there was no dispute about the succession. But in the early years of James' reign there were a number of 'plots' either real or alleged, and any of these if they had been successful would have brought the succession question to the fore. They might have either overthrown James or resulted in his death. As it was, the question was not seriously open.

The New King

Turning to James himself, as King of Scotland he had been successful by the standards of his time. James had been on the throne since he was thirteen months old, active in government and political leadership since the age of eleven, and in effective charge, running his own government and ruling Scotland, since he was about nineteen. So that at the age of nearly thirty-seven he was an 'old king', anyway an old hand at the business of kingship. As a result he had pretty set ideas about the practice as well as the theory of it. His theories—about the 'divine right' of kings—of which a great deal is made in some of the older books on this period, probably made less difference than some of James' practices, which had been successful in Scotland but were to prove less so when he came to try them out in England. Secondly, in Scotland James had had a good deal of trouble with various factions among the nobility, both protestant and Roman Catholic; he had got the better of them all. He had also had trouble with the Presbyterian church leaders; he had eventually defeated them too, and he had re-introduced a modified form of episcopacy, that is church government by bishops, though the Scottish church remained in other respects Calvinist in matters of doctrine and worship. It was these practical concrete victories that James had won, though he had

had to fight hard for them, which confirmed him in taking a very exalted view of the rights and duties of a king—the right of the monarch over all his subjects, over the church and over any other groups and institutions in his realm. Although James re-introduced episcopalian church government in Scotland and was an 'Erastian', that is believed in the supremacy of the state over the church, he remained to the end of his days a firm believer in the Calvinist dogma of 'predestination'. Throughout his reign, as under Elizabeth, it continued to be the official doctrine of the Anglican Church that everyone ever born into the world has been fore-ordained by God to salvation or damnation from the beginning of time, and that neither good conduct nor priestly ministrations can save the damned. As we shall see, there is an important contrast here with his son, Charles I.

The next fact to notice about James' Scottish background is that he came from a much poorer and economically less 'developed' country than England. The total royal revenue in Scotland is estimated to have been only one-fifth or one-sixth of the ordinary royal revenue in England (excluding parliamentary taxation). When James came down in 1603 he expected to find he was much richer than he had been before. And he brought with him a considerable number of 'hungry Scots', as they have come to be known. A good deal of the unpopularity of his government was due to the Scottish favourites whom he installed in England, rather than to the King personally, though naturally he was blamed for the antagonism aroused by these Scotsmen. The last important fact about James' experience in Scotland is that although he had ruled the country for many years, by most standards successfully, there were no institutions in Scotland with the power and the prestige corresponding either to the English parliament or to the English 'common law' and legal system.

James was better educated than most kings both before his time and since. Though this may not have helped him to get on with everybody, he was a scholar, if not an intellectual. He was sociable, though not towards ordinary people, and also an outdoor man and fond of sport. James had a deep and genuine love of peace. His worst fault was that he was an extremely bad judge of other people and of their suitability for different positions. It is wrong to say that James made no effort to adapt himself to English conditions, that he was completely set in his ways by the time he left Scotland and that this accounts for all his troubles here. He did make an attempt on some questions. And there were some points on which he showed himself to be more enlightened than his subjects, for example in his campaign during the early years of his reign for a complete legislative and administrative union of the two countries, not merely a union of the Crowns of England and Scotland. He fought a losing battle over this; for the time being, little beyond a personal union of the Crowns was achieved. There was only partial common citizenship, for those born after 1603 (the King won this much by a decision from the Judges in 1608), but more was blocked by vested interests and suspicions on both sides.

The System of Government

When we turn to the English political scene in 1603, the first point to emphasise is the very great degree of continuity, for example in the institutions of government. Much of what, in the previous book in this series, has been described as the system and structure of government under the Tudors, also holds good here.

The central government can be divided into five main branches. At the centre, responsible for policies being carried out and for the general efficiency of administration, the executive consisted of the King himself, the Privy Council and the two Secretaries of State. The Council and the Secretaries each had their own staff of clerks. In the days when almost all the official documents were hand-written (normally only Acts of Parliament and royal Proclamations were published in print), many junior officials and clerks spent most of their time copying these out. Different branches of the government used different styles of handwriting, and these styles had to be learnt by those who wanted to become writing clerks or officials. The King could be approached direct by his subjects through the Masters of Requests who presented petitions to him, but he normally referred these to his legal or financial advisers, and his orders were normally issued through one of the Secretaries of State. And—if he were making a grant—it would usually have to be confirmed by passing the three 'seals', that is first being written out and having the Signet Seal (in the charge of the Secretary of State) attached to it, next re-written and authenticated by the Privy Seal, and finally written out a third time and passing the Great Seal. Usually the last two stages were formalities, though they made it more expensive to obtain a grant or other formal document from the King, since all the officials involved at each stage had to be paid fees by the person or institution hoping to receive the grant.

The royal Household no longer played the crucial part in royal government which it had done in the Middle Ages. Then the 'Wardrobe' and the 'Chamber', its two main branches, had often acted as royal treasuries and supply departments, especially during the wars with France and Scotland. By 1603, although there was still no distinction between the King's personal income and the public revenue of the Crown, the Household departments were no longer acting in this way. They were responsible for little outside the royal Court itself. But the Court still had some political importance and, what is more, its upkeep was very costly in relation to the Crown's total income and expenditure.

The financial departments were also law courts. Much the most important was the Exchequer, which was responsible for over three-quarters of the royal revenues. Still independent of it were the Court of Wards, in charge of the King's main revenues as a feudal overlord, and the Duchy of Lancaster, responsible for his estates as Duke of Lancaster (a title which had been in the hands of the Crown since the beginning of the Lancastrian dynasty in 1399). Although there was no regular system of public credit and no official 'paper money', a large proportion of the revenues did not in fact pass through any of these departments in cash but only in an accounting sense, and were credited to the spending departments of government or to those who were owed money by the King.

The law courts formed a larger part of the government than in more recent times. They were also more closely or at any rate more openly involved with politics. The most important were the three 'common law' courts (King's Bench, Common Pleas and

Exchequer), Chancery, and the Star Chamber. As we shall see, some of the differences and rivalries between the various courts were politically important. The Privy Council itself also exercised powers of a judicial kind, although it was not a regularly constituted part of the legal system, not what contemporaries called 'a court of record'. The two regional councils, in Wales and the north, combined administrative with legal duties. Here too, as in the finance departments, the officials and under-clerks were largely dependent for their living on fees and gratuities (that is extra, informal 'tips') from members of the public (or from officials of other government departments) who, as litigants, suitors, tax-collectors, treasurers and so on, were making use of their services. This meant that all through the government the King's servants had an interest in ensuring that as much business as possible went through their own respective departments. The more business, the more fees, gratuities and other payments; the more fees, etc. the larger the officials' incomes would be. In some cases, this meant deliberately encouraging law suits or competing for legal business; in others, keeping up the level of royal spending or trying to influence the ways the royal revenues were paid in, or what they were spent on.

Finally there were some departments neither belonging to the household nor organised as courts of law. The Mint was responsible for the coinage of money, the Ordnance Office for weapons and munitions of war. The Navy was the largest and easily the most important of these departments, though the scale of its activities declined when the long war with Spain was ended by a compromise peace in 1604.

By modern standards English government throughout the seventeenth century was ramshackle, inefficient, wasteful and corrupt. Compared with other European countries at the time, or with governments in other civilisations at a similar stage of development, however, it was not too bad. Indeed after over a century of Tudor rule, James inherited one of the best governed (or by our standards, least badly governed) states in Europe. But the quality of a government depended then even more than it does today on the intelligence, character and standards of those at the top. This meant a deterioration under James, followed by some improvement under Charles I's Personal Rule, something like a breakdown during the Civil Wars, then a more efficient phase under the Republic in the middle of the century, followed by a partial relapse again under Charles II. Even so, the standards of efficiency were probably rather higher in 1688 than in 1603 and of honesty at least no lower. As we shall see, the way the government worked and the kind of men who served in it have a considerable bearing on our main subject—the struggle for power between Crown and Parliament.

The use of councils as both legal and executive bodies had been the dominant feature of Elizabethan government, from the Queen and the Privy Council at the centre downwards and outwards. One difference here is that James, unlike Elizabeth, sometimes sat in Council; this was perhaps a mistake of tactics—it may reflect James' sense of insecurity compared with his predecessor. Another is that, in trying to please his friends and win more support, he just about doubled the size of the Council. As a result there was a tendency for more divisions to emerge within it, also for an inner ring to take shape; with 25–30 or more members it became too large a body to conduct business effectively.

Turning to another aspect of the central government, the church continued to be dominated by a very close partnership between the royal government and the episcopal hierarchy. The principal instruments of this were the Courts of High Commission for the two ecclesiastical provinces of Canterbury and York, of which Privy Councillors as well as the archbishops and bishops and ecclesiastical lawyers and officials were members. The church was headed in James' early years by the right-hand man of Elizabeth's last Archbishop, Whitgift, who himself died the year after the Queen. His successor, Richard Bancroft, had been Whitgift's police chief in the anti-Puritan campaign of Elizabeth's latter years.

Other institutions of central government where the same continuity with Tudor rule can be seen are the Court of Star Chamber, and the two regional councils in Wales and the north, where there is very little change, except in details. The same is true in the government of Ireland, under a Lord Deputy (the King's viceroy) and a Council, with one or two subordinate regional councils in the out-lying provinces. The only important change here is that the un-successful war of liberation which the Irish had been waging since the later 1590s against English over-rule, was brought to a close with a decisive English victory in 1603, within the last few days of Queen Elizabeth's reign. This meant that Ireland cost the English government a great deal less than it had been doing, because the drain of heavy military expenditure was brought to an end. But victory brought its own problems; they were political rather than military. It soon became clear that the religious and the social cleavages in Ireland were deeper than ever.

Local Government

In order to understand how England was governed in the early seventeenth century, we must not limit ourselves to considering how things worked at the centre. We must look at local govern-ment and institutions. Here the first unit to take is the county. For military purposes the key officer in the county was the Lord Lieutenant; one man could be Lord Lieutenant for more than one county—in 1603 about half these posts were held by Privy Council-lors. They had mainly military duties; Lords Lieutenant were in charge of the militia, and they also exercised a political influence, for instance over parliamentary elections. But if the Lord Lieu-tenant was a Councillor or held an important office at Court, he was likely to be an absentee, not resident in his county, and the main job of running its military organisation then devolved on his subordinates—the Deputy Lieutenants, who were chosen by the Lords Lieutenant but with a royal veto. They were usually peers of the second rank or greater gentry. The Deputy Lieutenants and a number of other gentry in each county were responsible for the administration of justice in their capacity as Justices of the Peace.

The commission of the peace was the backbone of local govern-ment in Tudor and Stuart England. Sometimes there were separate commissions for the towns in a county, but often they included several of the same men. The foremost J.P. in each county held an office called keeper of the rolls (*custos rotulorum*); this and being a member of the 'quorum', one of whom had to be present at any sessional meeting, carried additional prestige. But these offices were all unpaid; they were Crown appointments but part-time and 'amateur'. In the early Middle Ages the Sheriff had been the leading officer of each county. Now his duties were largely ceremonial. He still had charge of some, very small ancient revenues of the Crown; his most important duties were the overseeing of parliamentary elections and the selection of jurymen. Often he too had a deputy who did most of the work for him.

An important function of local government was the collection of taxes. This was normally done by special commissions, but these commissions would usually include the men who were Sheriffs, J.P.s, and the officers of any towns in the county. For taxation purposes the county was split up into units called divisions, with a special sub-commission in charge of administering tax collection in each of them. Otherwise, the next unit of local government was the hundred, the sub-division of the county; each hundred was overseen for judicial purposes by a group of J.P.s, and it had as its executive officer below them a High Constable. Each parish (the smallest unit of local government, into which the hundreds were divided) had a Petty Constable. The sort who feature in Shakespeare's plays as comic characters—Dogberry and Verges—are, one imagines, Petty rather than High Constables.

Juries were another important part of local government as well as of the legal system. The very large number of people (men that is) who had some share in local government can be estimated from those who were eligible to be constables, churchwardens, overseers of the poor in their parishes, and from those liable for jury service. Even so of course, a great many, including probably over half the adult males in the country, roughly speaking the poorer half, were not eligible for these posts and had no part in local government at all.

The government of the corporate towns, or 'boroughs', was in theory distinct from all this. The boroughs were normally run by a mayor and a body of aldermen—that is a 'corporation'. Sometimes they were just ruled by a bailiff; sometimes the mayor and aldermen had to share power with a common council consisting of all the freemen of the borough or their representatives. But in practice many of the smaller boroughs, which by our standards were only villages, were dominated by one or more of the nearby great landowners, as was the case in the countryside. Only the City of London, which was a law unto itself, and a few of the other larger towns were not in fact dependent on neighbouring landowners in this way. Still, for taxation, police, judicial, and other aspects of local government London and the boroughs were outside the hierarchy of county, division, hundred and parish.

The strength and efficiency of royal government also depended on various officials who acted as 'go-betweens'. Their job was to carry messages, orders, reports and so on between the central government and these local officials. The officers of the royal postal service, the Sergeants-at-Arms, and the Messengers, who also had the job of making arrests and bringing people up for examination before the Council in London, were the most important of these. They were few in number, especially when we remember the lack of any professional police force or any regular peacetime standing army, apart from the King's two bodies of household guards (the Yeomen of the Guard and the smaller but socially more exclusive corps, the Gentlemen Pensioners). They can be distinguished from the local officers we have been talking about in that they were paid, and their appointment was on a different basis.

Compared with France there were very few permanent, paid officials in the country, that is away from the centre of government. There were some, mainly officers connected with the collection of various revenues. We shall discuss the different revenues of the Crown a little later, but the customs staffs in the various seaport towns and certain other revenue officers are the main exception to the fact that the English government had no paid local officials. In any case these men usually came from the locality where they worked, and were not sent down there from London or moved about the country, in the way that modern civil servants (inland revenue officials, etc.) are; or that some local officials of the royal government were in seventeenth-century France.

Clientage

The structure of central and local government in early seventeenth-century England is to be seen against the background of personal and social relationships which had grown up in the sixteenth but persisted into the early seventeenth century. This relationship is discussed most fully by J. E. Neale in his essay, 'The Elizabethan Political Scene' (reprinted in his *Essays in Elizabethan History*) and his book *The Elizabethan House of Commons*. He gives it the name of 'clientage'. This system went right through society; lesser men attached themselves to greater men, becoming their clients. Looked at from the point of view of the greater men, the system can be called 'patronage'. The king at the very top of the pyramid is the greatest patron of all. People who are near to the king—councillors, favourites, ministers, courtiers, bishops and so on—enjoy power and wealth and prestige by being near to him; they in turn dispense favours and patronage to other people, that is to say to their friends, relatives and clients. The Privy Councillors, the judges, and the top officials in the government patronise their clients, just as they themselves in one sense can be thought of as the king's clients as well as his servants. One feature of the administrative system in the sixteenth and seventeenth centuries is that many people who begin as the private employees of councillors and favourites transfer to royal service, making a diagonal switch and spiralling up the social and administrative ladders.

It is difficult to be certain just how widespread this relationship was. All servants and most employees were dependent on somebody else, and many wage-earners lived in the household as a member of the 'family' of their employer. The family was then far more the basic economic as well as social unit, although it was possible to be somebody's client without necessarily working for them. Clientage derived from ancient medieval traditions of employment, apprenticeship and guild regulations, and was also related to the more recent semi-military connections between greater and lesser men, which are now generally regarded as having been rather discreditable—that is to say the system of 'retaining'. Members of the nobility keeping armed and uniformed men in their service was one of the evils that the Tudors had helped to eradicate. Actually it had faded away as much as it had been stamped out. By the accession of James I the clients of a nobleman were not like retainers a hundred years or so earlier. They did not turn out in uniform with arms on his behalf, though they did still sometimes take part in local brawls and quarrels, and might interfere in parliamentary elections where their lord or patron was an interested party. Generally speaking, retaining and the whole pattern of social relations of which it was a symptom, had been transformed into a civilianised and perhaps rather more civilised form, under the system of clientage. A very good example of this is to be seen in *King Lear*; Gloucester's bastard son, Edmund, becomes the client of Kent and he later switches his allegiance to Cornwall. Edmund, with the disadvantage of his birth to overcome, is deliberately portrayed by Shakespeare as a caricature of the rootless, ruthless Machiavellian climber who uses his patrons as rungs by which he mounts the clientage ladder, kicking away the one below as he successfully gets his footing on the rung above.

The patronage system was extremely important in the law and the church, as well as in government service. On the other hand in these and the other professions and in business, men could rise on account of their qualifications and experience, and not merely by having the right connections. Patronage was very closely linked to birth. The inner circle of top people in seventeenth-century England was largely occupied by those who had been born into it; to rise into it was possible but difficult and unusual. The use of money was the standard way of getting into this charmed circle for those who did not have the right connections by birth or marriage. But it was not easy even to buy a way in without the aid of patronage, without becoming somebody's client or dependant at least in the initial stages.

Corruption

Any system of administration based on such relationships and without proper rules for entry and promotion by merit or seniority, gives great scope for nepotism and corruption. One of the most striking features of early seventeenth-century government, judged by twentieth-century standards, is its widespread—and in some respects quite staggering—corruption. But this must be related to other factors in England at that time. First of all there was a long-term fall in the value of money or 'inflation' which had begun in the 1510s–20s and was to go on until about 1630, over which 100–120 years the value of money fell—historians argue how much —some would say three, some four, some five, some sixfold. Secondly, the inadequacy of the official salaries paid by the Crown led to the complete dependence of officials on fees and gratuities, sometimes even on bribes received from members of the public making use of their respective courts and departments, and on favours or perquisites obtained from the Crown. Finally until the nineteenth century there was no fully developed idea of the 'public service'. The service of the King or Queen of England was not really different in kind from the private service of a nobleman, a London company, a great churchman, a college or some other ecclesiastical or educational institution. Once it had been acquired, an office under the Crown was often treated like any other piece of property. It might be held on trust for life, unless it was grossly misused. Offices in England were never openly heritable as in France, though in practice they were very nearly so, through the use of reversions—that is the right to succeed after the present holder; in this way an office could be passed on to the holder's son or son-in-law or younger brother. And apart from this, there was a widespread assumption that within very broad limits an office could be made use of to the holder's maximum advantage. Notions of service and duty to the public that are basic to the modern state, only existed in embryo. People still thought largely in terms of personal loyalty to the sovereign, although some political thinkers and some men engaged in the practical work of government were beginning to distinguish between the private service of the king and the public service of the state. As we shall see, this idea developed considerably in the course of the century.

It seems likely that the system had been deteriorating, that the amount of corruption had been on the increase in the last years of Elizabeth. Some historians have ascribed this to the old age of the Queen herself and of her great minister Lord Burghley, who died a few years before she did, and to the fact that the new men— Burghley's son Robert Cecil, and others—were less scrupulous. There seems to have been a slackening in restraint from above, and an increase of corruption at all levels; there was also fiercer

o

competition for positions that would be influential in the new reign that it was realised must soon come. Not all historians of Tudor England agree about this. But on the whole it looks as if there was a decline in scrupulousness, that the generation coming to power in Elizabeth's last years is more ruthless than the older men had been. So there again 1603 is not a clear dividing line. However the situation did get rapidly worse under James, because of his lack of restraint. The new King seems to have felt that since he had inherited a kingdom much richer than that in which he had grown up, he could afford to indulge his own expensive tastes and also his desire to be generous to his friends and supporters. This contributed to a disastrous worsening in the Crown's financial position, and so weakened its bargaining power in relation to Parliament.

Court Politics

The politics of James I's Court would not matter if the wealth and standing of rival individuals and groups alone had been at issue. But these rivalries also involved different policies. In the years 1603–8, Robert Cecil shared power under the King with other groups in the Privy Council. These consisted of the Howards (the Earls of Nottingham, Suffolk and Northampton) and other peers who held office and whose influence had been growing before the end of Elizabeth's reign, also to a lesser extent a group of Scottish favourites who were unpopular because of the offices and other rewards they received, but were not politically very important. Cecil's predominant position in the government was partly due to the position he had built up in Elizabeth's last years, to the fall of his great rival the Earl of Essex in 1601, and to Elizabeth's untrusting, rather ambivalent attitude towards Sir Walter Ralegh. James shared this attitude; indeed Ralegh was made the scapegoat for the first 'plot' of the reign. Besides, James preferred Cecil to anybody else as a man who would do the donkey-work of government for him. During the years 1609–12 Cecil, who had by then become Earl of Salisbury, continued to share power with the Howards; he now had to share it rather more with the King's favourites, particularly with Robert Carr (later made Viscount Rochester and then Earl of Somerset). Carr never had complete control over royal patronage, or decided the major issues of royal policy; he is important as a favourite, not as a statesman. But from 1610 on Salisbury's influence with the King began to decline; as we shall see, there were political reasons for this. The whole period from the fall of Essex in 1601 to Salisbury's death in 1612 is sometimes mis-called '*regnum Cecilianum*' (the Cecil kingdom), as it was described by some contemporaries. But this exaggerates the extent and completeness of Salisbury's control over the government, even at the peak of his power from 1608, when he became Lord Treasurer and an earl, to 1610. Personal ambition apart, Salisbury may be said to have stood for a policy of peace and neutrality abroad and financial reform at home. At the same time, his religious position was definitely protestant, and he would have preferred the Crown to co-operate with Parliament rather than to do without it.

For two years after Salisbury's death James tried to do without a principal Secretary, but the King was too lazy for this experiment to succeed. Until 1615 influence in James' government was divided between the Howards, especially the Earls of Northampton (until his death in 1614) and Suffolk, and Carr. But during these years there also emerged what can be called an 'opposition' group inside the Privy Council. The most important members of this comprised Archbishop Abbot, who had succeeded Bancroft in 1611, the Lord Chancellor, one of the Secretaries of State (from 1614), and one or two great peers who were members of the Council but not very active in administration. The next favourite, who succeeded Carr, was originally put forward by this opposition group as a candidate for the King's favour, to counterbalance the influence of Carr and the Howards.

In the next few years, 1616–18, the Howards, particularly the Earl of Suffolk, had to share power with this new favourite George Villiers, the younger son of a gentry family from Leicestershire, who was soon created Earl of Buckingham. The opposition group in the Council who had pushed Villiers forward quickly came to regret this. They were left behind, indeed completely eclipsed by his influence over the King, and the fact that he was taken into James' favour did not mean that their policies were adopted, or that they were all restored to favour. By and large, the Howards stood for a pro-Spanish, pro-catholic and anti-parliamentary policy; the opposition group for a more positively protestant home and foreign policy, and for a more sustained attempt to reach agreement with Parliament. No coherent policy can be ascribed to Carr beyond that of maintaining his own position, and even in this he was soon to fail.

The years 1618–28, that is the last seven of James' reign and the first three and a half of Charles', saw the predominance of Villiers in both Court and government. He was soon created a marquis, and subsequently Duke of Buckingham, the first non-royal duke since the execution of Norfolk in 1572. In these years the rule of a single faction—really of one man, his family and supporters— was more complete than that of the Cecils at the height of their power under Elizabeth or James. Particularly in the years 1623–8 Buckingham had an almost complete monopoly of royal patronage, of influence at Court, of royal favour, and even of control over government policies. A certain amount of opposition was kept up rather intermittently by some of the nobles in the Council and Archbishop Abbot, and—arising out of a quarrel about foreign policy—by an ex-ambassador, John Digby Earl of Bristol. But this was not at all effective. For the politics of the Court Buckingham's assassination in August 1628, is more important than the King's death in 1625, because Buckingham dominated Charles just as completely as he had James, though in a different way.

In terms of the policies which he supported, Buckingham's influence is more complicated than that of the other politicians we have been discussing. To begin with, he seems to have fallen in with the King's own preferences; he was also just intelligent enough—which Carr was not—to take advice and make use of other far abler men than himself, who either were already in the government or had joined it as a result of his influence. But as he became more firmly established, he came to have his own views on policy. Until 1623 he seems to have favoured the old 'Howard' scheme of a Spanish marriage alliance, which James himself had long hankered after. From 1624 until his death, however, he was the leader of the 'war party', standing for active intervention against Spain and later—on behalf of the Huguenots—against

France too. The reasons for this reversal will be discussed later. Again, Buckingham had sufficient intelligence to see that his war policy required co-operation with Parliament; he could not see that his own position, his incompetence as a war minister and— from 1625 on—his master's religious policy rendered this co-operation all but impossible.

This short outline of Court politics under James I and in the early years of Charles I, leaves out of account three very able and remarkable men. The first of these is Francis Bacon, the great scientific theorist and philosopher, who was a member of the government on the legal side from 1607 to 1621. The second is the greatest lawyer of the early seventeenth century, the champion and also the historian and codifier of the English common law, Sir Edward Coke; he held legal offices, latterly as a judge, from the 1590s to 1616. The third is less well known but scarcely less important—Lionel Cranfield, who had made his way up in the London business world with the traditional career of an apprentice who married his master's daughter and then took over the business. He became wealthy, went into government at the middle level in the customs service in 1613, and then held a series of senior financial posts from 1617 to 1624. These men were abler than any of those we have been discussing so far except Robert Cecil; but none of them ever held the King's favour as steadily and enjoyed his confidence in the way that Cecil had done, as later the Howards, and finally above all Villiers did. Their constructive influence was weakened by the fact that Bacon and Coke were personal rivals, and to some extent neutralised each other, especially in the disastrous middle years of the reign from about 1611 to 1616. Even after that, although Bacon was in high office and Coke had been thrown out of the government, Bacon never enjoyed a firm position in his own right; he was always completely dependent on the backing of Buckingham. The same is true of Cranfield. He had first risen in the government as a client of the Howards, but had then transferred his allegiance to Buckingham, who had pushed him forward and, as we shall see, made use of him in certain measures of reform. But just as Bacon was sacrificed by Buckingham in the Parliament of 1621, so too was Cranfield by Buckingham and Charles in that of 1624. Therefore throughout this period, only Robert Cecil from 1603 to 1610 had both the political and the intellectual qualities required of a statesman, as well as that close continuous influence over the King which was vital in order to be able to put consistent policies into effect. And even in the case of Cecil there were grave limitations on his power, as the story of the 1610 Parliament and his resulting loss of James' confidence shows. From the end of Cecil's life there is almost a divorce between formal responsibility at the top of the government, that is between the people who hold the major offices, and the enjoyment of actual power and influence. There is certainly a failure of integration or adjustment between the King's Court and the government of the country, between the monarch in his private and public capacities. Under Charles I this failure of integration probably helped to save England from successful royal absolutism. Under James the results are less dramatic, but they help to create an atmosphere of intrigue, jobbery and corruption, and to explain the lack of any consistent policies to deal with the situations and problems which arose.

Court Morality

The moral tone of the royal Court is important because it was inseparable from the government's standing in the country. The first feature to note here is James' reckless extravagance—his indulgence in luxury on clothing, jewels, feasting and masques, also his generosity in granting people pensions and making presents to both Englishmen and Scotsmen. The next is the great scandals of his reign, some of which affected people high in James' favour and his government. One of these involved Robert Carr, Earl of Somerset, James' major favourite before Villiers. Somerset was only enabled to marry the Countess of Essex as he wished, after faked evidence had been used in the divorce case brought against her first husband. A courtier who had spoken out against this, Sir Thomas Overbury, was arrested on false charges and then murdered in the Tower of London on the orders of Lady Essex (now Somerset)—she was the more serious criminal of the two. This came to light in 1615–16 and resulted in the fall of the Somersets, as even James was forced to take proceedings against them. In 1618 James' next leading minister, the Earl of Suffolk, and his wife were disgraced as a result of his being charged with bribery and other corrupt practices in his capacity as Lord Treasurer, with her acting as his accessory. There was also another divorce case involving one of the Secretaries of State and a branch of the Cecil family about that time. These were more than just sensational stories for the seventeenth-century equivalent of modern Sunday newpapers; they touched the highest people in the land. Although the King took action against the guilty parties when he was forced to do so, he was himself discredited by having befriended and promoted such people.

Another feature of the Court which had some political importance was James' obvious partiality for handsome and pleasant-mannered young men. There is no proof that while he was King of England James I was actually a homosexual, though his latest and most reliable biographer has no doubt that he had been at one time when he was younger. It may not seem to be the historian's business to pry into the private morals of James I, who has been in his grave for over three hundred years. But the answer is that, whether or not he was a practising homosexual, James' weakness for young men did influence the course of politics and indeed of English history, particularly through his infatuation with Buckingham. There was the factor of James' emotional deprivations. He lost his eldest son in 1612; his daughter married and went abroad in 1613; and his wife died in 1619, although he did not have very much in common with her and she differed from him in religion, having been converted to Rome; his surviving son, Prince Charles, was a withdrawn and unsympathetic boy with whom he had no warm relationship. It could be argued that Villiers to some extent satisfied James' need for a son, that it was more like a father–son relationship than a strictly homosexual one. Queen Elizabeth had of course been interested in handsome men, but she had never in the last resort allowed this to disturb her political judgment and that meant ultimately her reliance on the Cecils. The difference is that after Salisbury died James did allow his political judgment to be very seriously distorted by these partialities. Another feature of the Court's moral attitude concerns the way in which money was raised on an increasing scale by the sale of titles of honour, including peerages, and of offices in the government. The title of baronet was indeed invented simply in order to be sold. This upset many people because it conflicted with the social conventions of the time.

Even in the worst years, during the middle of James' reign, people still made some distinction between what was permissible, though by our standards it may have constituted corruption, and what even they regarded as impermissible. Bribes were distinguished from gratuities and perquisites; the fall of Bacon in 1621 illustrates this. It was thought particularly bad that Bacon had accepted presents from suitors in his own law court (Chancery). It was considered to be worse for a judge to accept such gifts than for a 'ministerial' or, as we should say administrative officer, to do so. In fact almost any leading man of the time could have been found equally guilty in substance, if not in form.

Another particularly shocking feature by modern standards, is that several leading men in James' government, including Salisbury himself and some of the Howards, were in receipt of pensions from the King of Spain. James eventually got to know of this, but he did nothing about it, except in the case of a much less important man, who happened to be in command of the naval squadron in the English channel; he was sacked, partly because in his case there was an obvious military risk. But the notion that a foreign government could in effect pay a retaining fee to leading members of a friendly government to keep them well-disposed (England and Spain being at peace after 1604) was considered fairly normal by the standards of the time. England was not the only country where this practice went on.

In the general tone of the government and in standards of official conduct, the years from the end of Salisbury's life to 1618 were probably the worst. This applies both as regards the means which the King used to raise money and the extent of official corruption. Although Buckingham's rule brought great evils and conflicts, there was a partial clean-up in the years from 1618 on. This was partly because there was less scope for corruption with the monopoly control of a single faction, though the favourite himself and his family took shameless advantage of their strategic position. It was also due to the work of Cranfield; while dependent on Buckingham, none the less within the limits which this imposed he tried to reform the government and to put the Crown's finances on a sounder footing.

All these features of James' régime are important less in themselves than because they were materially and morally damaging to the Crown's position taken in conjunction with other trends in England at this time.

Social Groups and Classes

Let us now consider the main social groups in the country with whom the Crown had to deal, starting at the top of the social ladder.

Landowners. The peerage had been reduced in numbers because Queen Elizabeth had hardly created any new peers for the last thirty years of her reign. So at James' accession there were only some sixty lay peers of the realm (that is peers of England with seats in the House of Lords: Irish and Scottish peers had titles but did not sit in the English House of Lords), plus the twenty-six bishops. Very few important members of the peerage could trace their ancestry as peers further back than the sixteenth century; those who could do so included the Howards and the Percies, Earls of Northumberland. James at once began to create more peers; by 1630 the size of this small closed group had doubled; it had passed the 100 mark by James' death. It is debatable whether James or Charles made the right men into peers. Some of the older families, even some of the ones who had been raised into the peerage by the Tudors, were jealous at the cheapening of their order and at the Stuart kings' reliance on new men in the government and at Court. On the other hand, the influx of mercantile families, and of men who had made their money and got to the top in administration and the law, as well as in trade, probably strengthened the actual quality of the House of Lords and the peerage.

The House of Lords was the political forum of the peers, particularly of those who did not hold positions at Court. Normally it acted as a moderating influence on the House of Commons, and inside the Lords the bishops provided a valuable block of regular government supporters. But since the number of bishops was fixed, they counted for progressively less as the House of Lords was enlarged by the creation of more peers. By the 1620s the House of Lords itself was deeply divided in its political attitude, especially towards Buckingham; this can be seen in the parliaments of 1625 and 1626, and in its temporary alliance with the House of Commons against the Crown in 1628. In general the influence of the House of Lords seems to have been declining in relation to that of the Commons. This is partly because the peers spent an excessive amount of their time on private business, putting through private bill legislation concerned with members of the peerage and their families. But there may be other reasons. Some historians have suggested that the peers were becoming relatively less wealthy compared with the gentry, and that this accounts for the decline of the House of Lords; this theory has neither been substantiated nor disproved. At any rate socially and politically the peerage was still extremely important. But the House of Lords counts for less as an institution than the peerage does as a social group in the country. This continues to be true right through the seventeenth and into the eighteenth century.

The landed gentry was a much larger class, to be numbered in thousands but even so only a tiny proportion out of a total population of somewhere between three-and-a-half and five millions in England and Wales. At the local level their political forum was the commission of the peace, and at the central level the House of Commons. Well over three-quarters of the members of any House of Commons in this period were of gentry origin socially; they sat for the majority of the 'borough' as well as the fewer but more esteemed 'county' seats. However, many of them owed their seats to the patronage of peers, and many commoners sitting as M.P.s were in fact sons and younger brothers of peers, some of whom would later succeed to peerages themselves. So these two groups or classes were in practice less distinct from each other than appears at first sight.

Some peers and gentry made money in coalmining, metal industries or commerce. But for the vast majority, land—in the form of profits from agriculture and rent from their tenants—was the basis of their wealth. Their social and political preponderance, too, rested on landownership, through control over their tenants as well as their servants and other employees, through the traditional respect accorded them, and through their grip on local government. A small freeholder, even though technically independent, would naturally hesitate to offend a neighbouring great landowner by opposing him politically. Hence changes in the fortunes, and consequently in the outlook of the landed classes, would have effects through the whole political and social structure of the country.

The remaining M.P.s were drawn from other social classes, but many of them, such as lawyers and royal officials, had professional qualifications which would make them rank socially with the gentry. A surprisingly large proportion of the leaders among the House of Commons' opposition were not just country gentlemen, but had some other position or experience: Sir Edwyn Sandys was a merchant and company promoter, Coke a lawyer, John Pym an official in the revenue service.

Lawyers. The lawyers were the only sizeable professional class in early Stuart England, with the exception of the clergy (who will be discussed below). But the law was not a united profession. The divisions within it correspond approximately to the two main types of 'common' and 'civil' law. Common law rested partly on custom and tradition, partly on statute (Acts of Parliament), but it was largely 'case-law', that is based on previous judicial decisions. Thus it was not founded on any collection of written codes, as were the 'canon law' of the catholic church and the civil law taught in the universities, which was based on the codes inherited by Europe from the Roman Empire. In that it was customary and judge-made, common law was also different from statute, which depended on positive enactment. By 1603 it was more generally accepted than it had been a century earlier that statute was the highest form of law in England, since an Act of Parliament could alter what was legal and illegal, which no judicial decision properly could.

The great majority of lawyers were educated at the four 'Inns of

Court' and the smaller 'Chancery Inns' in London, which were sometimes jointly described as 'the third university' of the kingdom. Those so trained, that is the common lawyers, had an intense professional *esprit de corps*; the Inns also acted like a finishing school, giving a smattering of legal training and a veneer of social polish to many members of the gentry who did not stay long enough to qualify and become barristers. Oliver Cromwell is an example of someone who spent a year or so at one of the Inns of Court.

The differences between the various law courts are a little more complicated. There were the common law courts proper (King's Bench, Common Pleas and the Exchequer), the equity courts (Chancery and Requests), and the prerogative courts (Star Chamber, the Councils of Wales and the North, the Privy Council in its judicial capacity). In all these, those who practised were common lawyers trained at the Inns of Court, though they might still have differences of interest because the courts were of different types. Then there were the ecclesiastical courts (such as High Commission and those responsible for the probate of wills) and a few miscellaneous ones (such as Admiralty for cases involving overseas trade). The university-trained civil lawyers practised only in the last two groups.

Disputes within the legal profession could be politically important. The amount of activity in a particular court determined the income of the officers in it, because of the way in which they were paid by fees. An increase or decrease in the amount of legal business, reflecting royal preferences or policies, was inseparably bound up with the bread and butter rivalries inside the legal profession, especially between those practising in the common law courts and those in the rest. It is a mistake to identify the common lawyers with the political opposition in the early years of James' reign; they were not always against royal policy, or necessarily allied with the opposition members of the House of Commons. To some extent such an alliance did take shape in the course of James' and Charles' reigns, as a result of royal policy—or royal blunders.

Big Business. Agriculture was easily the largest single source of wealth in the country at this time. England was not industrialised or economically 'developed' as it has come to be in the last two hundred years. At the same time a small group of business men enjoyed great wealth and exercised considerable political influence. Its members mainly consisted of export merchants, plus a few financiers, and a very few industrialists; socially this *élite* of the commercial world corresponded to an oligarchy within the City of London and a few cosmopolitans who lived in this country. London towered over any other town as a business centre, for instance in the export of woollen textiles—the largest single branch of English overseas trade. The population of London was at least fifteen times that of any other town. The next biggest were Norwich, Bristol and York. One recent estimate suggests that the population of London (including the suburbs, and not limited to the City as a unit of government) was nearer a half than a quarter of a million, and that the second town in the country (Norwich) had only 15,000. Remembering that the total population of England and Wales was probably between three-and-a-half and five millions, the capital may well have accounted for about a twelfth of it. The government of the City of London under the Lord Mayor, Aldermen, Common Councillors, and Sheriffs, was far more independent than that of any other town; its independence was a reality because of the City's great wealth, whereas that of many of the boroughs was not. This gave the Londoners political bargaining strength in their relations with the Crown which often needed to borrow money from them. As a social group, the mercantile *élite* can be bracketed with the greater gentry; they had very little in common with the main body of the urban middle class. Many of them were knighted under James, some even became peers; they were often Members of Parliament. Most of them acquired landed estates, especially in the counties near London, and their descendants in effect became established members of the gentry or even the nobility.

The Urban Middle Class. Then there were various middle-class groups who had some part in the processes of government, but can hardly be described as having shared in ruling the country. The bulk of the middle class proper in the towns—the bourgeoisie as it is called by many social and economic writers—comprised the smaller merchants, the retailers, the master-craftsmen, skilled and semi-professional workers like apothecaries, law clerks, junior officials, and some self-employed artisans. Members of this class might in some cases have the parliamentary vote or enjoy a share in local government, depending on the situation in particular boroughs. The franchise—that is the right to vote—varied very widely. In some boroughs most householders had it, in others only members of the governing body, or corporation; this was true from the origins of these boroughs in the Middle Ages to the first Reform Act of 1832 which standardised the borough franchise. In the counties it was limited to those owning 40s. worth a year of freehold land. In London men of lesser wealth could play some part both in the government of the City through choosing the Common Council and in the great London companies, which were the descendants of the guilds; but fewer of them had the parliamentary vote. Many local offices in cities and towns, such as bailiffs, beadles, criers, were filled by men of this standing.

The Rural Middle Class. In the country the next social group to consider is the lesser gentry—men who were styled Gentlemen as opposed to being Knights or Esquires. They could seldom hope to be Members of Parliament, and not normally J.P.s (if they became such, they were automatically given a social 'leg-up' and became Esquires). Apart from the title to be a gentleman, which gave them some (rather theoretical) equality with all other members of the gentle and noble classes (including the greatest peers of the realm), their wealth and way of life differed very little from that of the prosperous yeomanry, the well-to-do freeholders and tenant farmers in the counties. This is a distinction of social status rather than wealth or economic position. In many counties of England the yeomanry were prospering in this period and were often as rich as, or richer than, many of the lesser gentry. Indeed even the class socially below the yeomen, the 'husbandmen' or upper level of the peasantry, included some who were quite well off, again often prosperous tenant farmers; other husbandmen were very poor indeed, though some would be forty-shilling freeholders. Remembering the inflation and the consequent fall in the value of money, 40s. was not worth nearly as much as it had been when this franchise was fixed in the fifteenth century, so that many more people had the vote in the counties than would have done previously or if no inflation had occurred. In local government the lesser gentry, the yeoman and the better-to-do husbandmen acted as jurymen, constables, overseers of the poor, churchwardens. A few village craftsmen may have taken some share in local government at this level.

The Masses. Then we come to the classes in the country comprising well over half the population who had no share at all in public affairs, who as historians of the eighteenth century would say, were outside the 'political nation'. These include the bulk of the poorer peasantry, almost all servants, most semi-skilled and all unskilled workers. The size of the proletariat, that is the pure wage-earning class—people who had no property at all but were entirely dependent on wages for their living—is debatable: historians do not agree about it. This class was certainly growing, not only in London and other towns but in the countryside, due to the enclosure movement of the sixteenth century and even more to the commercialisation and general development of agriculture, and the growth of population. The speed of this transformation should not be over-rated. Social stratifications and class divisions were certainly very marked in early seventeenth-century England, but were not the same as those which prevailed later. Many of the poorer classes depended on wages or casual earnings in the textile industry; so they were very easily affected by ups and downs in England's exports of cloth as well as by economic fluctuations at home. Increases in the price of grain (for flour, to be made into bread) could easily have a catastrophic effect on them, pushing them over the borderline between poverty and destitution, and in years of bad harvest there was always a danger of mass starvation. On the other hand these dangers were reduced by the fact that most people were not dependent on wage-earning alone. Mixed occupations can be found within the same family, and often one man had more than one occupation; he might be a part-time wage-earning employee, also be self-employed, and be a small-holder; many wage-earners were also peasants with some land of their own.

These social classes, all of whom were normally outside politics, and most of whom were on the borderline of the subsistence level, are in the background to the political history of the century. Every now and again they come on to the scene, as in the riots against enclosures in the east midlands in 1607, in the west country around 1630, and, as we shall see, with much more effect in the 1640s. But they did not normally operate as a factor in politics. Their existence is reflected in the concern shown by Crown and Parliament alike over the price of corn, the administration of the Tudor code of poor relief, and the general problem of security against discontent which, if unheeded and allowed to become desperate, might erupt in social upheaval.

By modern standards, class divisions in seventeenth-century England were rigid, clear-cut and difficult to cross; but they could be crossed. Some men rose meteorically, such as George Villiers from gentleman to duke, Cranfield from apprentice to earl; the son of a tanner became lord chief justice, and the son of a husbandman a judge. But these are untypical; more characteristic of the age were yeomen and merchants, lawyers and officials who ended their days as gentry, and whose descendants remained in the gentry class. Other families went downhill, but the commonest reason for the disappearance of families from the gentry and other politically active classes was simply that they died out in the male line. Although the population was probably still rising, if not as fast as in the sixteenth century, the appallingly high death rate which kept it at a level of only about a twelfth of today's, was the most effective provision against hereditary rigidity. Even so, compared with what we know today, the social system was very rigid, and great inequalities of wealth and status were of its essence.

1 A yeoman's house.
This stone-built yeoman's house in Northamptonshire is luxurious by comparison with the kind of peasant dwelling shown below.

2 A peasant's hovel.

3 Landscape with a Coach by Jacob Esselens.
Travel by private coach was an expensive luxury, but after the Restoration it came to be regarded as a point of social prestige.

4 Sir Thomas Aston at the death-bed of his first wife, by John Souch, 1635. This death-bed scene is a reminder of the lower standards of hygiene and medical knowledge which contributed to the very high rates of infant and maternal mortality.

2 : Sources of Conflict (1603–29)

WE must now consider some of the ways in which tension and conflict arose in England during these years. This means that we turn from a mainly static picture of what the country was like to one of movement in both thought and action.

Religion

The Church of England had been established in the sixteenth century, as a result first of Henry VIII's breach with Rome, secondly of the protestant reformation under Edward VI, and thirdly of the Elizabethan church settlement. Ever since its inception the Church of England had been fighting a war on two fronts. We need to review the state of this conflict at the accession of James I.

The Catholics

The Roman Catholics, those who continued to give their adherence to the Papacy, constituted a strong element in parts of the country, especially in the north-west, some districts of the west midlands, and Cornwall. But practising Roman Catholics ('recusants', as those who would not come to Church of England services were called) were now only a small minority in the country as a whole. The Papal Bull of 1570 excommunicating Elizabeth, the Spanish-trained Jesuit missionaries sent over to reconvert England, the various plots involving the Spanish government, Mary Queen of Scots, or both, and finally the Armada and the Spanish War, had led to growing pressure on the Queen. Powerful protestant forces in Parliament and even in her Council demanded increasingly severe treatment of the catholics. The sheltering of Jesuits and other priests from the Continent came to be identified with treason against the Queen and the state; recusants were

D

subjected to a growing burden of penalties. Against a background of recent events like the Marian burnings, Alva's 'Council of Blood' in the Netherlands and the Massacre of St Bartholomew in France (1572), the protestant attitude is understandable. The forces of counter-reformation catholicism were indeed waging an implacable ideological war to exterminate protestantism and to recover the whole of western Europe for the Roman Church. And even by the standards of the time, their methods often seemed bloody and unscrupulous.

Since the 1580s there had been a presumption that catholics were a potential Spanish 'fifth column'. The main forms of discrimination against them were actual persecution for attending their own form of worship, the hunting of catholic priests and their execution—not as priests but as traitors, if they were captured, and a penal tax on recusant property-owners. By 1600 at least, this equation of catholics with fifth columnists was quite unreal. Most of the English Roman Catholics had not supported Spain in the Elizabethan war, even passively, and by the early years of James this was beginning to be recognised. Unfortunately the English catholics had hoped for more out of James than they were to get; over the years he had conducted an intermittent intellectual and diplomatic flirtation with Rome. The disillusionment felt by catholics when he did nothing to better their lot, led to the conspiracies against him, the rather feeble 'Watson's plot' of 1603 and the much more famous 'Gunpowder plot' of 1604–5— a daring, and until the last minute well-planned scheme to blow up the parliament buildings with the King, Lords and Commons in them, and then to seize power by an armed *coup d'état*. These ventures were the work of a desperate minority; and it is noteworthy that James and Robert Cecil wished to show only that the Jesuits were implicated in the Gunpowder plot. Since Guy Fawkes and Co. had had a Jesuit confessor who had known of their design for mass murder but had neither dissuaded them from it nor warned the authorities, there was some justification for this. It also reflected the policy of the King and Archbishop Bancroft, which aimed at playing on the division between the 'seculars' (that is, those priests who were not members of religious orders) and the 'regulars' (the Jesuits and members of other such orders). They tried to devise an oath of allegiance which catholic laymen and even 'seculars' could take; they used the penal fines on recusants as a form of pressure to encourage this. At their maximum of £20 a month, or confiscation of two-thirds of people's property for non-payment, these could obviously be crippling, but they were seldom fully exacted.

However these fine-drawn distinctions were wasted on most people. To the average protestant Englishman (almost regardless of education or social position) the 'Powder Plot', as it was called, provided irrefutable confirmation of his prejudices and suspicions. If these were the methods of the diehard catholics, were penal fines and civic disabilities so harsh and unreasonable? Once again, anti-catholic fears and hatreds might have died down with the gradual passing of time, if nothing had happened to re-inflame them. No doubt these feelings of people in the seventeenth century had some of the same psychological origins as anti-Jewish, anti-Negro and anti-Communist feelings have had in various countries in our own time. The search for some distinct group, to serve as a scapegoat for the ills of society, is a deep and age-old human trait. Yet in each case there is also a specific, historical explanation for the way such feelings are directed, and the form which they take. Anti-Popery was to be revived, indeed intensified by a series of developments in the course of the century. First came the outbreak of a major religious war on the Continent, which the catholics at first looked like winning. Then followed the Irish Rebellion of 1641 and Charles I's subsequent attempt to get Irish catholic help in the English Civil War. Later still catholicism became identified with the influence of another foreign power—France, and with attempts to erect a despotism on the French model.

Whether protestantism necessarily led towards parliamentary rights and constitutional liberties is debatable. Some historians argue that the basic protestant belief in every individual seeking the truth direct for himself in the word of God—that is, the Bible— rather than through a hierarchical priesthood, gave the protestant churches an inherent secular and popular bias from the first. On this view, the movements for constitutional government, even those in the direction of democracy which arose in seventeenth-century England, were a perfectly logical consequence of the sixteenth-century protestant reformation. On the other hand, there had been representative assemblies and popular movements in Europe long before the reformation, while in the sixteenth and seventeenth centuries there were some protestant countries where the systems of government were in fact just as absolute and as utterly undemocratic as those in the catholic countries of Europe. Still less were the great majority of seventeenth-century protestants 'liberal' in any meaningful, modern sense. But as a matter of historical fact, by and large the identification made by many protestants at the time, and by whig, liberal and rationalist historians since, was correct. Protestantism *was* on the whole allied to the cause of parliamentary government and the rule of law, catholicism to that of foreign intervention and absolute monarchy. In particular the radical wing of English protestantism, the Puritan movement, having found itself increasingly at odds with the Crown and the bishops had, as early as the 1570s and 1580s, used the House of Commons as an alternative platform from which to campaign for further religious changes. In so doing it had perhaps helped to strengthen the House of Commons' position more—in the short run—than the Commons had advanced the cause of Puritanism. In these circumstances, it is tragic but not surprising that many English catholics who were neither agents of Spain—or later of France—nor would-be subverters of the constitution, were harshly, sometimes cruelly victimised for persisting in their faith. More remarkable, in this general atmosphere of fear and hatred, are the few signs of humaneness and rationality, of kindness and tolerance, which cut across these ideological divisions and point the way towards a less credulous and so less ferocious future.

The Church of England

Turning to the Anglican establishment, the only officially recognised church in the land, the first point to remember is that by 1603 only men well over fifty could remember a time before the Elizabethan settlement of 1559. The average expectation of life being about thirty, that meant very few. The Church of England had come of age; by the test of success it was there, it existed and it worked. The main problems which confronted James and his church leaders were what policies to follow towards the catholics and the other opposition group, the Puritans—most of whom were still *inside* the church. At the same time as coping with the catholic danger, Elizabeth and her bishops had had many great struggles with the Puritans, and by the end of the reign had succeeded in curbing their power.

The other great problem was the poverty of the church itself, and especially of the lesser clergy in it. There was a crying need for better-educated clergy, and for the removal of certain abuses, such as the holding of more than one living or parish (pluralism), and clergy living away from their parishes (non-residence). To solve these problems a living wage had to be provided for parsons, most of whom were now married men with families. Except for the added difficulty of having to provide for a married instead of a celibate clergy, none of these problems was new; all went back long before the Reformation. But the struggle to raise the standard of the clergy was now bound up with the battle inside the church between the hierarchy and the Puritans. The King and the bishops had one remedy for clerical poverty, namely to halt the process by which church lands and thus their revenues were passing more and more into the hands of laymen. The Puritans, backed by some members of the House of Commons, had another; put very simply it was to re-distribute wealth within the church, by an attack on the property and income of the bishops and the deans and chapters of cathedrals. James did halt the alienation of church revenues which Elizabeth had resorted to when she had been short of money; and he backed his archbishop, Bancroft, against even the moderate Puritans.

The Puritans

The first difficulty in discussing Puritans and Puritanism is that of definition. Historians do not agree either on who they were or what their movement stood for. Perhaps here we should simply think of them as the more extreme wing of the protestant movement in England, those who felt that the Anglican Church was more or less on the right lines in its sixteenth-century settlement, but that traces of catholicism lingered in it. So although it was no longer formally subject to Rome, in their eyes the church was still tainted with popery, and needed to be made more strictly protestant. One of the central, and most effective Puritan demands was for a 'preaching ministry', that is a church of resident parsons who would really instruct their flocks. Puritans criticised the 'dumb dogs' of the establishment, who were either so ill-educated or so mistrusted by the episcopate that printed 'Homilies' had to be provided for them to read out from the pulpit, instead of their trying to preach proper sermons.

The most important distinction within the Puritan movement was between 'Separatists', 'Presbyterians' and 'Episcopalians'. The Separatists wanted to split off from the church and set up independent congregations of their own. They were few in number, mostly of humble social origin, and had been effectively hunted down in the latter years of Elizabeth; some of the remainder were in exile in the Netherlands by the early years of James' reign. To understand the severity with which these unfortunate people were treated, we have to remember that practically no one could yet imagine different churches or religious groups living amicably together in a single state. It was still widely believed both that religious disunity was an evil in itself—an affront to God—and that it inevitably led to civil strife. The memory of the so-called Wars of Religion in sixteenth-century Germany and France was much in people's minds. This was an added reason for the unpopularity of Roman Catholics; with the Separatists it might appear to be the only reason—otherwise they seem harmless enough. But besides this inability to conceive of successful co-existence between different religions, some of these extreme Puritan sects reminded people of another sixteenth-century phenomenon—the German 'Anabaptists' who had actually set up a communistic republic in Munster (1533–5) before it was savagely suppressed. Not all Separatists even believed in adult baptism, the most distinctive tenet of sixteenth- and seventeenth-century Anabaptists, let alone shared their other beliefs. But, as with the Munster commune, they drew their strength from artisans and other workpeople, and seemed a potential threat to the social order. There was also the memory of Ket's rebellion in Norfolk (1549) to underline the connection between extreme protestantism and popular social protest. Just as respectable middle-class Presbyterians looked anti-monarchist and 'democratic' to Elizabeth and James I, so Baptists and Separatists sometimes looked like anarchists and communists to men of property—protestant and catholic alike.

A more influential group of Puritan clergy inclined to a form of 'presbyterianism' on the model of the Scottish and Genevan churches but wanted to work for this from within the church. The more moderate, Episcopalian or Anglican Puritans, accepted the broad outlines of the Elizabethan settlement and did not want to introduce such a system of church government by presbyters and elders. But they were still Puritans in wanting to make the Church of England more protestant than it was, and were very much on their guard against any tendencies towards catholicism or any compromise with Rome. Then there were the laymen who supported the Puritans. Some of them went as far as the Presbyterians, but if they did so, it was with a different view of the proper relations between church and state; this, like the attitude of James himself on these matters, is best described as 'Erastian'. At the Hampton Court conference in 1604, James and Bancroft could have reached a compromise with the moderate Puritans, and so have isolated the few extremists. James failed to do this because he did not appreciate that these moderates were different from the extreme Scottish-type Presbyterians. He pre-judged the issue, uttering his famous platitude of political theory 'No bishop, no king'. This was to overlook the fact that the Puritans he was dealing with at that time were not against bishops as such, so that their wanting to get rid of them as a step towards overthrowing the monarchy did not arise.

After this, the Puritans had to make a choice. They could stand firm and be expelled, if they refused to subscribe to the doctrines of the Church of England, that is they could become Separatists. The number of Puritan clergymen who did so is disputed; this is partly a question of how to define deprivation for nonconformity.

Some historians say as few as 50, others as many as 300, but in any case this was only a small proportion out of a total of between 5,000 and 8,000 clergy. Alternatively they could conform outwardly but keep up a clandestine opposition from within the church. Lastly they could really conform and get on with advancing their careers. A more systematic anti-Puritan policy in the church, which had already begun under Archbishop Whitgift in the latter years of Elizabeth, was continued. However, this policy was checked by the death of Bancroft in 1610 and the appointment of George Abbot, who was that paradoxical mixture a Calvinist episcopalian, like the King himself. So there was less fundamental change in 1604 than might appear. There was no intensive drive against the moderate Puritans inside the church, no attempt to swing the Church of England away from protestantism towards some compromise with catholicism, until later, with the victory of a new 'High-Church' party in Charles I's reign. Only then did these 'Low-Church' Anglicans and moderate Puritans come into direct collision with the Crown and the hierarchy. This new High-Church party was taking shape during the course of James' reign. Its leading and most eloquent theorist was Bishop Lancelot Andrewes; the advancement of the more industrious, if more pedestrian, figure William Laud was delayed by James because he was afraid of precipitating a frontal conflict within the church. So that in religious matters, because of the different attitudes of James and Charles towards the Church of England and the opposition to it, 1625 is a more important date than it is in political history.

One result of the church settlement of 1604 was the famous translation of the Bible, the fruit of co-operation between the bishops and the conformist or moderate Puritans. This resulted in the 'Authorised Version' which became the most widely read book in the English-speaking world. Another was a continued drive against clerical poverty and against sub-standard clergy. The success of this is debatable; historians differ markedly in their estimates of Bancroft's achievement here. Whatever the truth about this, the divisions within the Church of England and the question of whether or not it could embrace the whole population, remained unsolved in James' reign, but were perhaps not yet insoluble.

The Law

Some of the jurisdictional clashes between different courts and groups of lawyers had political importance. The use of legal orders called 'prohibitions' by the common law courts, to stop cases proceeding in the other courts, led to a series of disputes, for instance as to whether cases about tithes (the payment of a tenth of people's produce or income to the church) should be heard in the Court of Common Pleas or in the church courts. The years 1605–10 saw a battle between Bancroft and the common lawyers which reached its climax towards the end of that period, in a struggle between the Archbishop and the Chief Justice, Edward Coke. Coke was not a Puritan; identification of the common law and Puritan interests, in so far as it was ever more than fragmentary, was a result of this struggle, not the cause of it. The battle was resumed in 1611 between Coke and the next Archbishop, Abbot; so it was not because Bancroft was anti-Puritan, since Abbot was himself a strong Calvinist.

Coke also got into trouble as a champion of the common law and of the limitations on the King's right to govern by issuing proclamations. These were used to fill in the gaps between parliamentary legislation by proclaiming that various laws should be enforced. There was a dispute about the exact legal position, both as a result of the repeal of Henry VIII's Act of Proclamations and as to whether new offences at law could be created by proclamation; this was more important than it would otherwise have been because from 1607 onwards very few Acts reached the statute book, that is became law. Partly in order to circumvent this dispute, Coke was promoted; he was really 'kicked upstairs' from Common Pleas to the Court of King's Bench, where he would have less scope for interfering in these matters, in 1613. In the struggle which developed, especially between him and Bacon, two rival views of the judges' role, indeed of the whole judicial arm of government, were at issue. Coke believed that the judges should be constitutional arbiters, holding the balance between Crown and Parliament and laying down what the law was. Bacon, a champion of Chancery and of the King's discretion as exercised through his Lord

Chancellor, held that the judges should be 'lions under the throne', that is servants of the King who merely happened to have judicial rather than executive duties. This battle was mixed up with personal rivalries and dislikes. Nor is it clear how far Coke wanted to go in erecting something like a body of fundamental law—comparable to the American Constitution. Again historians differ on this point, but whatever the truth about Coke's intentions, what matters is the political collision which resulted from this dispute.

In other respects King James had had some successes with the judges. We have already mentioned the common citizenship for people born in England and Scotland after 1603; he also won an important case concerning his right to levy extra customs duties—a test action over a cargo of currants imported by a merchant called Bate, in 1606. This probably made him all the angrier when he was defied by Coke. There were other indecisive legal skirmishes, between the common lawyers and the Council in the Marches of Wales; they even attacked the Court of Star Chamber. These prerogative courts were declining in popularity compared with the sixteenth century, perhaps due to their very success in helping to remedy the unsettled conditions which had made them necessary. In many people's eyes this may have removed the continued justification for their existence.

Coke was on weak ground in his final quarrel as Chief Justice. This was not against a prerogative or a church court but with the Court of Chancery, presided over by Lord Chancellor Ellesmere with Bacon as his grey eminence in the background. It was a dispute primarily over legal business, but involving royal interests. This arose over 'commendams', grants of church livings and their revenues to persons other than regular incumbents; in this particular case a bishop was in trouble for being a pluralist. The question was whether since it involved a private patron's property right, the case should be heard in one of the common law courts, or since the prerogative was involved, in Chancery. James decided to act as a final arbiter; he fancied himself as a sort of personal Court of appeal in these disputes. He ruled in favour of Chancery, and all the common law Judges except Coke gave way. It is not surprising that in 1616 James suspended Coke from all his judicial functions; the Chief Justice was told to go away into the country and re-write some objectionable passages in his law reports—the re-writing of history is not something new, invented by totalitarian governments in the twentieth century. In November Coke, still proving obdurate, was sacked from the bench. He is a most unlikeable historical personage, in his private as well as his public life, but an important one; as we shall see, he appears again in the parliaments of the 1620s. But even after the dismissal of Coke, it is wrong to think of all common lawyers as swinging into opposition; a number of extremely able ones continued to support the Crown, and did so at all stages right through the century. Lawyers were particularly easy for the Crown to win over, by the promise of judgeships and other legal offices—easier on the whole than other opposition leaders.

The significance of Coke's dismissal in 1616 is that it marks the end of any kind of three-cornered constitutional debate: that is between Crown, Parliament, and Common Law. From then on, Coke's attempt to erect the common law into a kind of independent 'third force' collapsed. Common lawyers either supported the Crown, or they tended to work with the parliamentary opposition, as Coke himself did. Further sackings of judges, who showed excessive independence—another Chief Justice in 1626, a third in 1634, and the suspension of the senior Exchequer judge in 1629—only underline this fact. Lawyers had to choose one way or the other, and those who stayed in the government conformed rather more nearly, though not perhaps completely, to Bacon's ideal of lions under the throne.

Crown and Parliament; Grievances and Supply

The constitutional struggle itself was easily the most important source of conflict, but it involves many of the other problems of early Stuart England which we have already considered. During the years 1603–29 Parliament was actually sitting (this is including adjournments of only a week or less, but excluding longer gaps between sessions) for about three years and four months—or approximately an eighth of the time. There was still something occasional and extraordinary, rather than ordinary and routine, about a parliamentary session; it was not yet a regular part of government. This was reflected in the financial assumptions which were still generally made but were becoming increasingly unrealistic, that the Crown should 'live of its own'. This assumed that the King should be able to manage in peacetime on his ordinary revenues without having recourse to parliamentary taxation or other extraordinary means of raising money.

The Royal Revenue System

The first question to ask ourselves about James' and Charles' relations with their parliaments, is why the King could not live on his own income. James was burdened with a body of debt, some of which was inherited, from the costs of the Spanish war, the Irish war, and aid for the Netherlands against Spain. He was extravagant personally—spending money on himself and his family and on his friends—reflecting his general inability to say No to people he liked. Then there was what may be called the inelasticity of the Crown's revenue system, on the in-comings side. We need to look at this a little more fully.

One traditional source of revenue was that from Crown lands. These were very inefficiently run, and though some improvement was achieved under Salisbury, they continued to bring in less than they should have done. Another consisted of feudal dues, the King's rights as a feudal overlord. The most important of these was his right to enjoy the guardianship or 'Wardship' of those of his tenants who died leaving heirs under age, and to arrange the marriages of their female heirs. Either the estates of those in wardship could be managed direct, and the profits collected on the King's behalf, or the wardship, including the right to manage the property, could be sold for a lump sum. There was also 'purveyance', the King's right to supply his Household at less than market prices. These forms of taxation were particularly unpopular with the landowning classes, on whom wardship fell directly, while purveyance was also felt or at least expressed as more of a grievance by them than by other classes; these revenues became still more hated if they were rigorously exacted. Next, based on royal prerogative but not on 'feudal' rights, there were monopolies, that is royal grants of the sole right to manufacture, distribute or sell particular commodities, and various devices for raising revenue by selling licences and exemptions. These were especially unpopular with business-men and ordinary people in their capacity as consumers. Monopolies had been heavily attacked in Elizabeth's last Parliament, and the Queen had actually promised to recall them, without however surrendering her right to make such grants. There was a further objection in that monopolies were extremely wasteful; they brought very little revenue in to the Crown relative to the amount they cost the subject, the difference going into the pockets of the monopolists and the middlemen, or the 'projectors' as they were known.

The Customs were the best in the sense of being the Crown's most elastic source of ordinary revenue. The great debate here was how far the King had a right to adjust the rates of Customs duties and the range of goods which were dutiable without parliamentary consent. The Tudors had already done this a little, and as a result of the legal decision already referred to in 1606, James did it a good deal more, setting up a new branch of Customs duties, called the 'New Impositions'. The profits of justice (from fines on offenders and from fees paid by users of the law courts), smaller traditional feudal and prerogative revenues, clerical taxation, and penal taxes on recusant catholics, were all useful if they were pushed to the maximum, but they could hardly be decisive in enabling the King to pay his way.

Then there are what have come to be called the 'extraordinary' revenues. Among these were the taxes voted in parliament; they were assessed on landed rather than commercial wealth and had not kept up with the inflation, and so were bringing in less than they should have done. Parliament had a traditional right to discuss grievances, and with determined leaders it could get the Crown to make reforms and grant concessions in return for voting such taxes—Subsidies, Tenths and Fifteenths as they were called. The calculation of people's wealth on which the levying of these taxes was based had become hopelessly out of date; they were not reassessed on fresh valuations nearly often enough, and this meant that more subsidies had to be voted than earlier in the sixteenth century, in order to yield the same real value to the Crown. Non-parliamentary taxes, which the Crown had a right to raise, included an extra tax in wartime for the Navy called 'Ship-Money'. The Crown also had a more dubious right to compel people to lend it money. Sometimes these loans were in practice forced, though in theory voluntary; 'Benevolences', a kind of compulsory capital levy, had been illegal since the end of the fifteenth century, but forced loans came to much the same thing. On the other hand, if the Crown overdid the levying of forced loans, it would become harder to raise genuine loans at interest, from the financiers and moneyed men who might otherwise be able and willing to lend. The Crown was becoming increasingly dependent in these years on the London money market, and in particular on a small group of large-scale financiers; these included the syndicates who were managing the Customs, paying the Crown a fixed rent and making their profit from the amount by which the duties exceeded this—the system known as farming. The Customs farmers were important primarily because they lent large sums of money to the Crown on the security of the duties which they themselves were about to collect. The Crown could also raise money by the sale of capital assets: timber, jewels, and above all land. Here there was a vicious circle, because obviously the more land that was sold, the smaller the Crown's income from land would be. It might have been in the Crown's interest to sell off all its lands at a good price, but only if it could have established other reliable forms of regular revenue. The sale of titles, honours, and offices was a minor source of revenue under James, but like monopolies caused more bad feeling than it was worth.

We need to ask ourselves why this revenue system was so laggard, why the Crown was in such a disadvantageous position as a result of 80 or 100 years of gradual inflation. First of all, the law and custom of the land were on the whole unfavourable to arbitrary royal action. Although the Tudors had got some extra customs duties, this was not clearly established; despite the New Impositions there was a widespread feeling that a limit existed to what the Crown could properly do without parliament. Second, there were the interests of royal officials, many of whom took their cut out of the Crown's revenues. They often had a vested interest in preserving archaic methods of revenue collection and accounting; also many had a vested interest in keeping expenditure up when the government ought to have been trying to cut it down. Then there is the fact that the law was simply unenforceable without the co-operation of the propertied classes in town and country; this applies particularly to the Crown's dependence on the nobility and gentry as magistrates in the countryside and on the Aldermen and other governors of the City.

Compared either with modern Britain or with other countries in Europe at the same date England was then an extremely under-taxed country. The money which the French Kings got from the *gabelle*, their tax on salt (then needed in every home, to preserve food) alone exceeded the entire royal revenue in England.

The Rise of the Commons

Parliament's position and importance in the country was not only a matter of finance. Parliament, and especially the House of Commons, had been developing its own procedure, growing as an institution in the sixteenth century. The use of larger parliamentary committees, and particularly the practice of the whole House sitting as a committee with its own elected chairman instead of the Speaker, made it more difficult for the Crown to control its proceedings through the Privy Councillors sitting in the House. The Speaker was becoming less effective as a royal nominee, less able to manage the House as the King wished; and when the House was in committee, he was not in the chair at all. The House of Commons established control over its own privileges, and over disputed elections. Two cases which strengthened this control were decided in 1604—those of Shirley and of Goodwin *versus* Fortescue. The Commons also succeeded in widening their right of free speech in 1621, when for the first time they discussed foreign policy; in 1624 they did so again without the King even trying to stop them.

There is also the difference of personalities. Elizabeth's later parliaments had been deferring to her as a grand old lady; there was a certain feeling of frustration, even of pent-up aggressiveness in parliament, which even a very tactful king would have had difficulty in handling. In fact the situation was worsened by James' tactlessness and by his choice of Councillors, too few of whom were eligible for election to the Commons. At the end of Elizabeth I's reign, there were 6 commoners in a Council of 13; in 1603 James had 8 and by 1613 only 5 commoners in a Council about twice that size. Nor did all those who were eligible obtain seats: only 2–3 Councillors sat as M.P.s in James' first Parliament, and 4 in his second. In the last parliaments of his reign and the first of Charles' (1621–6) the numbers were better than this; in those of 1628–9 and 1640 they were down to the level of 3–4 again. But it was not just a matter of numbers. Those who were elected proved less capable of guiding and controlling the House than their Elizabethan predecessors.

Then there were the continued religious divisions. Despite the defeat of the Puritans in the 1580s and 90s, and the outcome of the Hampton Court conference, the House of Commons was still favourable to them. It would be a mistake to say that all M.P.s or even the majority were Puritans; but the House of Commons had a kind of Puritan, or anyway militantly protestant bias. Some historians argue that this gave them a source of moral and religious strength which they would otherwise have lacked. It certainly meant that their proceedings were not merely based on selfish class interests, but were permeated by an ideology, a view of life and of society.

Social changes which had been in progress during the sixteenth century and were still going on, were reflected in the membership of the House. More and more of the later Elizabethan M.P.s were educated men, wealthier and more sophisticated. This is bound up with the controversy as to whether or not the gentry, as a class, were rising in relation to other social classes in the country. Without accepting the views of some historians, whose evidence is not supported by closer investigation, it seems likely that the gentry had been gaining at the expense of the Crown, the church, and possibly the poorer classes. Real wages had certainly been falling in the course of the sixteenth century and were probably still at best stationary in the early seventeenth; so we need not suppose that

5 The Somerset House Conference, 1604, arranged the treaty to end the war with Spain, begun in the 1580s: English representatives are on the right, with Robert Cecil in front, the Spaniards are on the left.

King Powhatan comands C: Smith to be slaine, his daughter Pokahontas beggs his life his thankfullnes and how he subiected 39 of their kings. reade ý history.

6 Adventures in America. Captain John Smith, author and explorer, was captured by Indians and about to be executed, when Princess Pocahontas begged his life from her father King Powhatan. Pocahontas was later converted to Christianity and came to live in England.

7 Hatfield House, Hertfordshire.
Built for Robert Cecil when he was chief minister of James I, Hatfield is a typical Elizabethan–Jacobean mansion, in appearance a mixture of gothic and renaissance influences.

8 The Queen's House, Greenwich.
The Queen's House, built by Inigo Jones for Henrietta Maria about 20 years later than Hatfield House, shows the classical simplicity of the 'Palladian' style.

the peerage was declining in order to agree that the gentry were rising. The contrary argument is that the opposition in the Commons reflected the growing desperation of gentry who were in decline—that is, in acute economic difficulties, because they could not make ends meet as 'mere' landowners, and who wanted to share in the profits of office and the other benefits of Court favour. This is very hard to square with what is known of the Commons membership in Elizabeth's or the early Stuart reigns.

Over-emphasis on the part played by either 'rising' or 'declining' gentry in the House of Commons means neglecting the many reasonably affluent M.P.s whose fortunes remained more or less level. It also involves the assumption—equally unwise in history or in present-day affairs—that the same economic motives impel everyone in the same political direction. There was, however, a certain jealousy or feeling of resentment, on the part of the 'Country'—the Members of Parliament who did not have any connection with the royal Court or the government, against the 'Court' —those who had offices or were connected with the government in one way or other. This tension is an important factor, and a theme which runs right through seventeenth-century politics. The natural, perhaps inevitable, antagonism between Court and Country was heightened by the moral disapproval aroused by James I's Court, and by the religious character of the parliamentary opposition. Material jealousy was here yoked with self-righteousness, making a formidable political instrument.

James' Early Parliaments

The successive parliaments of this period provide many specific instances of these general trends. James' first Parliament was largely taken up with grievances and disputes, but a certain amount of useful, uncontroversial business was put through. This House of Commons more or less told the King that it was going to be more outspoken, stand up for its rights more vigorously than its immediate predecessors had with Elizabeth. In general it can be said of the early sessions of James' first Parliament (1604-7) that relations with the Crown tended to worsen, but there was no decisive clash.

E

The sessions of 1610 saw a more serious collision, with finance as the central issue. The King's total debt had doubled in the first five years of his reign; on the other hand Salisbury had succeeded in halving it again in the years 1608–10, partly as a result of the New Impositions, partly through an economy drive. Salisbury now took the initiative in setting the King's finances on a sounder footing; it was a good moment to choose, just because the King was not in acute need. He put forward a series of compromise proposals which have become known as the 'Great Contract'. This failed, because the terms could not be agreed on. The King was to give up wardship, his debts were to be settled, and a new tax on land was to be voted to him. Some of the King's other advisers were against his surrendering any of his prerogatives, and tried to undermine Salisbury's position; many Members of Parliament were very reluctant to vote any regular tax on property, fearing that the Crown would thereby become independent of Parliament altogether. They had the constant example of other representative institutions on the Continent, particularly in France, before them; also many M.P.s were not prepared to overlook the question of the Impositions' legality. One member made a notable speech in which he brought the issue of sovereignty into the forefront, asking who had the final say in making the law and levying taxes—the King alone, or the King in Parliament?

The failure of this compromise led to the dissolution of James' first Parliament, the decline of Salisbury's influence, the worsening of the financial situation, and an era of many financial projects and devices. Besides those already mentioned, the latter included a disastrous interference with the export trade in cloth. The King, advised by Alderman Cockayne, tried to prohibit the export of all cloth except in its fully finished, instead of in its semi-finished state, in order to reap higher customs dues. There was a boycott on the part of the buyers in the Netherlands; Cockayne's new syndicate, who had taken over the management of the trade from the traditional 'Merchant Adventurers', did not have the resources of capital to carry on; there was a catastrophic fall in cloth exports, and so in the Crown's customs revenue. The King had to give way and the previous system was restored—a great deal of ill-will as well as material loss and hardship having been incurred in the process.

For practical purposes James ruled without parliament for over ten years after the failure of the Great Contract. True, one was called in 1614, but it has become known to history as the 'Addled' Parliament, because it only sat for a short time and achieved nothing at all. It failed both because of a number of disputes and because it was sabotaged from both sides. A group within the Privy Council, including the influential Howard family, were against the King trying to co-operate with parliament. And several Members at this time showed themselves unwilling to meet the King even halfway; they were particularly resentful because they believed—perhaps mistakenly—that he had been interfering with elections, and over a speech by one of the bishops in the House of Lords, criticising them. The same issues as in the previous Parliament, such as monopolies and impositions, were again brought up by the Commons before they would consider voting money.

For several years after this James did without parliament (Elizabeth had on occasion gone for about five years without calling it). He relied heavily on the advice of the Howards until 1618; thereafter Buckingham was in the ascendant. James also took counsel frequently with the Spanish ambassador in London, Sarmiento Count Gondomar, who encouraged him in his attitude of trying to rule without parliament, and offered the prospect of a marriage alliance between a Spanish princess and James' son, Charles. The payment of a very large dowry would contribute towards keeping the Crown financially independent of Parliament.

During the six-and-a-half-year interval between the Addled Parliament and the next one, many grievances arose which found no outlet. The most important were those which affected the classes represented in the Commons. Cockayne's project has already been mentioned. Trade had scarcely recovered after this scheme had been wound up when there was a disastrous slump in the cloth industry, due to the effects of the European war on English exports. Although James could not be blamed for it, this was even more serious for all those involved in the sale and manufacture of cloth, and indirectly for the producers—the sheep-farmers. English exports plummeted down; there was widespread distress as a result of unemployment, and the whole country seemed to many people to be threatened with total ruin. Meanwhile from 1617–18 on, a limited campaign of financial reform was set on foot under Cranfield, at first a junior minister and client of Buckingham, but then Lord Treasurer (1621–4). This was comparable to, but in some ways perhaps more thorough than that conducted by Salisbury in the years 1608–10. One difficulty was that this economy campaign, especially the part affecting the spending side of government, was quite incompatible with an active foreign policy, which might involve intervention in the European conflict.

Foreign Policy

Suspicion of James' foreign policy because of its pro-Spanish aspect grew, particularly from 1618 on. To go back to the beginning of the reign, the peace which had wound up the long Elizabethan war with Spain in 1604, had on balance been popular, or at any rate had come to be accepted as reasonable. It was disliked by a few freebooters who lived by privateering—or licensed piracy, and by a few naval and military commanders disappointed in their ambitions of leading more expeditions against Spain or the Indies, men such as Ralegh. The peace was opposed too by those, again like Ralegh, who genuinely wanted to found English colonies in South or North America, none having up to this date succeeded.

James' main fault in foreign relations was an exaggerated idea of what he could get by diplomatic bargaining in relation to England's actual strength. This was especially true of his plans for a marriage alliance with the great house of Habsburg, the rulers both of Austria and the Holy Roman Empire, and of the Spanish empire, which included most of South America and the West Indies as well as much of Italy and the southern Netherlands (modern Belgium). In this situation a state of acute tension arose on the outbreak of what was to become a long and general war in Europe, the Thirty Years War (1618–48). Roughly speaking, James hoped that if England stayed out of it, he would be able to keep Spain out; if England did not come to the support of the protestant (especially the Calvinist) princes of Germany or of the independent northern Netherlands, then Spain would not come in on the catholic side in alliance with the other, Austrian Habsburgs. This meant that James did not go to the aid of his son-in-law, Frederick when he lost the kingdom of Bohemia, shortly after rashly accepting it from the local nobility (who were in revolt against the centralising, pro-German and anti-Czech policy of the Emperor, as well as against his militantly counter-reformation religious policy). As a result of his intervention Frederick subsequently also lost his own territory, the Palatinate, which was invaded by Spanish forces. In the early 1620s the war became more general. Fighting was also resumed between Spain and the Netherlands after a twelve-years' truce from 1609, and soon Denmark came in on the side of the German protestants. Despite this, the whole of the Palatinate was conquered and occupied, and the Danes were defeated.

Except against the Dutch, the armies of the counter-reformation were everywhere victorious. The very existence of European protestantism seemed to be threatened; and in England there was a mounting demand for intervention, very similar to the demand in the 1570s and 1580s that Elizabeth should do more to help the Netherlands in their struggle for independence against Spain. The situation was complicated by another factor. In the early years of James' reign, under the great King Henry IV, France acted as an effective counter to Spain in the European balance of power. This was not true from Henry's assassination in 1610 until Louis XIII's coming of age and the establishment of Cardinal Richelieu as his chief minister in 1624. Since the domestic condition of France was too disordered for her to counter-balance Spain effectively during this interval, more of an onus rested on England to resist Spain, that is if Habsburg power was to be resisted at all. James was eventually persuaded that he should help his son-in-law and the protestants in Germany with money and 'volunteers' (again this kind of 'cold war' situation is not something new in our own century). The House of Commons on the other hand wanted a maritime and colonial war against Spain, and were much less enthusiastic about intervention in Germany. They also insisted on discussing these problems of foreign policy and military strategy,

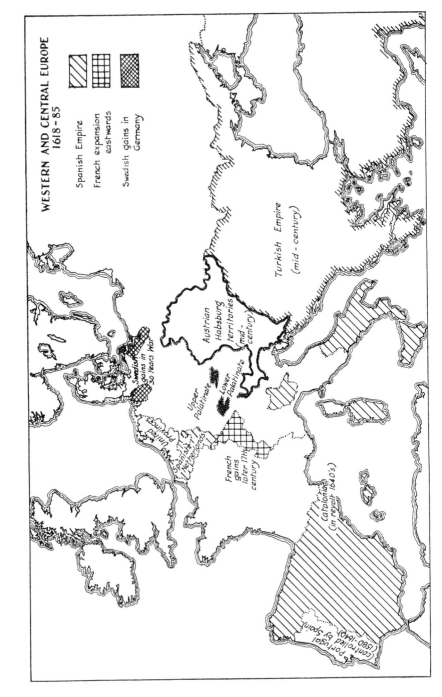

WESTERN AND CENTRAL EUROPE
1618–85

Spanish Empire

French expansion eastwards

Swedish gains in Germany

Turkish Empire
(mid-century)

Austrian
Habsburg
Territories
(mid-century)

Upper
Palatinate

Lower
Palatinate

Swedish
gains in
30 Years War

United
Provinces

Spanish
Netherlands

French gains
later 17th century

Catalonia
(in revolt 1640's)

Portugal
(controlled by Spain)
(1580-1640)

which had previously been a matter only for the King or Queen and the Council. However parliament's willingness to vote the extra taxes needed once a policy of intervention had been decided on, might involve giving way here, remedying some of their other grievances, or possibly both.

James' Last Parliaments

The 1621 Parliament, the first effective one for over ten years, voted sufficient money for only very limited intervention in Europe, and made it clear that they would not vote more until a number of grievances had been remedied. On some issues, the King, advised by his favourite Buckingham, gave way. The worst of the monopolies were disowned, some of the 'projectors' were sacrificed, and a Bill was framed against monopolies in general. Various measures of administrative reform were not resisted, some even being supported by the government's spokesmen in the House. The attack on Lord Chancellor Bacon was allowed to proceed; indeed the King expressed himself deeply shocked at the way in which Bacon had accepted presents or bribes, and supported the proceedings against him. But on other matters there was complete deadlock. The King's continued pro-Spanish foreign policy had led to a deepening suspicion that he was following a pro-catholic policy at home too. The Commons particularly disliked what they believed to be the over-lenient way in which recusants were being treated and the lax enforcement of the penal laws against catholics. Against the continental background—the mounting challenge of the counter-reformation, backed by the armed might of Spain—this attitude was less unreasoning and intolerant than it may seem to us today.

Then there was the issue of 'free speech'. This idea goes back to parliament's origins, in the Middle Ages, as a part of the King's Court and Council. Members, like judges or other people within the royal Court, had a special 'liberty' from ordinary processes of law while carrying out their duties and a special right, indeed an obligation, to advise the King freely and honestly. Privilege of M.P.s and free speech in parliament had been a frequent source of trouble between Crown and Parliament under the Tudors, with the Commons generally widening the scope of both. In fact

Members were quite often arrested after a parliament had been dissolved, for what they had said in it. But arrest during a session, for anything less than treason or some other serious crime, was agreed to be a breach of privilege. Between two sessions of a parliament, the position was less clear. In theory two separate questions, in practice free speech and privilege tended to go together. The Crown's strongest critics in the Commons were particularly keen to widen parliamentary privilege, sometimes for discreditable reasons (to escape ordinary legal proceedings against themselves) but mainly to serve the constitutional principle of free speech. In 1621 foreign affairs were linked to discussion of religion and supply; this came to the fore at the end of the first session in the spring, and again in the second session at the end of the year. And it was on these issues that the Parliament was dissolved by the King— and a page of protest torn from its Journals by his own hand— without a single Act having become law, except for a small grant of money at the beginning.

The Parliament of 1624, the last of James' reign, was preceded by an abrupt switch in foreign policy. In 1623 the attempt to bring about a Spanish marriage alliance reached its absurd, even fantastic climax, with an unofficial, impromptu trip across Europe by Prince Charles—the suitor for the hand of the Spanish princess—accompanied by Buckingham. They galloped through France incognito, complete with false beards, and arrived at the Spanish Court, only to find that they were the victims of Spanish diplomatic finesse. They had to cool their heels in Madrid, and Charles could not even speak to the girl he had come to marry. The Spaniards, who had perhaps never taken the marriage project seriously, had totally out-manoeuvred them, and the King's misgivings about this wild trip were well justified. Though he got his favourite and his son back safely, the whole adventure was a humiliating fiasco. As a result of this, Charles and Buckingham—two proud and hot-headed young men—were violently disillusioned with Spain and swung strongly in the opposite direction, in favour of active intervention against her. James, who was a man of peace and fancied himself as the great arbiter of Europe holding the balance between its warring factions, was bullied into reluctant agreement.

So the final Parliament of his reign met in an atmosphere where the Court party had been converted to the foreign policy of the opposition, and there was a measure of agreement between Crown and Parliament. This should not make us miss the point that Parliament was still gaining ground. This time the Act against monopolies did reach the statute book; it was the first substantial limitation on the royal prerogative during the century. In addition foreign policy was discussed freely, with the King making no serious attempt to prevent it; the money voted was tied to specific expenditure, and the House of Commons even appointed people to see that the taxes were spent for the right purposes. Administrative reform was an issue again. This was related to an attack which had been brewing against Lord Treasurer Cranfield (now Earl of Middlesex). He was unpopular because his financial reforms had affected the interests of many people at Court and in the government; he had also got a bad name in the country for corruption—certainly he had behaved high-handedly and had made large personal profits while in office. Cranfield stood for a policy of economy in government spending which was incompatible with an active foreign policy, let alone intervention in the war, to which Charles and Buckingham had now become converted. So they encouraged the Commons to proceed with his impeachment (that is he was charged by the Commons before the House of Lords sitting as judges on him). In practice Cranfield was made the scapegoat for various abuses and unpopular features of government policy; as with Bacon, many of the charges against him could have been brought against almost any statesman of the time.

Parliament and the King accepted the principle of indirect intervention in Germany and of a maritime war against Spain. Negotiations were begun for a royal marriage alliance with France instead of Spain. The King and the Prince both promised Parliament that catholic worship would only be allowed for the Princess and her household staff, whereas the Spaniards had always held out for a general toleration of catholics. In fact the French marriage treaty did include a secret clause promising toleration for all English catholics. Thus James and Charles practised a deliberate deceit; yet since this clause was never implemented, their pledge to the French was also broken. The apparent harmony between Crown and Commons in 1624 should not disguise the fact that Parliament was still asserting itself more and more. But it did provide a slightly more hopeful background to the new reign.

Charles I's Early Parliaments

In some ways there was as marked a contrast in personality between James and Charles as there had been between Elizabeth and James twenty odd years earlier. Unlike his father Charles I was not a scholar, still less an intellectual. At first entirely overshadowed by his elder brother, he had had a difficult and unhappy childhood, with physical handicaps which the state of medical knowledge at the time did nothing to reduce; perhaps the rigidity and the weaknesses in his character, the fact that he was a difficult man to deal with, can be explained in psychological terms. Certainly he was less of a theorist than his father, but in some ways he was more rigid in his ideas. Basically he was not a man of strong character, and he needed to lean on other people; nor was he a good negotiator, not being flexible enough in outlook or reliable when he had agreed to a compromise. However these features of Charles' character were not widely known in 1625, so his reign started reasonably well.

In the first Parliament there was increasing criticism of the mismanagement of the war, the misuse of the money that had been raised and the misconduct of military and naval operations. This was inevitably aimed at Buckingham, who as Lord Admiral was in charge of the Navy. This Parliament also saw disputes about the size of the money grant that should be voted, and its allocation, and about the customs duties; the House of Commons, or many of its members, had still not really accepted the legality of the Impositions. Their mistrust of Buckingham meant in fact mistrust of the King, although for some time they did not express this; indeed many Members would not even allow themselves to see it. But as a kind of gesture to express these feelings and their resentment over the Impositions, they refused to vote the King that branch of the traditional customs duties known as 'Tonnage and Poundage'. Since the late fifteenth century these had been voted to successive sovereigns for life, in the first Parliament of each reign—James had got them for life in 1604. Instead they voted them to Charles for one year only; this was a clear and deliberate blow, and he took it as a personal slight.

The other important issue which emerged in this Parliament was a renewed religious conflict. The House of Commons not merely criticised excessive leniency in the Crown's treatment of the catholics, but now also attacked the new High Church party within the Church of England, the group known to history as the Arminians. They are so named after a Dutch theologian, some of whose theoretical ideas they took over, but they are important in their own right as a group in the Church of England and for their part in political and religious disputes. They were attacked in the Commons for their allegedly catholic leanings in matters of doctrine and liturgy (the forms of church services). In doctrine their worst offence was their questioning of the doctrine of 'predestination'. The Arminians' emphasis on priests' vestments, church ornaments and elaborate ritual in services symbolised their inner leaning back towards catholicism. In general they put more emphasis on the role of the priesthood and of the sacraments, less on prayer and sermons than the Puritans and the 'Low-Church' Anglicans. Few protestants could grasp that the Arminians were catholic, without being Roman or 'popish', though they included a few—as we should say—'fellow travellers' with Rome. They were the spiritual ancestors of the modern Anglo-Catholic party in the Church of England, though most Anglicans were later to accept some of their practices and beliefs. The Arminians' unpopularity was only an aspect of the fear and hatred aroused by popery, which as we have seen had some rational grounds but were swollen and inflamed by an element of mass hysteria. Their political views intensified their unpopularity. Some Arminians exalted royal power and prerogative in their sermons and writings, magnifying the powers of the king as against the traditional laws of the land and the place of parliament. Even so, despite these disputes, Charles probably made a tactical mistake in dissolving his first Parliament so quickly, since none of his later ones were potentially so tractable.

In the second Parliament of his reign (in 1626) the King's financial needs were correspondingly greater, since the war was being

conducted on a larger scale. There had been a completely unsuccessful expedition against Cadiz in south-western Spain, and this
led to a direct attack on the favourite. The King had used his prerogative before the session began to try to remove the active
leaders of opposition in the Commons by making them sheriffs,
which meant that they had to be resident in their counties and so
could not be Members of Parliament. But as a result, the most
responsible leaders who had been conducting business in the House
in the previous session were removed and leadership passed to
more extreme and less experienced men, in particular to a fiery,
eloquent Cornish knight with a bad sense of tactics, Sir John Eliot.
The King's position was also weakened by a split in the House of
Lords; an anti-Buckingham party had emerged, including the head
of the Howard family the Earl of Arundel, and the ex-ambassador
in Madrid, the Earl of Bristol, whom Buckingham tried to make a
scapegoat for the Spanish marriage fiasco in 1623. Again Charles
failed to get either his vote of Tonnage and Poundage (even for one
year this time) or a parliamentary subsidy. Instead the Commons,
led by Eliot, proceeded to try to impeach Buckingham himself—the
very weapon he and Charles had so complacently encouraged them
to use against the unfortunate Cranfield in 1624, when even James
had warned them of the dangers of such a precedent. It was this direct
attack on his favourite and principal adviser which led to Charles
dissolving his second Parliament, again without anything—except
ill will—having come of it. It is probably true that there was an
element of suspicion and ignorance on both sides which better
liaison might have dispelled; the Commons were unnecessarily
suspicious of the King's foreign policy, and the King did little to
take them into his confidence.

Between this Parliament and the next which followed it two
years later, there were several important developments. The first
was the levying of a forced loan on a larger scale than had ever
yet been achieved; it was equivalent to several subsidies. But this
was raised at the cost of over seventy members of the gentry being
jailed for refusing to contribute. As a result, Sir Thomas Darnel
and four other knights, who had been so imprisoned, brought an
action at common law against the Crown for arbitrary arrest;

their counsel demanded that a writ of habeas corpus should be issued, that is a summons for their appearance in court, to be charged with a specific offence, and that otherwise they should be released. This, like Bate's case in 1606, is one of the most famous legal disputes involving constitutional principles in the early Stuart period. The 'Five Knights' lost their case. As with Bate and his cargo of currants, the Judges found for the Crown, but the opposition's views had been given a good airing.

Then there were developments arising out of the actual conduct of the war. The overseas expeditions, and the preparations for more such ventures, meant that troops were billeted on a large scale on ordinary families in parts of the south of England, and martial law had to be imposed, because the discipline of the troops and the seamen, whose pay was often heavily in arrears, was so bad. The fleet which had put to sea in 1626 was in such a bad state that when a wind blew up, it was shattered and had to put back to port, and no expedition could be undertaken that year. At the same time, by an almost incredible degree of ineptitude in foreign policy, Buckingham and the King, while they were still at war with Spain, had become simultaneously involved in war with France. This had arisen out of a series of disputes, including a trivial quarrel between Buckingham and the Queen Mother of France who had rejected his advances! The English claim to search French neutral shipping in the Channel was more serious (this issue was to cause trouble between Britain and neutrals in most of the wars we were engaged in for the next three hundred years). England was now aligned on the side of the French protestant minority, the Huguenots, who were holding out against the French Crown in the western port of La Rochelle. And in this respect, the French war appealed to the militant protestants in the House of Commons. Yet in terms of the European balance of power, or of helping the protestants in Germany and the Netherlands against the forces of the Habsburgs and the counter-reformation, it was madness for England to dissipate her energies in a war against France, which was potentially the only real counter to Spain.

The Commons would probably have accepted this switch of foreign policy, if a successful blow had been struck to help the

French protestants. But the expedition that was mounted in 1627 to the Isle of Rhé off La Rochelle, though on a larger scale than that against Cadiz two years before, was an even bigger failure. There was a general feeling of national humiliation; people compared it to the loss of Calais in 1558. The other development was the continued collection of customs duties that were illegal in the eyes of the Commons. The Tonnage and Poundage dues having been voted for one year only in 1625, from 1626 on the King was collecting them without constitutional authority, while the Impositions were still queried by many Members, although they had been collected since the early years of James' reign. However Buckingham and other Councillors advised the King not to continue this course of rule without parliament, but to go back to a more conciliatory policy; this is the background to Charles' third Parliament which met in 1628.

The Crisis of 1628–9

As in 1624, at first there was a slightly more conciliatory atmosphere. The Commons were under the leadership of Sir Thomas Wentworth, a very practical man, concerned to root out failures and abuses in the royal government but not to attack the King's powers. He was a member of the Yorkshire gentry, a wealthy landowner, who had already twice offered his services to the Crown but had been excluded by Charles from the previous Parliament and had actually been in prison briefly for refusing the forced loan. Their other leader was Sir Edward Coke, the elderly champion of the common law, who was obsessed by the need to find legal and historic precedents for political actions. The House framed a Bill of Rights against the grievances of non-parliamentary taxation, arbitrary arrest and imprisonment, billeting of troops and martial law, but it became clear that quite apart from the King, the House of Lords would not pass this into law. So the Commons, still under the leadership of Coke and Wentworth, changed their tactics and framed a Petition of Right, designed not to make new laws, but to state what the existing law was, and to get the King's agreement that it should be observed. Success in winning support for the Petition from the Lords made it extremely difficult for the King to refuse his assent. While the Petition was going forward, the Commons refrained from renewing their attack on Buckingham, and they voted five subsidies, which although inadequate and scarcely more than the forced loan had raised, was none the less the largest sum they had voted since the end of Elizabeth's reign. They still did not face the fact that the sort of war that they wanted—effective measures against Spain and to restore Frederick to the Palatinate—would require very much larger supplies than this. Suspicion that the money would be mis-spent as long as Buckingham was at the head of the government, and resentment at the King's delays and hedging over the Petition of Right, brought this moderation and restraint to an abrupt end. Eliot and Coke led a violent attack on Buckingham's policies and on the favourite personally, and there was a renewed attack on the Arminians and their continued promotion in the church. Satisfaction on these issues was virtually made a condition of Tonnage and Poundage being voted. At this point, in the middle of the summer of 1628, the House of Commons began to move ahead of the House of Lords in the lengths to which they were carrying their opposition to the Crown; the King chose a strategic moment to adjourn this Parliament, but—recognising perhaps its earlier moderation—he did not yet dissolve it.

Between the first and second sessions of this third Parliament of Charles I there were several developments which had important effects in the years to come. In August Buckingham was murdered by a disappointed unemployed officer, who had persuaded himself that it was his mission to rid the kingdom of this pest. This brought to an end the rule of a single faction in the King's government and at Court. The government was once more divided between cliques or factions, jockeying for control and acting as rivals for the King's favour, for no one man ever again had the undisputed control which Buckingham had enjoyed in the last years of James' and the first years of Charles' reigns. This inevitably brought the King himself more to the forefront; he had his favourite advisers, ministers he relied on more than others, but never one with the same combination of personal and political ascendancy as Buckingham.

In this situation new leaders rapidly emerged as the dominant faction in the Council. Their immediate importance is that they favoured a reversal of the country's foreign policy, back to a pro-Spanish policy, such as had been followed earlier in James' reign; some of this group were secret Roman Catholics or at least catholic sympathisers. Meanwhile Wentworth, disillusioned with the more extreme features of the Commons' attack on the Crown, had accepted a peerage. Shortly after the death of Buckingham he entered the government, taking charge of the King's affairs in the north of England as President of the Council at York. In France the port of La Rochelle, the last major stronghold of the Huguenot rebels, fell to Richelieu and the royal army. This meant the end, for practical purposes, of the English attempt to intervene in the French civil war and paved the way for restoring peace with France. During these months a number of merchants conducted a campaign of resistance to the payment of Tonnage and Poundage, and in some cases to that of Impositions too. As we shall see, this was complicated by the fact that one or two of those involved were also M.P.s in the Parliament which was still in being. Another noteworthy feature of these months is that Charles continued to promote Arminians in the church; this may look like deliberate provocation of the Puritans and other protestants, but it was probably due more to insensitiveness towards public opinion than to calculated defiance of it. However it was now made abundantly clear that these High-Churchmen had the direct personal backing of the King. The crucial appointment was that of William Laud, to be Bishop of London. He was less of an Arminian in doctrine, but in full agreement with them in matters of discipline and ritual, and shared their views of the church's political function. Since Archbishop Abbot was out of favour, this was the key position in the church.

In the 1629 session of Parliament Charles tried to get his grant of Tonnage and Poundage. But the surviving records make it perfectly clear that he was determined these duties should go on being collected whether they were voted by parliament or not. The position was slightly different with the Impositions. They continued to be queried by some Members of Parliament, but the King preferred to levy them by prerogative (backed with legal precedent) rather than to seek parliamentary authority for doing so. There was a continuous battle over these issues. There was a renewed and still sharper attack on the Arminians, and now there was also a new issue—that of parliamentary privilege. This arose because those M.P.s who had refused to pay Customs duties had had their goods confiscated by the King's officers. Eliot and others claimed that even between sessions this was a breach of privilege. At the same time the King's new chief minister, Lord Treasurer Weston (later created Earl of Portland), was attacked, as epitomising the pro-Spanish, pro-catholic and arbitrary tendencies which the House saw in the King's policies.

Rumours that the King would adjourn or suddenly dissolve the Parliament, led to a plan by Eliot and several other Members to pass a series of resolutions before the King could end the sitting. This led to the famous, if disorderly, scene on the 2nd March when the Speaker, who wanted to obey the King's orders and stop the proceedings of the House, was forcibly held in his chair by two of Eliot's younger and more stalwart supporters. The three resolutions drafted by Eliot a day or two earlier were put to the House and carried. One of these was against Arminianism, equating it with crypto-popery and indeed with treason; the other two were against the levying and the payment of Tonnage and Poundage without parliamentary authority. This too was equated with treason, which at this date was technically—as it still is theoretically, according to English law—against the sovereign and not against the state or the country in general. This made it all rather unreal, and depended on the firmly held fiction that it was not the King who was doing wrong but only his evil Councillors. These resolutions had no constitutional validity; they were not 'Acts' of Parliament, but simply expressions of the Commons' views. They alienated a number of moderates in Parliament and in the country; they were not in any way approved of by the House of Lords. Eliot's plan may have been a tactical error, and it certainly gave the King his chance. Charles dissolved Parliament, while many people felt, if not that he had been hard done by, at least that the militant wing of the opposition had behaved unreasonably.

The after effects of this dissolution are important, in order to

F

understand what happened in the next ten years. The King issued a proclamation, making it clear that he would not call another parliament at all until he felt that the House of Commons had come to its senses, that is until the Members had come round to his way of thinking. Rumours that another parliament was to be called, circulated from time to time in the years 1629–34, although in a second proclamation issued soon after the dissolution Charles made it an offence even to repeat such reports. By 1636 or 1637 it was clear that the King would only call another parliament if and when he was compelled by financial necessity; it was also clear by then, that when parliament did assemble, there would be a day of reckoning compared with which 1621 or 1628 would be quite tame.

Eliot and his associates were proceeded against by the ordinary process of law. The judges again on the whole acted on the King's behalf, finding for instance that parliamentary privilege did not cover the plan which had culminated in the scene on March 2nd. Refusing to submit and beg the King's pardon, Eliot died in prison in 1632. Wentworth and others had already gone over to the King, Coke died of old age. These changes meant that another less well known man, who had acquired much useful experience in the 1620s, was the natural leader of the parliamentary opposition when the House eventually did re-assemble many years later. This was a Somerset gentleman with government experience in the Exchequer, John Pym. The resistance to payment of customs duties which some merchants had tried to stage quickly collapsed. Again the judges supported the Crown, and faced with the possibility of not trading at all, or else trading on the King's terms, the merchants chose the latter. Not merely were the customs duties collected, but there was a partial commercial recovery. Soon after— peace being made with Spain (1630) as well as France—there was a minor trade boom, and the amount of revenue which the King got from the customs rose to a higher level than ever before.

Historians have argued as to whether or not, towards the end of the 1620s and particularly in 1628–9, Parliament was 'bidding for sovereignty'. That is, whether it was trying to alter the balance of political power in the country, to wrest decisive control from the Crown. Charles' third Parliament can be portrayed as an aggressive, offensive body, and this view of it has been taken by some recent historians. On the other hand, the Petition of Right is an extremely moderate document. The subsequent dispute about whether or not the King's levying of Tonnage and Poundage and the Impositions, and his other methods of raising money in the years which followed, constituted a breach of the Petition's condemnation of non-parliamentary taxation, does not alter its essentially conservative character. Indeed at this time the great majority, if not all of the King's opponents in the Commons, almost certainly still thought of themselves as upholding what they believed to be the ancient, balanced constitution of England, against the King's encroachments in the direction of arbitrary government. In this they believed that he was being misled by his advisers, rather than being personally at fault. Because looking back, we can see that they were to a large extent deceiving themselves about Charles, and because it is very doubtful how far this mixed or balanced constitution had ever in fact existed, this does not detract from their sincerity. Nor does it disprove that their intention was conservative, even if the King's reactions were forcing them to move in the direction of radical, perhaps revolutionary measures. Only in reaction to the King's attitude, to the suspicion which was generated by his policies, his reliance first on Buckingham and then on the revived pro-Spanish faction in the Council, did the Commons become more aggressive over religion, more reluctant to vote taxes and readier to attack the collection of money which they had not voted. Their attitude towards royal ministers was still only negative: they claimed the right to impeach those whom they thought were misleading the King, but they did not yet claim a veto on whom the King should employ. On the other hand, if we take the sequence of parliaments from 1621 to 1629, although they were not all equally difficult from the King's point of view, each one seems in a different way to assert its position a little more than the one before. In terms of the politics of the Court, the death of Buckingham marks a dividing line; in the affairs of the nation, the dissolution of Charles I's third Parliament provides a point at which to pause.

3 : The Personal Rule of Charles I (1629–40)

THE first point to notice about the personal government of Charles I, sometimes called the 'eleven years' tyranny', is that the King's rule without parliament was in itself only of limited significance. As we have seen, King James had gone without a parliament from 1610 to 1614 and again from 1614 to 1621. An interval of over seven years under Cardinal Wolsey early in Henry VIII's reign was the longest recorded break between meetings since parliament had become a recognised institution of government in the late thirteenth–early fourteenth century. The eleven years' interval was in particularly sharp contrast to the period of frequent Parliaments in 1621–9. Otherwise it is important to remember that the government of the country was carried on as before, by the King and his Council, the usual machinery of the law and the revenue courts, and the various conciliar courts at the centre and in the provinces. The ordinary system of local government continued to work as before, and was not affected merely by the absence of parliament. We need to look more closely at several other features of the Personal Rule in order to understand what it was like.

Divisions in the Government

First of all, within the government, as a result of the removal of Buckingham, there was a revival of factional politics—that is, the rivalry of individuals and groups, such as we saw particularly in the middle years of James' reign. The difference here is that some of the individuals are rather more worthy protagonists, standing for different policies as well as for personal and group interests.

The first phase can be said to extend from 1628 to 1634, and is marked by the ascendancy in the King's counsels of Lord Treasurer Weston. He had himself made his way to the top as a client of the

Duke of Buckingham. But soon after the death of his patron, Weston reversed Buckingham's foreign policy and became the leader of the pro-Spanish group; associated with him, though not a close friend, was the Earl of Arundel, head of the Howard family which had a traditional pro-Spanish bias going back at least to the beginning of the century. In his early years as Lord Treasurer Weston did achieve some limited success in raising the King's revenues, but more in reducing expenditure. He was of course helped here by the restoration of peace, first with France and then with Spain. Weston was vulnerable to attack firstly because he was personally corrupt, though not perhaps on quite the same shameless scale as Lord Treasurer Suffolk in 1614–18; secondly because he was a secret Roman Catholic sympathiser—he declared himself a catholic openly only on his deathbed. He was most closely associated in the Council with Francis Cottington, the Chancellor of the Exchequer whom he had promoted, just as Buckingham had promoted him. Cottington had begun his official career as a junior diplomat in Spain and was not only pro-Spanish in politics, but was also attracted to the Spanish way of life in general. In the last years of Lord Treasurer Weston's life Cottington clearly was hoping to succeed him; how much Weston tried to ensure this happening is less clear. These two were later joined by Francis Windebank, who became Secretary of State in 1632; he had originated as a client of Laud, but by 1634–5 was switching his allegiance to Cottington, or so it seemed to his previous patron.

Then there was the great partnership of William Laud, the Bishop of London, who was made Archbishop of Canterbury in 1633, and Thomas Wentworth, the Lord President of the Council in the North, who was appointed the King's representative in Ireland as Lord Deputy in 1632, and took up this post in 1633. He was created Earl of Strafford in 1640. Their friendship was taking shape by 1630 and was a firm alliance by 1632–3. In the later 1630s Laud was the King's most important single minister, but he was never really 'prime minister' (a term which only began to be used—and then always in a derogatory sense—late in the century), in the way that, say, Robert Cecil had been under James, or that, as we shall see, Clarendon and then Danby were to be under Charles II.

Laud did not hold any of the great lay offices of state, though he was a Privy Councillor and on most of the important Council committees. Nor did he ever have a monopoly of royal patronage of appointments in the government. In short, Charles I's government during these years was never that of a single faction. Weston predominated at first, then Laud. Wentworth was less effective, as a partner in the Council and at Court, than he might have been with his great abilities and strength of character, because he was largely absent from the centre of affairs—first at York and then in Ireland.

In their general attitude towards the government of the country, Laud and Wentworth had a policy which was not fully shared by the King himself. A confusion is made in a number of books which equate the policy of Laud and Wentworth with that of Charles and his régime. In their letters to each other these two refer to their belief in 'Thorough'. By this they meant a higher standard of honesty and efficiency, and sometimes a greater degree of ruthlessness, in order to put the King's affairs on a sounder footing; certainly it implied a tougher line with critics and opponents of the Crown. Thorough related to the means necessary to achieve a 'clean-up' of the machinery and personnel of government, more than to their ultimate objectives. In long-term aims the champions of Thorough were probably nearer to Charles than they were in the matter of means. Charles' trouble was that he willed the end without always willing the means to achieve it; he wanted to be an absolute ruler without all the bother and unpleasantness involved. This was to be disastrous for him, but perhaps the country had reason to be thankful for it.

Then there was the group at Court centred on the Queen, Henrietta Maria, the French princess whom Charles had married in 1625. She became much more influential politically after the death of Buckingham; this was because her personal relations with her husband were greatly improved. They came to be a very devoted married couple, but unfortunately Charles, again like his father, was not able to separate his private affections from his political judgments, and the group of courtiers round the Queen became one of the most influential elements in the Court and government. Both directly and through them the Queen on the whole exercised a baneful political influence on the King. She instinctively preferred absolutist to constitutional methods, and she caused many people to associate the Crown with the catholic cause. The friends and favourites of Charles and Henrietta were for the most part a more respectable lot than under James. There was not the same disreputable moral tone to Charles' Court, but on the other hand many of their favourites were equally parasitical and unpopular in the country, and were associated with some of the most vicious and detested features of Charles' régime.

Although they occupied a rather uneasy place in it, there were still some old-fashioned protestants in Charles' government. Such men had in most cases begun their political careers under James, some even under Elizabeth; they supported a strong royal government, but were not in favour of absolute monarchy, 'Thorough', or any signs of a pro-catholic or pro-Spanish policy. There were also several peers in the government, who held positions on the Council but were not active members of the administration. They were relatively detached from royal policies and often cool towards some of their colleagues. Again these men included some who had formed the opposition first to Carr and the Howards, then to Buckingham, in the 1610s and 1620s.

Thus it is quite impossible to equate the King's government or its policies with Thorough, as personified by Laud and Wentworth. If these two men had had anything like complete control of the government for ten or even for five years, if they had enjoyed the unqualified support of the King, the story of England then and in the years which followed would have been very different. It is at least possible that one, or both of them together, would have succeeded in erecting an English version of the type of despotism which Richelieu was creating in these very years for the monarchy in France. For example, neither of them had direct and continuous control over the King's finances and the means used to raise money, or over the conduct of foreign affairs.

We must now turn to the other aspects of Charles' Personal Rule which help to explain its nature and also help to explain the causes of its downfall.

Finance

This must be related to the chronic inadequacy of the Crown's ordinary revenues. The King was still unable to 'live of his own', even in peacetime, and his financial measures were aimed at overcoming this difficulty, since after 1629 he was determined not to have to seek parliament's aid. This was achieved primarily by extending the customs duties beyond even the New Impositions achieved under Salisbury. A further duty was brought in which became known as the 'new New Impositions'; there were revised rates on the goods already dutiable; there were extra duties on particular products, both on those exported outside the country and on some shipped round the coasts. (One such was the very important coal trade between Newcastle and London, this fuel mainly being used domestically, to keep the Londoners warm, and not for industrial purposes.) In addition, the rents payable by the 'farmers', those business syndicates who managed the older branches of the Customs for the King, were greatly increased in the later 1630s. This was less sensational than Charles' other financial measures, but in terms of hard cash—and sound credit—it was more important.

One of the most notorious means used to raise money was the hunting up of ancient, medieval precedents for extra feudal rights by which the King could raise money in the form of taxes or capital levies. Thus technically all gentlemen worth £40 p.a. or above in freehold land were supposed to be knighted at the King's coronation if they were not so already. This was quite archaic and unreal, and had not been operative for a long time. It was suddenly enforced in the early 1630s, and the equivalent of more than two parliamentary subsidies raised from the gentry by these 'compositions for knighthood', or fines for having failed to come forward to be knighted back in 1626. Then there was a campaign connected with the administration of the royal forests to prove that large numbers of landowners had encroached on their boundaries. Going right back to the reign of Edward I over three hundred years before, the King's lawyers found out what the boundaries of the forests should have been, and then fined all those who had allegedly encroached on them. A number of other small additional taxes belong more or less in this category. With the possible exception of the knighthood fines, the unpopularity incurred was out of proportion to the financial results achieved.

There was a more systematic attempt than under James to use economic 'controls' over particular industries, and various types of monopoly as revenue-raising devices. Technically these got round the Monopolies Act of 1624 by being granted to companies rather than to individuals; that exception had been made in the Act to preserve the rights of the monopoly trading companies and the interests of the City of London. Even measures for administrative reform were, by the taking of 'compositions' from offenders, turned into a means of getting in a little extra money. Some of these controls and monopolies constituted a double, even a triple grievance. There was the actual burden of additional taxation, fees or licence charges; some were also a positive inhibition on economic enterprise in town and country, for they included controls over urban and rural building and the iron industry, besides an older one over the manufacture of cloth exercised by officials called Aulnagers. Monopolies in the actual production of some goods—that for making soap being the most notorious—hit people as consumers in two ways: they had, or said they had, to pay more for less satisfactory products, and the grievance was intensified by the fact that the monopolists and others involved in these projects made far more out of them than the Crown did. It was a very uneconomical way of raising money, considering the amount of hostility it aroused.

Besides the Customs, some of the King's other existing, legitimate revenues were used more efficiently to bring in a larger yield. The revenues of the Court of Wards were very strikingly increased; its net yield to the Crown doubled in the last fifteen years of its effective existence, that is between the mid-1620s and 1640. There was also an attempt to use fines in the law courts, especially in Star Chamber, for political purposes, and to raise revenue. The amount achieved here too was insignificant, but brought great resentment. An outrageously heavy fine of £70,000 (later cut to a composition of £12,000) was imposed on the City of London for allegedly failing

to carry out their obligations for the colonisation of London-
derry in northern Ireland, for which it had been granted a charter
in the reign of James. As we shall see, this was a part of the rather
complicated story of Ireland's place in English seventeenth-century
history.

Despite the unpopularity incurred by these measures and the
limited success of some, taken as a whole they did improve the
Crown's financial position. So did Portland's campaign to reduce
royal spending and his determination to preserve peace. If we compare the early 1630s with the position by 1639–40, ordinary royal
revenues had been raised by over 40 per cent., possibly by nearer
50 per cent., from just over £600,000 to nearer £900,000 a year. But
this was still not enough. The economy drive achieved very little,
for example in the royal household. The subsidies which had been
granted in 1628 failed to pay for the war which had ended in
1629–30; they were used to pay off the debts incurred earlier
during the war. Even in the middle 1630s the King was still burdened with large debts; he had to go on borrowing in order to make
ends meet, and his finances came to depend on his ability to do so.
That is to say, he got to the point where he was borrowing money
partly to pay off his previous debts. As under James, the sale of
capital assets was another expedient. A great deal of land was sold
by the Crown in the first ten years of Charles' reign, but this was
ended when Archbishop Laud took temporary charge of royal
finance in 1635. The sale of titles and offices by the Crown was
stopped at the death of Buckingham, and only resumed when the
position became desperate again some ten years later. Outwardly
however the King's finances were in a healthier state by 1635, and
they continued to be until 1638.

Ship Money

The position seemed better than it really was partly because the
costs of the Navy were by this time being wholly borne by a new,
extraordinary tax. By 1636–8 Ship Money, the most notorious and
important financial device of the Personal Rule, looked as if it was
going to become permanent. There were good precedents from the
sixteenth century and even from James' reign for raising this levy

from the coastal towns and counties in time of war or obvious national emergency. When Charles started raising it to build a new fleet in 1634, some of his ministers were ready to argue that an emergency existed. They pointed to the naval strength of the Netherlands, France and Spain, the threats to English shipping arising from the war in Europe (in which England was by then a neutral) and to the fisheries round our coasts because of poaching by the Dutch fishing fleets, and also the defiance by foreign ships of the English King's historic claim to overlordship on the narrow seas round his country. They argued that all these factors fully justified the levying of Ship Money. But by 1636 the tax had been extended from the coastal areas to the whole country, and it was clearly becoming a regular form of revenue, even though the country was still at peace. The real issue was whether the King could raise this additional tax, on the grounds that he alone was the judge of what constituted a 'national emergency'. It was this issue which led to the third of the great early Stuart constitutional law cases—that of John Hampden.

Hampden had refused to pay the small amount of Ship Money for which he was assessed. He was a wealthy Buckinghamshire gentleman who had connections with many other members of the parliamentary opposition. He was not alone in refusing to pay, but the King chose to bring an action against him rather than against two of the peers, both Puritans, who had refused to pay and had advised their tenants to do the same. Hampden could be tried as a commoner in the ordinary courts, but they could only be tried before a special court composed of other peers. Before this, Charles had got the judges to approve in principle his Ship Money levy, once in 1635 and again in 1637. This technique of getting the judges to give theoretical verdicts in advance on doubtful legal issues, had been practised on occasions by other sovereigns including James, but it had always been unpopular. There was a strong tradition in English common law that the judges should decide particular cases on their merits as and when they were brought before them, and that they should not give general rulings in advance.

Hampden's case was eventually heard before all twelve of the common law judges. His leading counsel, Oliver St John, was a barrister who was also connected with the opposition groups by ties of family and friendship as well as political outlook. St John argued that, even though it was the King's prerogative to decide whether there was an emergency or not, in this particular instance (since Ship Money had first been raised in 1634 and was still being collected in 1637) there had been plenty of time for the King to call a parliament, and therefore he should have done so if he wanted extra taxes to meet such an emergency. If it were a matter of a sudden crisis of a few weeks, then he could raise money without parliament; but if it were of several years' duration, the case for this fell to the ground, because it was impossible to argue that he had not had time to call a parliament since 1634. St John did not deny that the King was the judge of whether or not an emergency existed; that is to say, in technical legal terms, he did what is called pleading a 'demurrer'—to admit the facts but to argue none the less that his client was in the right. On the King's side there were slightly varied arguments; in general it was maintained that the King had an absolute discretionary power in all matters relating to defence and the security of the kingdom; some of the King's counsel went further in the direction of exalting his prerogative in their arguments than others. This was also true of the judges giving their verdicts. Seven of them found for the King, five on moderate grounds but two on grounds which if translated into political fact would have given him absolute over-riding power, indeed complete, unchecked and despotic control over every aspect of the national life. Two of them, Croke and Hutton (whose names deserve to be remembered along with those of the better-known parliamentary champions in the constitutional struggle), found for Hampden. This was a bold thing to do, and it gave courage to three others to find in his favour on more technical grounds, for example that the summons had been to provide a ship or part of one, and not money to pay for ships. This meant that the final verdict was only seven to five—a very near thing. It was regarded by many people as a moral defeat for the King, and is generally held to have led to a decline in the standing of Charles' régime. However, in 1638 and even into 1639 Ship Money still continued to be collected over most of the country, though with greater difficulty than before. It was only in 1640 that there was a general break-down in its collection, due to an almost total refusal to pay; the nearest comparison with this is the 'tax-payers' strike' staged against Wolsey in the 1520s, when he tried to raise a large non-parliamentary tax, mis-called the Amicable Grant. But by 1640 there were many other influences at work to undermine the position of Charles and his government, besides the outcome of Hampden's case, and this is only one of several factors which help to account for the altered situation.

Foreign Affairs

In foreign policy, the activities of Charles I, like those of his father, appeared to many of his subjects as pro-Spanish and not in the country's best interests. Although the question of a marriage alliance was not at issue in these years (the future Charles II was only born in 1630), there was a return to the policy of trying to recover the Palatinate by diplomacy rather than by war for Frederick the King's brother-in-law, and then for his son and heir, Charles' nephew. The King entered into a series of tortuous diplomatic negotiations, which even included plans for an alliance with Spain to partition the Netherlands as the price of the Palatinate's restoration. But the European powers realised that Charles was not in a position to intervene on a large scale because of his desire to avoid calling parliament. He was thus in a weak bargaining position, since he could not offer to do as much as he wanted in return. Roughly speaking, from 1630 to 1637 the main leanings of the English government were pro-Spanish. Then there was an interval in 1637–8, when the policy of a French alignment was temporarily in the ascendant. This alliance nearly succeeded but again not quite, because Richelieu realised just as well as the Spaniards that Charles was not in a position to offer enough in return for what he wanted. Policy then swung back to being pro-Spanish, though despite the Ship Money building programme England could not prevent a Spanish fleet, which had taken shelter off the Kent coast, from being overwhelmed by the Dutch in 1639. The details of these manoeuvres are unimportant since their effects were negligible and did nothing to help the Palatinate or the European protestants in general, though a small volunteer army had been sent to Germany in the early 1630s.

Charles managed to avoid additional war expenditure, but he aroused a great deal of suspicion in the country. This was particularly so in relation to the progress of the war in Germany. The victories which the Habsburg and catholic forces won during the late 1620s culminated in the Edict of Restitution of 1629; by this lands which had belonged to the church before the Reformation were to be taken back from their lay owners and restored to the church. There was a real fear that Charles was thinking of doing much the same in England. This is an example of how people identified the constitutional and religious conflicts in England between Crown and Parliament, between Puritans and the church hierarchy, with the great ideological war which was raging on the Continent. The intervention of Gustavus Adolphus, the King of Sweden, in the early 1630s as the new champion of the protestant cause raised the morale of the militant protestants in England; Gustavus' death in battle (November 1632) was greatly mourned. By 1634–5 it was clear that the war was going to have an indecisive outcome. With the entry of France on the side of the Netherlands and the German protestants, it became much less of a straightforward religious conflict, and more of a struggle for power like earlier and later European wars. Most people did not see this at first; the role of France was not very clearly appreciated. And Charles continued to be criticised for not committing England to the protestant side, despite the fact that it was no longer a war of catholic versus protestant, since one of the two greatest catholic powers was now fighting in alliance with the German and Dutch Calvinists.

Charles I's government was seldom united on foreign policy. The possible alternative policies corresponded approximately to the rival factions in his government, as had often been the case under James, and even more so under Elizabeth. Weston, Cottington and their group can be thought of as pro-Spanish. One of the Secretaries of State favoured a general protestant alliance, but not at the cost of losing the King's favour, so he did little to implement it. At first favouring the anti-Richelieu faction inside France and so lacking much influence, the Queen's group aimed at a French alliance. The second Secretary, Windebank, veered between the first and third of these alternatives. Laud and Wentworth favoured English neutrality, at least non-belligerency; they were well disposed towards Spain, but they did not want a positive alliance involving entry into the war. Foreign policy was still perhaps seen by many people both in the government and in the country at large as more of a religious question than it actually was. The period from the Reformation to about 1630 is one when national conflicts in Europe correspond most closely to religious divisions; and although this was no longer true to the same extent, there was a time-lag before people of strong religious views realised this. Nor was it at first seen that the recovery of France under Richelieu was leading to a change in the whole European pattern, coinciding as it did with the decline of Spain which was hastened by the long war with the Netherlands and also from 1635 by the war with France. Spain's decline was accelerating and thus altering the whole balance of power. The independence of other countries would soon be threatened by France instead. Moreover the Dutch were already greater colonial and commercial rivals of England than the Spaniards were. James I had been pressed to make a firmer stand against them over English trading rights in the Far East: for Puritan merchants there was a real clash of interests here, between protestant unity and their pockets.

Religion: Laud and the Puritans

The religious developments in England during these years can almost be spelled out in the name of one man—William Laud. But here, unlike the case with 'Thorough' on the political side, he was closely backed by the King. Laud was less interested in the High Church doctrines of the Arminians—indeed he was prepared to ban some doctrinal debate in the church altogether—and more in questions of ceremony, ritual, organisation and church discipline. He defeated the bishops who opposed him, and the whole episcopal hierarchy became increasingly identified with his policies; this is especially true after he became Archbishop of Canterbury in place of Abbot in 1633. Laud conducted a campaign against the only other bishop of any standing, who represented middle-of-the-road Elizabethan protestantism but was a rather worldly man, John Williams, Bishop of Lincoln. He and Laud had been rivals in James' reign; Williams had actually been a senior member of the government in the early 1620s—yet another of Buckingham's clients who had been discarded by the favourite when it suited him. Laud harried him with a series of charges, some less ill-founded than others, and eventually Williams was imprisoned.

The first aspect of Laud's work which deserves notice here is his renewal of Bancroft's campaign for a better paid and educated, more obedient and orthodox clergy. The results were limited; only a very few laymen helped Laud by giving back church property, or by securing a larger yield for the clergy from tithes and other revenues. Many more were frightened off by the fear of a general campaign to recover church property, such as was proceeding in Germany and—as we shall see—the King was also attempting in Scotland and Wentworth in Ireland. This can be seen in conflicts over tithes, notably between the church and the City of London, which fought a successful delaying action to avoid having their tithes re-rated so that they would represent a genuine one-tenth of people's annual incomes. The Londoners and citizens of other towns preferred to keep the established clergy on short commons and to spend the money instead on 'lecturers' whom they could appoint, to deliver extra sermons, usually of a Puritan character. The system of advowsons, that is the right to appoint parsons to parish livings, was another source of trouble. This and the 'impropriation', or lay ownership of tithes, led to a clash between Laud and a group of Puritans who had a rival scheme to recover church property. They organised a syndicate called the 'Feoffees for Impropriations' who bought up tithes and livings which came on the market and then installed firm Puritans. Laud had their activities broken up by a series of legal charges in 1632–3; he was in favour of recovering church wealth but not in order to install Puritan ministers.

Laud made full use of all the disciplinary machinery of the church: archbishops' visitations, ecclesiastical courts, and at the centre the Court of High Commission, in order to impose this new orthodoxy. By doing so he greatly increased the unpopularity of these various institutions; anti-clericalism, or at least anti-ecclesiasticism, was intensified during these years. Perhaps more important still, not only among the clergy but also among laymen, middle-of-the-road protestants came to join the Puritans in opposition. Their disapproval of Laud's insistence on altars being raised and railed off at the east end of churches, and his other changes in the ordering of such matters, merged in their deeper fears of catholicism.

Neither Laud nor Charles I was a secret Roman Catholic, but both of them had illusions about the possibilities of reunion with the Church of Rome. They felt that the Papacy would be prepared to meet the Church of England halfway; Laud noted in his diary that he had been offered a cardinal's hat by an emissary from Rome, but had refused it 'till Rome be other than it is'. That in itself suggests that he did not make an unqualified refusal or rule out the possibility of some form of reunion at a future date. In this he was quite unrealistic about the terms that Rome would accept. It was also a disastrous miscalculation of the opposition, which was much stronger and more extensive than either Laud or Charles seems to have realised. In one way this was paradoxical. At Court the Roman Catholics were tolerated, enjoying immunity in the Queen's Household and at foreign embassies, while those in the country continued to be persecuted vigorously—the penal taxes on recusants were heavier than ever in these years. So that it was not in every way a pro-catholic policy, but it seemed like one, the more so since a few men in high office favoured greater leniency, and did what they could to stop the harrying of catholic priests. This looked especially suspicious in conjunction with the King's apparently pro-Spanish, anti-protestant foreign policy. Foreign and religious affairs are difficult to disentangle in these years; and they were not separated by most contemporaries.

The King's and Laud's religious policies also gave a new impetus to English colonisation overseas. Successful settlement on the east coast of North America had begun in the reign of James, with the foundation of Virginia in 1607. Although there was a religious element in this, it was mainly undertaken for other, more material

G

reasons. Some people wanted more land than they could acquire at home; others went from love of adventure, curiosity about the recently discovered new continents, hope of finding gold and silver mines as the Spaniards had done in Mexico and Peru. Then there were those who hoped for commercial profits, from exporting cloth and other English products to these colonies and bringing back goods which were not produced in this country. All this fitted in very well with the general economic ideas of the time. And, despite James I's dislike of the 'noxious weed', Virginia gradually began to show a profit through the production of tobacco. The colonial ventures of the 1620s and 1630s did not exclude such economic motives, but they had a much more clear-cut and definite religious aim, namely to get away from a Church of England to which many Puritan groups were increasingly opposed. Some who went to America were Separatists, a few of whom were already in exile in the Netherlands; these, the famous 'Pilgrim Fathers', founded the small colony of New Plymouth in the early 1620s, in order to separate completely from the Church of England and set up their own form of Puritan worship. Much more important is the foundation of the colony of Massachusetts Bay, at the end of the 1620s and in the early 1630s. This was the result of the emigration of a larger body of Puritans, who were not complete Separatists but wanted to reform the church—to take it over and set it in order—rather than to opt out of it altogether. Many thousands of people went to the various Puritan settlements in New England during the Personal Rule. But we must not overlook the fact that many thousands more, perhaps twice as many, went to the other English colonies of Virginia and the small West Indian islands; there was even a catholic 'refugee' colony established in Maryland.

Historians have argued a great deal about how important religion was in persuading people to emigrate in these years. Probably the majority went in hope of bettering their lot, namely for economic reasons, but a sufficiently dynamic minority went to the New England colonies largely for religious reasons, to give these colonies a distinctively Puritan character. This was to be very important in their subsequent relations with England, for they were always the pace-makers in asserting colonial rights against the

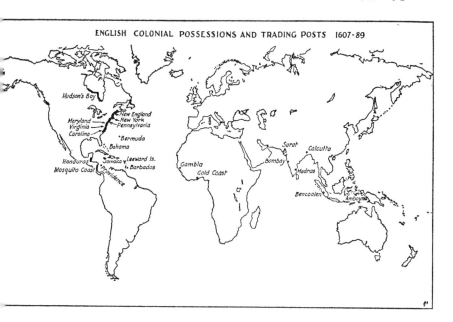

ENGLISH COLONIAL POSSESSIONS AND TRADING POSTS 1607-89

mother-country. It was to be important later in giving a distinctive character to the United States, at least until this one region was merged in the much larger whole. Many early New Englanders did not regard themselves as permanent exiles. They hoped, having shown how things should be done on a small scale over there, to return and do it on a larger scale at home. 'We shall be as a city upon a hill', said the Massachusetts leader, John Winthrop; and although he did not come back, several others did and played their part in the great events of the years 1640–60.

In the later 1630s these religious conflicts were sharpened. A series of prosecutions was undertaken, initiated by Laud and his supporters, against three Puritan pamphleteers—a barrister, a clergyman and a doctor. They were put in the pillory and had their ears cut off; the one who was regarded as a personal enemy by Laud, the lawyer William Prynne, was also branded on his cheeks SL, for seditious libeller. He had already been in trouble and had his ears clipped three years before, for attacking the theatre and thus the Queen—who took part in amateur theatricals. While sentences of such physical severity now seem only vicious to us, they were not seen in the same light at that time. The penalty for treason was death by disembowelling, while hangings and floggings were the mainstay of the criminal code. However, these prosecutions won a gratuitous amount of support for the Puritans, from people who would not otherwise have been inclined to their cause. This was especially so since the pamphleteers had been tried in Star Chamber, where Laud and other bishops on the Privy Council also sat as judges although they were themselves interested parties. So the persecution of the Puritans, the role of the bishops in the government, the alleged pro-catholic and the undoubted pro-Arminian tendencies of the King and the church hierarchy, and the favour shown to catholics at Court and in the government—all came together in these years, to give a great additional strength to Puritanism. It was a largely negative strength, an expression of what people were against. Many were becoming more and more opposed to the way the Church of England was going under Charles I and Laud and so found themselves in alliance with the Puritans without necessarily sharing the same positive aims. Some of the opposition leaders may have been astute enough to see this; others genuinely felt that Puritanism was gaining ground more than it actually was. Events in the next decade were to show that support for any one positive Puritan programme was much more limited than this negative opposition to the policies of the King and his Archbishop in the 1630s would have suggested. By their actual religious policies—and by what they seemed to stand for, Charles and Laud asked for trouble, and made the government's whole position much weaker than it would otherwise have been.

Wentworth in the North

The most forceful and probably the most gifted of Charles' ministers, Thomas Wentworth, better known as the Earl of Strafford, was not at the centre of affairs. He was important for different reasons. In the north of England, as President of the Council at York, for the most part he simply mirrored the policy of the central government. If anything he enforced it more efficiently and thoroughly—for instance in seeing that the Elizabethan laws for poor relief were properly executed, likewise the measures against wrongful enclosure of open and common fields which re-sulted in cottagers being driven off the land, so bringing about what contemporaries called 'depopulation'. The Council in the North, like that in the Marches of Wales, was becoming less acceptable in the early seventeenth century probably because of its own previous success. So a more forceful use of the Council now made it all the more unpopular. Wentworth also had a number of personal and family enemies among the Yorkshire gentry, and he made several more who resented the way in which he used the machinery of government to carry on these private feuds and to advance his own fortunes. Although he always tended to see his opponents as trouble-makers serving their own private interests, his enemies saw him in much the same light. Information about his private affairs which has only recently become available to his-torians, suggests that the old-fashioned contrast between a high-minded autocrat and his selfish opponents was overdrawn, and that he was just as interested in serving his own purposes and lining his pocket, as the people he was contending against.

Wentworth in Ireland

To understand the importance of Wentworth's work in Ireland a brief background sketch is necessary to explain what had been happening there before. The conquest of Ireland by the English had begun as early as the twelfth century, but only a small semi-circle of territory round Dublin, known as the 'Pale', had been colonised by English settlers during the Middle Ages and brought under permanent English rule. Ireland, we might say, had been in a state of semi-subjection for several centuries. And we should distinguish there between the vague overlordship, which was claimed and by the end of the fifteenth century had come to be exercised over most of the country, and the actual settlement by an English land-owning class which was still mainly limited to the Pale. During the sixteenth century, English overlordship was successfully asserted over the whole of Ireland; from 1540 the King of England claimed to be King of Ireland too. The area under effective English rule and settlement was enlarged especially in the centre and parts of the south. There also came to be a religious division between this

English colonial ruling class and the native Irish population, whose living standards and general way of life differed markedly from those of their occupiers, conquerors or 'civilisers'. The Irish, including almost all the native aristocracy, remained Roman Catholic when England first broke away from Rome under Henry VIII and subsequently became protestant. There was a series of rebellions or attempted wars of liberation (according to which way they are looked at) by the Irish in the sixteenth and seventeenth centuries. The most serious one coincided with the war against Spain, and had taxed the strength and resources of the Elizabethan state to the utmost. This, the last large-scale rebellion which had any serious chance of throwing the English out, was only finally put down in 1603 and the conquest of Ireland completed, just at the beginning of the Stuart dynasty in England.

The next phase in Irish history saw further colonisation of the north, in the province of Ulster. It was slightly different in character from previous settlement, in that the colonists included Scottish Presbyterians as well as people from England, and were drawn from different social classes. A whole alien minority, and not just a ruling class of landowners was thus established. And the Scots provided a further religious complication.

Even within the colonial upper class a division was apparent by the early seventeenth century, between the descendants of the older settlers, who were often known as the Anglo-Irish or the 'old English', and the newer settlers who had gone over under the Tudors or were still doing so under the Stuarts. This latter group, which included many officials and lawyers with government connections, had not had time to 'go native'; they were more strictly protestant, and had not inter-married or come to terms with the Irish way of life. By contrast, many of the old English had, as it were, become half-Irish themselves in their outlook and in some cases shared the catholic faith with the native Irish. Unless the English government in Ireland was to rule the country by undisguised military force they obviously needed to win enough support from some of these groups, to maintain the government on a peaceful footing. In the later 1620s a series of promises about land titles, feudal dues and so on, known as 'the Graces', had been issued as a concession to the old, Anglo-Irish settler group. Furthermore the Irish government had had no effective supervision from England, or leadership from the viceroy for several years, and it was in a very slack state; there was need for a firm hand. This was the background to Wentworth's arrival in 1633.

Wentworth soon called the Irish Parliament. It had not met for eighteen years, but this interval had far less significance than the breaks between parliaments in England. He played for time over the Graces, and did not in fact honour the promises which he had made. But he succeeded in getting quite large taxes voted and a number of laws put through. It was only as the sessions went on that the members became increasingly disillusioned. They realised that they had been fooled, and the Lord Deputy soon became just as unpopular with these older Anglo-Irish and, for slightly different reasons, with many of the newer settlers, as his predecessors had been. None the less he had made a successful start with this first Parliament in 1634.

The main features of Wentworth's rule in Ireland are important because of their bearing on events in England. First the process of colonisation was resumed, particularly in the west. Wentworth—rather high-handedly—dispossessed a number of landowners, including some old English as well as native Irish. Secondly, he followed a policy of recovering church lands; by contrast this was a direct attack on the interests of many of the new English, the recent settlers who had acquired property, which should have remained in the hands of the official protestant church, often by dubious means or for ridiculously low payments. Thirdly, under the influence of his friend Laud, he tried to swing the Anglican Church in Ireland towards Arminianism; he supported a very small High-Church minority, by-passing the moderate leaders including the Anglican primate. In this way he created a split within what was already a small minority. Yet at the same time, although as in England this policy of Arminianism was denounced as heading in a catholic direction and alienated many non-Puritan protestants, it did not go far enough to conciliate the Roman Catholic majority.

Meanwhile Wentworth conducted a purge of self-seekers and

corrupt officials inside the government, a clean-up such as he and Laud would have liked to see undertaken in England but never had the chance to attempt there. In the course of the next few years he quarrelled with most of the men who had been in control of the Irish government when he arrived, and he got rid of several, sometimes on rather questionable grounds. But at the same time, as in the north only on a larger scale, Wentworth and his friends were lining their own pockets very successfully. As against this, the King probably had better value for money, in that Wentworth raised the revenues considerably and made the Irish government self-supporting for the first time since the end of the Elizabethan war; he was even able to pay for a small regular army out of this surplus. If Wentworth did make a profit himself, it was not entirely at the expense of the King, as had all too often been true of reforming officials before. But the brittleness and essentially temporary quality of his achievement in Ireland is apparent when we look at what happened after he left. Within little over a year, in 1641, there was a major rebellion. He had succeeded in alienating most of the important English ruling groups from the royal government without really winning over the natives. It was they who rose in another desperate attempt to throw off English protestant overlordship and the occupation of the country by an alien settler class. Possibly Wentworth should not be blamed for this; if he had remained there in full control, this rebellion might never have happened. Certainly he did at least try to have a policy, which was more than any other Lord Deputy had done.

At the same time as all this, he was making a great many enemies in England. For one thing some of the people he antagonised in Ireland also had English interests, while others stirred up opposition to him through their friends and relatives in England. Also he refused favours, in the form of grants of land and offices in Ireland, to many important individuals, including several members of the peerage. Above all, by his Thorough policy in Ireland, he became identified with the toughest possible execution of the King's policies in general. He was felt to be straining the law and misusing the courts and other institutions of government, in order to enforce these policies, while his attempt to reform the administration alienated many officials. So although he was not in control of the King's government in England, except for a few months in 1639–40, he came increasingly to be thought of as its main champion because of what he was doing in Ireland. This seemed to many people suspiciously like a 'blue-print' for what he and the King would have liked to do in England if they were able.

In fact it was not because of anything in Ireland but because of events in Charles' other kingdom—Scotland—that the final crisis of the Personal Rule was precipitated.

Charles I and Scotland

One of James I's, or as he was in Scotland James VI's, most striking victories had been his success in preventing the abolition of bishops in the Scottish church. He had made other modifications in the religious system, making it less rigidly Presbyterian, and less independent of royal control. The peak of this achievement was reached in 1618, though the trend continued down to 1621; James then seems to have realised that he had gone about as far as he could without provoking overwhelming opposition. There was no attempt to force the Scottish church further away from its Presbyterian, Calvinist mould until the 1630s, when this policy of 'anglicanising', or making it more like the Church of England, was resumed. There had however been another measure early in Charles' reign called the Act of Revocation, which was aimed at recovering church property that had passed to laymen since the Reformation. Although this Act was later modified, it stirred up a great deal of opposition and resentment among those who stood to lose most, the nobility and the gentry (or 'lairds') of Scotland. Charles also twice remodelled the Scottish Privy Council and the central government, at the beginning of his reign and again when he went up for his belated coronation in Scotland (1633). He came to rely, for the execution of his policies, on a very small group of courtier-peers and on the newly promoted bishops. Many of the nobility were alienated from the King and his policy for these reasons and because he did not rely on them and give them offices in the government. They were ready to join the Presbyterian religious leaders in opposition to the King if an issue arose to bring them together.

Most of the Scottish nobles who continued to support the King were either catholics, and therefore regarded with the greatest suspicion by almost everyone else, or they had become absentees living at the English Court and had lost touch with opinion in Scotland.

For all these reasons, the issue of a new Prayer Book in 1637, based on that of the Church of England, was only the climax of a series of provocations. The opposition which it aroused cut across the divisions between clergy and laity, and between different social classes. Its use could not be enforced, so great was the resistance, some of it violent. The King persisted in his determination to have the new Prayer Book used, and the opposition came to a head in the winter of 1637–8. In February 1638 a document known as the National Covenant, in support of their traditional religious rights and political liberties, was drawn up and sworn to by vast numbers of the Scottish people. It was a direct defiance of Charles' authority. Thus he was forced to make a crucial decision: whether to admit that the opposition in Scotland was overwhelming, withdraw the Prayer Book and make some other concessions such as reducing the power of the bishops, or else be prepared to coerce the Scots by force. It was a fateful choice, and much in the subsequent history of England as well as Scotland followed from it. By some date in June 1638, Charles had taken his decision, which was to prove fatal to the whole system of the Personal Rule in all his three kingdoms, to raise an army to coerce the Scots. From then on the downfall of his régime can best be understood by a study of the sequence of the main events and the way these were related to each other. We cannot follow this story in its full detail here, but we must look at its essentials in order to understand what happened.

Weakness of Charles' position, 1638–9

Although the King had a revenue surplus and his finances seemed to be on a fairly sound footing in 1638, he did not have sufficient reserves and his credit was not good enough to enable him to wage war effectively against the Scots. It was not only a matter of running into debt on military expenditure. The King's whole financial system had become dependent on the willingness of his creditors, especially those in the City of London, to go on lending him money on the security of future revenues. But many of the revenues that he was raising in these years were not recognised as constitutional and legitimate by the parliamentary opposition. If another parliament were to be called, their future collection would be imperilled, and therefore the King's creditors would not regard them as acceptable securities for the repayment of the loans they were going to make him. This meant that the King's whole financial position could quickly become much more precarious; it was a delicate balance, which could easily be upset.

Moreover, the King's opponents had been heartened by the Hampden case and had also gained additional support from the attacks on the Puritan pamphleteers. They had managed to keep together since 1629 in various ways. Many Puritan peers, gentry and merchants—members of the constitutional opposition of the previous decade—were involved in colonial projects. John Pym for instance was the Treasurer of the Providence Island Company, a venture backed by several militant Puritans, to promote settlement but also to carry on privateering against Spain, in the Caribbean. There were also the more strictly ecclesiastical projects like the Feoffees for Impropriations already mentioned. The opposition included various family and regional groupings or connections. These consisted of peers and gentry who were brought together by ties of kinship and marriage, as well as by friendship and common beliefs, and included men who actually had positions in the government; Pym himself was a junior official until 1638 and there were some in higher posts. Others had friends or relatives in the government, such as those Council members who did not support the King and his Archbishop, any more than they did the policy of Thorough. So that when parliaments were summoned again in 1640, there was an organised opposition, which conducted election campaigns on a nation-wide basis. The long interval between parliaments did not therefore mean that opposition had been broken up.

Charles I's position was further weakened by the disagreements within his government, both in Scotland and in England, on how vigorously he should act against the Scottish resistance and the

English opposition. Several Councillors and lesser officials, such as those connected with the opposition groups, were against many features of the King's policy, besides armed coercion of the Scots, from which they dissociated themselves as far as they could. This helps to explain why Laud and Wentworth came to be so strongly associated in people's minds with the policy of coercing the Scots, and with a generally vigorous enforcement of the King's claims. In fact Charles had himself decided to use force against the Scots, and he would probably have followed this course even without the two champions of Thorough. So in that sense they were blamed unfairly and made the scapegoats for what was really the King's own policy.

Charles made two attempts to impose his will on his Scottish subjects, in the so-called 'Bishops' Wars' (1639 and 1640). He raised quite large armies, which in itself caused a great deal of resentment at the conscription of men and the billeting and extra taxes to maintain these troops on their way to the Scottish border. The King's forces and his reserves of money would at best have been barely sufficient to defeat the Scots, who were surprisingly united in their opposition to him. But at the same time, large sections of English public opinion either hoped that he would fail, or at any rate were apathetic and gave him no support.

In 1639 a truce was made without there having been any actual fighting; both sides showed some reluctance to push things to the point of armed conflict. Charles made some concessions. He allowed the Scottish religious system to revert to what it had been under his father, removing the bishops from effective power, recalling the offending Prayer Book, and giving way to other constitutional demands, such as granting the Scottish Parliament more independence from royal control. But he regarded all this simply as a way of gaining time. Unless they gave way, Charles was determined to make another attempt to coerce the Scots the following year, and this was the immediate cause of his undoing.

The Crisis of 1640

More important than the King's concessions in Scotland, which were in any case insincere, was his decision in the interval between these two 'campaigns' in the north, to call a parliament in England. This was the first of the two which met in 1640, the one known—with good reason compared to its successor—as the Short Parliament. The decision to call it is sometimes said to have been a serious miscalculation which is blamed on Wentworth, now recalled from Ireland in the hope that he could save the situation. After his Irish experiences, Wentworth perhaps had an over-optimistic view of how a parliament could be handled with firmness and dexterity; he thought that the same thing could be done in England. If so, this was an odd mistake for a man who had taken so prominent a part in the famous session of 1628. If, however, the King could no longer avoid having one by 1640, then the calling of the Short Parliament may not have been such a blunder. It was a potentially tractable body, with which the King might have come to terms; this is certainly true by contrast with its successor, the Long Parliament. More serious and more open to criticism is Charles' failure to negotiate and his over-hasty action in dissolving it. The Commons were presented with a series of demands—the King offered to abandon Ship Money in return for a vote of twelve subsidies. The House of Lords, or some of the King's supporters there, tried to put pressure on the Commons to vote these taxes, although it was regarded as a historic prerogative of the Lower House to take the initiative in matters of taxation. The Council was divided on how the Parliament should be handled. It has sometimes been argued that there was deliberate sabotage; at the very least there was a lack of tact and patience, and this Parliament was dissolved prematurely with nothing agreed, but not on the advice of Strafford (as he now was) or Laud in particular.

The second or Long Parliament of 1640 was forced on Charles I by a combination of circumstances. In August–September the Covenanters' army not only proved too formidable for the King to impose his will on the Scots, but actually invaded the north of England, and the royal forces were unable to stop them occupying Newcastle. A petition was presented by twelve peers, calling for another parliament as the only effective remedy both for the Scottish situation and the general grievances of the nation. Its signatories included some who were later to be among the King's supporters, as well as the more committed opposition leaders; and this made it the harder to resist. A few weeks later, the King summoned a 'Great Council' of all the peers, a body equivalent to the House of Lords without the Commons, in a final attempt to stave off another parliament. The Earl of Bristol, Buckingham's rival from the 1620s, at once took the lead in demanding that one should be called, but by then other factors had compelled Charles to accept the necessity of this. There was an almost complete financial collapse, due to the failure to raise further large loans in the City of London. Finally what might be called a 'peace party' emerged in the Council, among those who had been left in charge in London when Strafford and the King went up to York to conduct the campaign against the Scots. The members of this group were already preparing to make Laud and Strafford the scapegoats for the grievances of the eleven years' tyranny and the Crown's unpopular policies. At the same time there was a loss of nerve on the part of other Privy Councillors, a feeling that the whole edifice was about to topple down, and that they had better get out from under while they could.

Causes of the Collapse

Thus the weakness of Charles I and his régime in 1640 is due partly to the strength and surprising unity of his opponents. They enjoyed a much wider range of support both in England and in his other kingdoms than was to be the case when the Civil War came two years later. Correspondingly it was due to the narrowness of the support for the King and his government, and the half-heartedness of many who ought to have been among its strongest backers. Laud and Strafford were isolated; so was the Church of England hierarchy, which Laud of course had fashioned increasingly in his own image; and so was the royal Court, for Charles and Henrietta Maria were very cut off from the mainstream of public opinion. Neither the propertied, the traditional ruling classes in the country, nor the mass of the common people backed the King.

Some historians have advanced the theory that Charles did have

popular support, that the Personal Rule had seen enlightened experiments in social welfare policies. It is perfectly true that in the
years of economic distress (1629–32), due to bad trade conditions
coinciding with harvest failures at home, the King and his Council
had made a real effort to see that the laws concerning poor relief
were properly enforced. They also imposed a prohibition on the
export of corn while there was a scarcity at home, bullied em-
ployers into keeping on their workpeople even when there was no
work for them to do because of the slump, and used the full vigour
of the law against some profiteers. Perhaps their orders to J.P.s and
other local officials to levy poor 'rates', to find work for the willing
able-bodied poor, to flog the idle and to relieve the helpless were
more detailed and emphatic than those issued in previous crises.
Perhaps the response was better too. Historians are not agreed on
this, and until more research has been done into the nature and the
effects of the government's social policy, we can only reserve
judgment. In general it could be called a return to an Elizabethan
policy of 'paternal' state control, and it contrasts favourably with
the ineffectualness of James' government in the economic crisis of
the early 1620s. But there was never any question of anything like
a modern policy of social welfare; it would be a howler as well as
an anachronism to picture Charles I as a kind of 'Tory-Democrat'
born out of his time, a precursor of Disraeli and the modern Conservative Party. Disraeli may have persuaded himself so, but then
he was a statesman not a historian! As we shall see, the only
genuinely popular, democratic and even partially socialistic movements which did arise in seventeenth-century England, were at the
very opposite end of the political scale. They were an off-shoot
from the King's opponents during the Civil War and had no use
whatever for Charles or his policies. Yet, as with many popular
historical myths, there is just a grain of truth in the traditional
view of the Personal Rule. The King and his ministers did try to do
a little more for the poor than their immediate predecessors or successors; indeed Charles probably cared more for his ordinary subjects' welfare than most other British sovereigns before the
nineteenth century. But as a great economic historian R. H.
Tawney once wrote, Stuart social policy 'was too often smeared

with an odious trail of finance'. Even the drives against depopulation and profiteering degenerated into minor dodges for raising a little extra cash.

The people of England must have been singularly ungrateful to Charles if he had been ruling in the true interests of the poor and down-trodden. There is not a shred of evidence of popular support for the King when the real crisis came in 1640, or indeed in 1642. It is more plausible to argue the contrary, that the constitutional opposition of the upper and middle classes was actually being forced on by popular pressure in a still more radical direction. This cannot be proved, but a series of riots in London against Laud in the late spring of 1640 provides some evidence for it. At least this view is not in direct conflict with the known facts, as is the suggestion that the mass of the people supported the King.

Before we consider the story of the revolution which followed in the years 1640–2, it is worth estimating the nature of the movement against Charles and his system. It can be argued that the opponents of the King and his government wanted only limited, practical reform of what they regarded as the abuses of the previous eleven years: that is, the absence of parliaments, the Arminian policy in the church, the levying of Ship Money, the other unconstitutional financial measures, misuse of the prerogative courts, the over-prominence of the bishops in Star Chamber and the Council, and so on. Alternatively they may have wanted to curb the powers of the Crown, to reduce the King's freedom of action to a greater extent than was the case even before the Personal Rule, to alter the whole balance of Crown and Parliament in the Tudor constitution, and indeed to change the very basis as well as the institutions of government. Was it a limited, conservative revolt, or something more far-reaching and revolutionary? This involves a further question. The great seventeenth-century Royalist historian Hyde, Earl of Clarendon, believed that it was a deliberately planned revolution, indeed a conspiracy, by a group of desperate, disaffected men, many of whom may have been—so it has been suggested recently—in severe economic difficulties themselves. Alternatively the opposition may have developed from basically very conservative beginnings. Gradually, force of circumstances—the logic of the crisis itself and the march of events—may have forced them, often against their own wishes, to adopt radical, and eventually revolutionary policies, in order to secure their conservative objectives.

The truth probably lies between the two extremes. Many of those who supported the opposition in 1640–1 but later went over to the King, clearly believed that it was essentially conservative. They regarded Laud and the King as the innovators, and the opposition, including themselves, as standing for the traditional, balanced policies in church and state. If the inner group of opposition leaders—Pym and Hampden and their circle—were deliberate, conscious revolutionaries from the beginning, they certainly managed to deceive a lot of people, including a number of highly intelligent, gifted and able men. The most probable answer is that Pym, Hampden and their followers, were originally quite conservative, at least that they wished to be. But that they saw the way things were going, and realised sooner than other people that radical measures were needed to weaken the Crown, if their objectives were to be secured. In this way, they got out of step with many of their erstwhile allies, who were not prepared to use radical means even to secure conservative ends. This, as we shall see, offers a reasonable explanation of the events which were to follow in 1641–2, particularly of the division which appeared among the reformers.

4 : Civil War and Revolution (1640–9)

The Long Parliament

THE first session of the Long Parliament—the most momentous in all our history—lasted from the beginning of November 1640 to September 1641. That Parliament should remain sitting with breaks of only a few days for so many months was in itself without precedent. The first feature of the situation to notice during this session is the continued weakness of the King's political position. The second is the relative unity of the opposition. The third is the shakiness of the specific legal charges in the attack which the Commons mounted against the King's principal ministers and advisers, notably Laud and Strafford, but the force of the more general political ones. Strafford's arrest early in November was in itself a dramatic victory for Pym and his supporters; they believed that if they did not charge him with treason, he would have them accused of treasonable correspondence with the Scots, and there is some evidence that they were right. Certainly he was the only man on the King's side bold enough to advise Charles thus to strike the first blow, and able enough to have carried out such a policy if the King had been prepared to approve it. Another feature of these months, despite many concessions made by the King to the parliamentary reformers, is the continued growth of mutual suspicion between him and the opposition leaders. In particular Charles felt that the Commons were using the need for continued supplies to be voted for the Scottish army, if it were not simply to live off the north of England and desolate the occupied counties, as a form of blackmail, anyway to get more concessions out of him. The opposition leaders on the other hand believed that the King was temporising, as he had done with the Scots in 1638 and 1639, and simply waiting for his chance to strike back. More than once they feared an actual military coup might be attempted against them. Many were quite sincere in this belief; others probably knew that there was some evidence to suggest it, and decided that it made a good propaganda weapon.

The Long Parliament's positive achievements in its first session are very striking. They got rid of almost all their most dangerous enemies. The King's chief legal adviser, Finch, who had dragooned the judges over Ship Money in 1635 and 1637, fled abroad, along with Secretary of State Windebank, who was accused of leniency towards catholics. Strafford was impeached and imprisoned with the tacit support of the Lords. But despite a lengthy trial the following spring, his conviction was in doubt; and his execution was only achieved by the use of the procedure known as 'Attainder', that is the passing of an Act condemning him to death for treason. This was a legislative rather than a judicial way of getting rid of someone—and indicates that the political counts against him were as cogent as the strictly legal ones were dubious. 'Stone dead hath no fellow', said one parliamentarian leader to Hyde, the future historian of these events. Laud remained in prison with charges pending against him; elderly and demoralised, by this time he was obviously the less important of the two, and it was not a matter of removing a dangerous enemy but of taking revenge for his measures against the Puritans. Some of the other judges who had upheld the King's unlimited prerogative over Ship Money were also attacked. These steps were to punish those responsible for the excesses of the 1630s, also to prove to the King that he could not hope to repeat this kind of thing.

Two important measures concerned the future of Parliament itself. Together these were to make it impossible for the King ever to rule without it again. The Triennial Act laid down that there had to be a parliament at least once every three years and, if the King did not do anything about calling it, a procedure was laid down for having it summoned and elected without him, through the ordinary machinery of central and local government. An Act was later passed against the adjournment (for more than a few days) or the dissolution of the Parliament then sitting, without its own consent. At the time, the reasons for this were more financial than political.

The Crown's creditors, and those who were contemplating lending it money to be secured on revenues which had not yet been collected, would only continue to lend if they thought that Parliament was still going to be sitting. These revenues would then have a safe legal basis; otherwise repayment would not be assured. In the short run this Act limited the King's constitutional prerogative more than the Triennial Act, since it meant that he could not now legally get rid of the Long Parliament by his normal right of dissolution.

Several measures were passed against the unconstitutional taxation and other financial abuses of the 1630s. Ship Money was banned by statute; there were Acts against the misuse of the Forest laws, against the Compositions for Knighthood, and against monopolies. Also the monopolists were purged from the House of Commons, thereby depleting the King's already small following there. Some of the new Customs duties were suspended altogether; the traditional Tonnage and Poundage was voted for a few months only and then renewed for a few more, thus underlining as well as actually increasing the King's financial dependence on Parliament.

Measures were passed against some of the ecclesiastical policies of the 1630s. The Canons for church discipline, which Laud had passed in the spring of 1640, had marked the last triumph of Arminianism on the very eve of its overthrow. It was argued that, apart from anything else, the Convocation of the Church should not have remained sitting after the dissolution of the Short Parliament, so the Canons were automatically invalid.

A series of Acts was also passed, in the summer of 1641, which went a good deal further than merely attacking the abuses of the 1630s, or Charles' Personal Rule. These destroyed the very institutions of Tudor conciliar government: they included the abolition of Star Chamber, and the effective end of the Councils in the North and the Marches of Wales, the abolition of the judicial powers of the Privy Council (later resurrected for 'appeal' cases, in which form they survive to this day), and also the abolition of the Court of High Commission, which was linked of course with the attack on ecclesiastical abuses. These measures were far-reaching. Not only did they ensure that the régime without parliament could not be repeated but also that the whole machinery of autocratic monarchy could not be revived without a statutory or military counter-revolution.

The broad basis of agreement which had made these great achievements possible was not maintained, and a number of divisions developed within the ranks of the reformers during 1641. First of all there was the difficulty of preserving the fiction of attacking only the King's ministers and advisers and not the monarch himself. This applied particularly to the attacks on Laud and Strafford who had been closely associated with Charles and what he was trying to do, and had obviously enjoyed his full approval for their actions. The notion that 'the King can do no wrong', which was the fiction that the reformers wished to preserve, really implies—as is the case in Britain today—that the King or Queen cannot do very much at all, politically speaking. But in the seventeenth century when the King still effectively ruled the country as well as reigned over it, this was somewhat unrealistic. In fact Pym and Hampden were later to be criticised by William Walwyn, one of the leaders of the democratic party in the Civil War (the 'Levellers' as they became known), for having preserved this fiction even when fighting against the King. One of the most serious disagreements to emerge involved the powers of the Crown, and whether Parliament should restrict these further than they had in the legislation already passed up to the summer of 1641. Some wished to curb the King's powers and prerogatives, particularly his free choice of ministers and advisers, because they distrusted him and feared that he would try to reverse the reforms already achieved.

A religious division had also become apparent. The House of Commons had been overwhelmingly united in their attack on Laud and on Arminianism and the allegedly catholic tendencies of the previous régime, but very soon a split emerged. On one side were the extreme anti-episcopalian Puritans, the 'Root-and-Branch' party as they came to be known from a famous petition presented to the Commons and later embodied in a Bill, seeking to destroy the system of church government by bishops 'root and branch'. On the other side were the moderates, the Low-Church Anglicans and the episcopalian Puritans, who wanted to remove the abuses of the Laudian period but not to change the basic system of the Anglican Church as it had grown up and endured since the Elizabethan settlement.

The division among the once-united reformers may also have arisen from differing reactions to stirrings of popular discontent. There were anti-enclosure riots in several parts of the country during 1641; and the London 'mob' came out—apprentices, workmen and small tradesmen with some solid respectable citizens among them—in support of the extreme reformers, to demand the execution of Strafford and to support 'Root-and-Branch'. There were signs that a major upheaval might threaten the foundations of the social order. The disturbances in London were not for the most part 'proletarian', in the sense of being limited to the wage-earning working class; they were engineered by, and to some extent even composed of middle-class elements. But it can be argued that the division which developed in the two Houses of Parliament was affected by the different ways in which people reacted to this threat—whether real or imagined. The more conservative-minded may have felt that in the face of a real revolution, they should rally to the monarchy, and close their ranks against a danger far greater than that arising from their limited differences with the King. The other kind of reaction, personified by Pym and his supporters, was to try to canalise this popular movement, to make use of it in order to put additional pressure on the monarchy. They would thus seek further concessions, both to reduce the King's political powers and to put through a more radical religious settlement. It is also arguable that they may have felt obliged to act as they did in order to keep control of the popular movement, but too much should not be made of this. Some recent historians may have gone further than the evidence warrants here, but it should be taken into account in explaining the split within the reformers' ranks.

It is difficult to understand why Charles I, whose range of support was so narrow at the beginning of the Long Parliament, had recovered so much ground in about a year, by the autumn of 1641. It is partly to be explained by the divisions which we have just been discussing. There was the deepening religious rift, evident in a growing fear among many Anglicans of an attempt to impose some form of Presbyterianism, to root out bishops and abolish the use of the Prayer Book. There was also the debate over control of the government, which was sharpened by the outbreak of a rebellion in Ireland in the autumn of 1641. This was another attempt by the Irish to throw off English rule, beginning in the north of Ireland but soon spreading south. It was accompanied by atrocities; these however were grossly exaggerated, perhaps in some cases deliberately, to work up popular fears and hatreds. This rebellion raised the problem of who was to have charge of the armed forces which would be needed to suppress it. Parliament, or rather the more radical party led by Pym, would not think of trusting the King with command of an army; the King for his part would not consider surrendering one of his fundamental prerogatives, control over the armed forces. This issue was linked to other political and constitutional demands by the opposition, such as having something approaching a veto over the King's choice of Councillors and ministers. Fear of the masses may also have been intensifying during the last months of 1641.

All these divisions are apparent in the struggle over the famous document known as the Grand Remonstrance. This was passed through the Commons, then presented to the King and published. It was largely a catalogue of grievances against Charles, listing what had been wrong in the 1630s, what Parliament had already achieved in the previous session, and what remained for them to do. The debates on it were long and sometimes embittered; after the M.P.s had nearly come to blows among themselves, it was finally carried by only eleven votes (159–148), such was the evenness of the two sides at this time. This shows that the King had recovered, or at least that Pym and his allies had lost, a great deal of support.

The Coming of Civil War

It cannot be assumed that the final breach which led to the outbreak of civil war in the following year was already unavoidable, or inevitable. But it is fairly easy to see why the situation did get worse from then on. The news from Ireland became more serious.

The revolt spread from Ulster to the east and south, and the scale of the fighting—and of the atrocities committed by the rebels—grew, and in growing was still more exaggerated. Tens, even hundreds of thousands of Protestant settlers were said to have been ripped up, murdered, turned out into the snow to freeze or starve to death, and so on. But the real question could not be avoided: who should have command of the forces which practically everybody in England agreed must be raised in order to reconquer Ireland.

About this time the Puritan campaign against the bishops became more violent and extreme. The Londoners again turned out to demonstrate in large numbers. This time, the object of their intimidation was the bishops and the peers in general, for refusing to accede to a demand from the majority party in the Commons that the bishops should be expelled from their House. Then, as if to confirm and justify all their earlier suspicions that the King was only waiting for a favourable time to attempt a military coup, Charles, fearful for his wife's safety and goaded on by her, finally did try this. At the beginning of January 1642, he tried first to accuse of high treason and then to arrest five M.P.s and one peer. He came into the Commons in person with a large posse of armed men at his back. There was a famous scene, very different from that when Finch had had to be held in the chair in 1629. The Speaker, no longer the King's pliant nominee, protested that he was the servant of the House and could not tell him without their authorisation where the five had gone. Charles, failing to see them, exclaimed, 'I see all the birds are flown', and withdrew baffled. They had in fact, with only a matter of minutes to spare, taken refuge in the City of London, where the King did not dare to pursue them. There had been a political upheaval in London the month before; control had been wrested from the King's allies among the wealthy aldermen by the popular party, the Parliamentarian Puritans. This was now decisive, in providing the parliamentary opposition with the backing they needed; without the smaller revolution in London, the King might very well have seized the five (who included Pym and Hampden) and so broken the back of the opposition by force.

Until he attempted this act of violence, time and circumstances since the end of the Parliament's first session, had been on the King's side. He had been gaining ground. But this disastrous resort to force which was not carried through successfully, left him worse off than before, as is often the case in politics. Although Charles made one or two more minor concessions, such as agreeing to the exclusion of the bishops from the Lords and of all churchmen from civil offices, he lost a good deal of the middle-of-the-road, moderate support that he had regained at the time of the Grand Remonstrance.

After this, it is hard to see how war could have been avoided. The gulf of fear and suspicion was too deep to be bridged. Charles and his family left London—perhaps mistakenly, but the King had little alternative unless he was to give way altogether. He was not to return to his capital until he came as a prisoner, after the end of the Civil War. The final breach between the Crown and the majority in the Commons came on the question of control of the militia, the home defence forces. This was allegedly to secure the country against a possible Irish attack; in fact it was a struggle for control of such limited armed forces as did exist in the country. The English army in the north had by now been paid off, and the Scots had also gone home. The militia, though of little use without further weapons and training, was at this time about all there was in the way of an army. The question was whether the two Houses could legislate (by majority vote, as with passing ordinary Bills) in the King's absence. The crucial measure, known as the Militia Ordinance, was passed in February and March 1642, when the Commons and rather more reluctantly the Lords declared that in order to put the kingdom's defences under commanders they trusted and approved, this had the force of law. That was to give it the effect of a statute, although it had not been accepted and signed by the King, and so was not in the strict sense an Act of Parliament.

From March to August 1642 England drifted, or rather lurched towards civil war—the first major internal conflict involving more than one region of the country since the fifteenth century. One of the most interesting features of these months is the propaganda battle between the two sides. The King, now much more ably advised by Hyde and others who had rallied to him the previous autumn, on the whole tended to get the best of this paper warfare. Previously many people in the country had felt that it was Charles and his supporters who stood for innovations and novelties in church and state. Now Hyde and the King's other new Councillors were able to show that on the whole it was Parliament (or rather the majority of about three-fifths in the Commons and the small minority of peers who had remained in London) who were the innovators and were trying to make fundamental changes. The document put out by the Commons in the summer, the Nineteen Propositions, went a good deal beyond the Grand Remonstrance and in fact played into the King's hands in this respect, because it did seem to claim for Parliament a right to dictate to the King whom he should have as ministers. This was an attack on one of the central royal prerogatives. Most conservative-minded people in the upper classes still found such an idea unacceptable, though later generations were to come round to it. While this was going on, both sides pushed ahead with military preparations, making the clash all the more inevitable. Both said that they were only taking defensive steps against the other; but as is often the case in such a situation, once two sides begin to arm and mobilise, a direct clash becomes more, not less likely. Conflict broke out in August at the local level, for control of the militia and the machinery of government in individual counties, and for certain strategic towns and fortresses; general hostilities began in September.

Its Causes

There are many possible explanations as to why the Civil War began when and how it did. The unbridgeable gulf on political principles (the King's powers in relation to those of Parliament), the equally unbridgeable gulf on religious matters (between Root-and-Branch Puritans and Anglicans) provide two obvious ones. But these constitutional and ecclesiastical beliefs were probably only held strongly enough to have caused a resort to armed force by relatively small numbers on each side. Indeed it is most unlikely that more than a very small fraction of those involved had accepted that war was necessary, still less wanted war even as late as the summer of 1642. These differences alone could scarcely have produced a civil war dividing the country against itself. More important perhaps are the role of personality and the unfolding logic of the crisis: Charles' temperament and outlook, the fears and chronic mistrust which he generated in others, and on the opposite side the apparently aggressive intentions of Pym and his party. The war would hardly have come about when it did but for a whole sequence of events partly unrelated in themselves, including the Irish rebellion. Once things had got to a certain point, almost any move that either side made, short of some sweeping concession which was scarcely thinkable after January 1642, was likely to make the situation worse, to increase the mutual fears, intensify the suspicions, and make each side feel they must be ready for a sudden blow by the other, or even to get their blow in first. An alternative view has sometimes been advanced by Royalists and others, that despite his earlier mistakes, the King was on the whole the injured party and that the revolution was engineered by the inner ring of opposition leaders. This is the conspiracy theory. On this view it is extremely difficult to see why more people did not understand what was happening at the time. Neither does it fit in with the fact that Pym was definitely losing support in the autumn of 1641 precisely because he was going too fast and too far for many moderates; his policy at that time was quite inept if he was really such a calculating conspirator. The King's false moves too, notably the attempt on the Five Members, are difficult to square with this theory.

Then there are the various theories which emphasise social divisions as the main cause of the war. According to one of these, it was an upheaval by the middle class, a bourgeois revolution against a feudal monarchy. This was the old-fashioned Marxist view of the matter (and presumably still what is taught about the English Civil War in communist countries). An alternative view is that it was partly a middle-class revolution, partly the result of different responses by members of the upper classes to the threat of popular revolution from below.

Whatever interpretation one adopts, it is important to distinguish the different phases in this very crowded period, from 1639 to 1642.

A set of explanations which seems most convincing for one will not necessarily account for all of them. First there is the growing weakness of Charles' Personal Rule and its breakdown, with the fall of Strafford and Laud who with all their faults were the only figures of heroic stature in Charles' government. Next there are the limitations put on the King's powers, the destruction of the prerogative and conciliar machinery in 1641. Then there is the division which developed between the more moderate and the more extreme reformers in that year, exemplified in the split over the Grand Remonstrance. Finally after the King's attempt on the Five Members and the Militia Ordinance there are the events leading to the outbreak of fighting, when people actually had to take sides. This raises the question of how many wanted war, how many chose one side or other because they could not avoid doing so, and how many managed to remain uncommitted. These are the problems of 1642 and later to which we must now turn.

Its Nature

There are several different ways of looking at the Civil War which help to explain its nature. First there was a geographical division. A number of counties, such as Lancashire and parts of the midlands and south, were fairly evenly divided, and there were minorities in all counties; even in the most strongly Royalist areas there were some Parliamentarians, and vice versa. But broadly speaking, most of the east and south-east of England was Parliamentarian, and most of the north and west of England (and almost the whole of Wales) Royalist. That is, by and large the areas of the country which at this date were the more populous, the economically more advanced were for the Parliament; the economically more backward, the less populous were for the King.

Secondly there was a religious division which partly corresponded with this geographical one. There were individual exceptions here too; some Puritans can be found fighting for the King, some Anglicans for Parliament. But most strong Puritans were Parliamentarians; very few active ones supported the King. Nor can many strong Anglicans, who had no Puritan leanings, be found on Parliament's side. Despite the use made of the Papist-Arminian

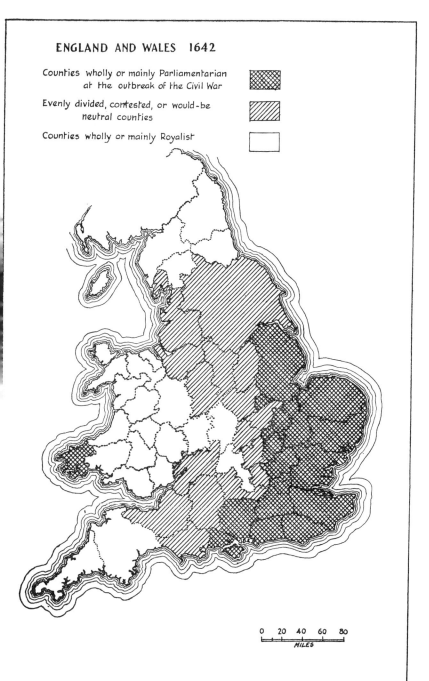

ENGLAND AND WALES 1642

Counties wholly or mainly Parliamentarian
at the outbreak of the Civil War

Evenly divided, contested, or would-be
neutral counties

Counties wholly or mainly Royalist

0 20 40 60 80
MILES

danger by Parliamentarian propaganda it did not amount to much. Arminianism was not a force with any following among the laity. As for the catholics, the King was well supplied with recruits from some districts where they were numerous, while a few wealthy individuals gave him generous financial help. Many more, who had no particular reason to love Charles and his government, would have liked to remain neutral. But they were all treated as enemies by Parliament and forced into the King's camp. The Roman Catholic menace was something of a myth, but gained greater credibility from the King's subsequent Irish policy. He began an incredibly foolish attempt to do a deal with the Irish catholic rebels, and even to use them against his enemies in England, which made the theory that he was all the time secretly trying to erect a catholic despotism seem more plausible than it otherwise would.

There were also significant social and economic divisions. Up to a point it was a war of town against country: London, most of the larger market and cloth-manufacturing towns and almost all the seaports, even in the otherwise Royalist areas of the north and west, were for the Parliament. The larger part of the rural areas, except in East Anglia, parts of the east midlands and the south-east were for the King. And up to a point, as one would expect from what has already been said, this corresponded to a class division. Although no social group was 100 per cent. on either side, they were divided in very varying proportions. The great majority of the peerage were for the King, and over the whole country probably a majority of the gentry too (though some historians who have studied the problem would not agree with this); whereas among those of the middle classes—merchants and yeomen and other such groups—who took sides at all the preponderance were for the Parliament. S. R. Gardiner, who was not disposed to adopt a class interpretation of the conflict, suggested that there was a real social division but that this was incomplete because it did not exactly correspond with the religious cleavage: upper-class Puritans being Parliamentarians and middle-class Anglicans Royalists. Among contemporary historians writing at or near the time, Clarendon put great emphasis on the fact of London, the clothing areas, the seaports and what he calls 'the middling sort' being Parliamentarian, and most of the old upper class—the peerage and the gentry—being for the King. Recent attempts made by some historians to show that there were differences of an economic character between the two sides within the gentry class (other than the regional differences already discussed) have not so far been proved. There is one possible exception, which it is hard to know how to interpret: relatively more Royalists may have been heavily in debt, or in embarrassed and less healthy financial circumstances.

Another division suggested recently, is that between the 'ins' and the 'outs', or Court and Country (using those terms in a political sense). According to this view, the Civil War was a conflict between people who were office-holders, had some connection with the royal Court or shared in the benefits of the previous régime, and those who were excluded from these advantages. This is closely linked to what has been described as the conspiracy theory of the revolution. Clearly there is an element of truth in this interpretation, but it cannot have constituted the main reason why most people took sides as they did, especially the rank and file. Even at the top, the Parliamentarians included a number of men who had held office or been in some way connected with the royal government. And for the Royalists the opposite is equally untenable. The numerous small gentry of the north and west of England were overwhelmingly Royalist when most, indeed the vast majority, of them had no connections with the Court, no advantages of holding office or enjoying similar perquisites before 1640 or even before 1642. This distinction may be truer of the merchants than of the landowners. Monopolists, tax-farmers and others with special privileges tended to be Royalists, and most others Parliamentarians.

Up to a point there was also a moral difference between the two sides, symbolised by the nicknames which they gave each other. This may only be another way of looking at the split between Puritan and Anglican (or catholic), between Town and Country, between middle class and nobility or between 'Country' and 'Court'. But just as no two of these divisions were quite the same and none followed directly from another, so too the moral difference existed in its own right. The Parliamentarians were called

'Roundheads' by their enemies, originally because some of the London troops had their hair cut so short that it could not be seen under their helmets, although many Parliamentarian officers, even strong Puritans like Oliver Cromwell wore their hair as long as any Royalist. The Royalists were called 'Cavaliers', and portrayed as mounted desperadoes who rode about plundering, raping and massacring. In general, the Parliamentarian troops were better behaved towards civilians than their opponents, but this may have been because they were usually better paid and supplied. Many Puritans certainly regarded their opponents as loose-living and immoral, if not damned. They in turn were often regarded as sanctimonious hypocrites, who condemned sexual immorality while encouraging the greater sins of greed, pride and rebellion.

There is a sense in which the war consisted of a large number of local and even personal conflicts coming together on a national scale. It involved the settling of many private and family feuds, very much of the kind that are found in the sixteenth century; it was in this narrower sense a war of cliques and factions, arising from the nature of family ties and from the system of clientage and patronage.

It is difficult to single out one factor among so many, to explain why people took sides as they did. But at least within the upper social groups (the gentry in particular), differences of political, or constitutional outlook were perhaps decisive. This kind of emphasis on people's general attitude towards the constitution and how the balance of power should be distributed, is supported by the fact that so many in the less developed and consequently more conservative parts of the country finally took the King's side. By contrast, those in the more developed, go-ahead parts were more for the Parliament precisely because by 1641–2 it was the party of change and innovation. This suggests that in 1642 many members of the upper classes who thought of the King as the upholder of the traditional system in church and state, rallied to him out of instinctive loyalty, while those who thought more rationally about it and recognised the need for further changes, tended to be Parliamentarians. With some this may have been a matter of temperament, with others of material interest or what they believed to be their interests; but it was also at least in men's conscious minds a matter of outlook and beliefs.

In addition there was a difference of age between the two sides, anyway among M.P.s and to a less marked extent among officials in the central government. The Parliamentarians tended on average to be older men than their Royalist opponents. One explanation of this, of youth being relatively speaking on the side of the King, may be that it was a reaction against the dominant Puritan tone of the late sixteenth and early seventeenth centuries on the part of the younger generation; if we look ahead, to the Restoration Court and social life, then that seems quite plausible. Or it may simply reflect the fact that after eleven years of Personal Rule a generation was growing up which could not remember a time before the rule of the King without parliament, before the dominance of Laud and the Arminians in the church. On this view, time was literally on the King's side. And it could even be argued that Pym was aware of this, and felt that it was better to precipitate the clash than to wait until the King gained more support if his system was maintained for longer.

The search for one all-embracing interpretation of the divisions in the Civil War is probably just as mistaken as the search for a single explanation of its causes. But this does not mean that we should abandon any attempt to offer explanations. Nor should we forget that it is possible to combine more than one of them; all but one or two of those which have been mentioned here are perfectly compatible with each other. Only historians who feel that everything must be ascribed to one particular theory or set of causes find it necessary to reject all the other possible interpretations; most of them in fact believe that the truth consists of some combination of these various hypotheses, and do not cling defiantly in the face of the evidence to any one of them. Nor because there is so much about people's motives, as well as their interests, that we can never know after over three hundred years, because we cannot know more than a small fraction of the whole truth and that only very imperfectly, do they therefore stop trying to explain what happened and take refuge in some defeatist answer, ascribing it all to a jumble of circumstances or to forces beyond our understanding.

I

The Course and Outcome of the War

Parliament's first and greatest asset was its possession of the capital, London, which provided it with the largest supply of ready money in the kingdom and also with a large number of men, especially potential infantry soldiers. Parliament also held most of the other seaports and controlled the Navy. Although business suffered much from the war, such overseas trade as continued was mainly under Parliament's control, and they collected the revenue from customs. They were also able to cut the King off from possible sources of supply overseas. Less important was their control of the iron industry—for making guns—in Kent and Sussex and parts of the midlands. Their possession of the capital besides being an asset psychologically, was also an advantage because it gave them actual possession of the various departments of state and the law courts in London and Westminster; moreover, many of the Parliamentarians had practical experience themselves both as M.P.s and in local government. A potential military advantage was that they were operating on interior lines, due to the geographical division of the country, as already described.

Parliament's main weakness was the political divisions among its supporters. It has been suggested that within the House of Commons in the years 1642–4 there was an approximate threefold grouping. The Peace Party wanted to make a compromise with the King almost before the war had begun and certainly before they had defeated him. The Middle Group, led by the great Parliamentarian statesman John Pym, aided by Hampden, stood for a definite attempt to win the war but not for the unconditional surrender of the King and his supporters, and were prepared to negotiate when the time seemed ripe. They managed to keep on reasonably good terms with Parliament's commander-in-chief the Earl of Essex (son of Elizabeth's ill-starred favourite). The War Party, people more extreme than Pym and his followers, believed that the King must be decisively defeated before negotiations could even be contemplated. One great difficulty among the Parliamentarians was their lack of clear, long-term objectives—whether they did really want to defeat the King, and if so, what they wanted to do then, whether to impose the Nineteen Propositions, make him accept some other set of peace terms, or try to get back to the situation as it had been in the summer of 1641. Very few members, even of the War Party, wanted to get rid of Charles I in the early years of the Civil War. Perhaps not more than two or three people in the House of Commons (out of over five hundred M.P.s, of whom about three hundred were Parliamentarians) were actually republicans; one of them was put in the Tower by Pym and his supporters in 1643. Parliament's other weakness in the early stages was their lack of good trained troops, especially cavalry.

Turning to the Royalist side, the King's greatest asset was or should have been united leadership under the sovereign himself. Historians are divided as to how good a commander-in-chief Charles made; he lacked decisiveness, he often took advice from too many different people and did not listen to the wisest. Even if authority was united on the King's side, counsel was deeply divided, particularly over the best way to win the war. There were those who favoured a direct, massive frontal attack on London, and others who preferred a gradual reduction of Parliament's supporting areas in the outlying parts of the country. Both these strategies were tried at once in 1643, when the King's forces did have the initiative, with the result that neither succeeded. The King undoubtedly had an initial superiority in the quality of his troops, notably of his cavalry and their leaders. Members of the nobility and gentry with their servants and tenants provided a body of dashing horsemen, under the leadership of the King's nephew Prince Rupert of the Palatinate, against whom the Parliamentarian forces at first proved quite unable to stand. The King had the further potential military advantage of strategic encirclement of the main parliamentary area round London.

Many of the King's weaknesses explain themselves from what we have seen of his and Parliament's sources of strength. But perhaps the worst was the division and rivalry among his Councillors and his generals, especially between his civil and military advisers, for instance on whether to seek outside help, from Ireland or the Continent. Secondly there was his lack of financial resources. The King had no regular sources of revenue comparable to the Customs duties, and he proved less successful than Parliament at collecting taxes from the counties that were in his power. And particularly in the latter stages of the war, he lacked sufficient supplies of steady second-line troops; the geographical division of the country gave Parliament the preponderance of manpower as well as wealth.

In the years 1642–4 the main military feature of the war is the even balance between the two sides. A number of indecisive battles were fought; local victories were won by both sides. The numbers of men engaged were small by later standards. Until 1645 no single army ever reached 20,000, while 5,000–10,000 was more typical; in the summer of 1644 three Parliamentarian armies united to besiege York totalled 26,000–27,000, but half these were Scots, and the Royalists never mustered more than about 18,000 for any single operation. Yet there were many small local forces and scattered garrisons as well as the main field armies, and by 1644–5 there must have been over 100,000 men in arms—adding the two sides together, but excluding Scots and Irish. Since the male population of fighting age (say 15 to 50 years old in those days) of England and Wales cannot have been much over one million, the combined effort was considerable. To achieve this, both sides had to resort to conscription for their infantry, though by 1645 Parliament had more cavalry than they could use. The other burdens—taxation, requisitioning of supplies and billeting—were probably even more resented by the non-combatant population than the forced levying of men. At no stage were the active political supporters of the two sides more than a minority in the country; only occasionally could they rely on spontaneous mass support. One memorable instance of this is the huge turn-out of Londoners—from all classes, women as well as men—to help repel Rupert in the autumn of 1642. Charles came nearest to victory then, and again in the mid-summer of 1643. But on each occasion he failed to press his advantage home and risk everything in a frontal attack on London. He could, however, have got considerably better peace terms then than later. There were two sets of negotiations, in the winters of 1642–3 and 1644–5. In both, especially the former, Charles would have been able to settle for better terms than had been contained in the

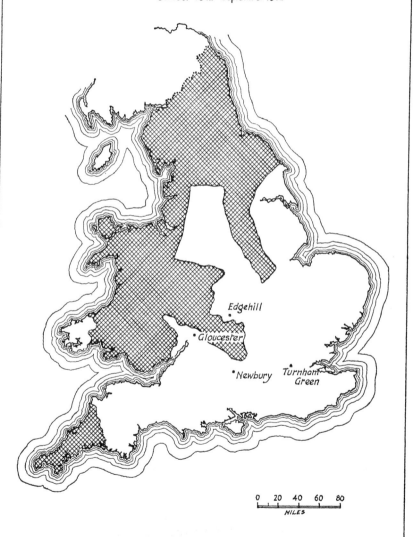

ENGLAND AND WALES 1642-3

Areas under the King's control,
       spring 1643.

Places named...... Main battles and sieges,
       October 1642 – September 1643

Edgehill

•*Gloucester*

•*Newbury*   *Turnham Green*

0 20 40 60 80

MILES

Nineteen Propositions of June 1642; in a sense therefore the war had so far proved favourable to his bargaining position.

Meanwhile the indecisiveness of the war, its miseries and hardships, the heavy financial burdens imposed on all classes, led to a great feeling of war-weariness in the country. The spread of neutralism now took a more threatening form with a large movement among the peasants of some districts, called the Clubmen (since they were said to have armed themselves with clubs), who defied the armies of both sides. The King seriously damaged his cause by making an alliance with the Irish; he even planned to bring Irish troops over to use in England. This caused far more additional hostility than it gained in military advantage. On the other side, despite many muddles and divisions and even military defeats Parliament made better use of the passing of time. As a result of divided authority and faulty strategy, their commander-in-chief was cut off and lost the whole of his infantry in Cornwall as late as the summer of 1644. As against this, Parliament built up a more efficient administrative and financial system. New taxes were introduced, including the Excise (a duty levied on home-produced as well as imported goods, even on basic foodstuffs for a time) and the 'Weekly Pay', later called the 'Assessment', a much more effective direct tax on wealth and property than there had ever been before; there were also heavy capital levies on Royalists and even on neutrals. Far greater sums of money were raised in taxation during the Civil War, especially on the parliamentary side, than had been, with so much complaint, under the early Stuarts. Tonnage and Poundage, the Impositions, subsidies, forced loans, even Ship Money shrank into relative insignificance compared with the amounts raised during these years.

Furthermore, whereas the threatened Irish intervention actually harmed the King, Parliament was greatly helped by the renewed military intervention of the Scots. They came back on to the scene in 1644, as a result of an agreement with Parliament. One effect of this was to make the divisions on the parliamentary side still more acute, but there is no doubt that it strengthened them militarily. The treaty with the Scots, known as the Solemn League and Covenant, was put through by some Parliamentarian leaders,

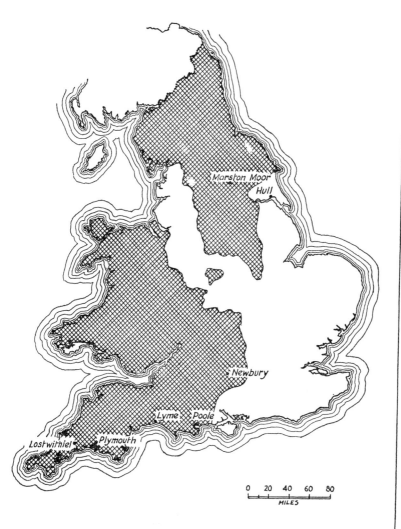

ENGLAND AND WALES 1643-4.

Areas under the King's control, mid-winter 1643-4

Places named..... Main battles and sieges of the summer of 1644

Marston Moor
Hull
Newbury
Lyme   Poole
Lostwithiel   Plymouth

0   20   40   60   80
MILES

including Pym and the younger Sir Henry Vane, who were not rigid Presbyterians. The Scots, however, considered that Parliament was now committed to introducing a Presbyterian system into England. The alliance certainly helped to shift the balance on the Parliamentarian side, and did lead to a modified Presbyterian church settlement. But at the same time, through the failure of Parliament's first set of generals to win decisive victory, and the death of their original leaders (notably Pym, and Hampden who died of wounds), a new radical party emerged. This was a much strengthened version of the small War Party of the earlier years. Many of its members were Puritans of a different type, in religion they were more like the Elizabethan Separatists, who believed in the right of each congregation to choose its minister and to worship according to its own choice. They believed in a state church, but a much more decentralised one than the Presbyterians wanted. Since they held that within certain limits every congregation should be independent, they came to be known as 'Independents'; in religious terms they were the ancestors of the modern Congregationalists. It is confusing that both the names Presbyterian and Independent were given to political groupings as well as to followers of particular religious systems at this time. The 'political Presbyterians' were, by and large, the moderates on the parliamentary side, who wanted to make a compromise peace with the King, the successors of the old Peace Party. The 'political Independents' were the new War Party, those who wanted a decisive victory over the King.

During 1644–5 Oliver Cromwell came to be increasingly important, because he was one of Parliament's most active and successful commanders and at the same time a leading member of the Independent party. Cromwell was an East Anglian gentleman; a backbencher in the 1628–9 Parliament, in 1640–2 he supported Pym on political questions but was a 'Root-and-Branch' man in religion. Militarily, his greatest contribution at first was as an organiser and a trainer of troops. He insisted that the cavalrymen at least should be respectable characters who knew what they were fighting for. As regards the officers, provided they were broadly Puritan in outlook, military capacity was to count for more than either their social origins or their exact doctrinal position. In helping to create an army of this kind, composed largely of Puritan volunteers and with promotion on merit, Cromwell was unconsciously a revolutionary. But in many other ways he was a conservative, and he was soon to come into conflict with the more radical elements in this army, for whose very existence he was largely responsible.

By the beginning of 1645 the parliamentary forces had been organised in the 'New Model Army' under one C. in C., Sir Thomas Fairfax. He had originally been one of their commanders in Yorkshire and in the purely military sense was probably the ablest man they had. At the same time on the political side, the Parliamentarians were becoming more and more divided. The Presbyterians or moderates, although their military leaders were mainly discredited, still commanded a majority in both Houses of Parliament; they were strengthened by alliances with the Scots and with the City of London. The Independents or radicals were a minority in Parliament but increasingly dominant in the Army; although Fairfax did not belong to this party, Cromwell, his second-in-command, and many other senior officers did. Besides these two parties, there were other Puritan sects. Their members were all more or less Separatists, and many went further than the Independents in their opposition to any state church, while some opposed any form of publicly organised religion; in political terms they were mostly supporters of the Independents rather than the Presbyterians.

The reasons why Parliament at last defeated the King decisively in 1645–6 are fairly clear. By this time they had a much larger army, whether or not it was better man for man. This was largely due to better financial organisation in the territory they controlled, and superior resources which can in turn be related to the geographical division of the country. Having inferior resources for a long war, the King's best hope had been in a speedy victory. He might possibly still have won in 1644, but his chances were far less good by then than in 1642–3. The royal armies in the north were defeated at Marston Moor in 1644, the King's own army in the midlands at Naseby in 1645, and his remaining forces in the west later in 1645 and 1646. Realising that further resistance was hopeless, in 1646 Charles surrendered to his old enemies the Scots, fleeing from his wartime capital at Oxford to reach them in the north.

ENGLAND AND WALES 1644-5

Areas still under the King's control,
late summer, 1645

Areas lost by the King since the mid-
-winter of 1644:5

Places named..... Main battles and sieges of summer 1645.

Newark

Naseby

Oxford

Winchester

Taunton   Langport

Corfe

0   20   40   60   80
MILES

The Search for a Settlement

The next important problem to consider is why no lasting agreement was reached, why there was a period of deadlock interspersed with tortuous intrigue and negotiations (1646–8). Of those involved, Charles who had deliberately given himself up to the Scots rather than to the English Parliamentarians, hoped to recover by diplomacy or intrigue what he had lost by the fortunes of war. The second party involved in this situation, the Scots, wanted to see their own church system imposed in England and they also wanted to be paid for their military help. Thirdly there was the Parliamentarian majority—the Presbyterians, who wanted a compromise constitutional settlement, something like the position of 1641, provided that the King would also accept their church system. Fourthly there were the Independents, a minority in Parliament but by this time dominant in the Army, which now had its own grievances. Both officers and men wanted guarantees that they would not be charged with actions committed during the war and that their large pay arrears would be settled. They also demanded religious liberty, at least for all Puritans, and they came to play an increasing part in politics, wanting a more secure settlement with the King and the Scots than the Presbyterians did. Charles tried to play off these groups against one another, particularly the Presbyterians against the Independents in order to see which would give him the better terms, and for a time he succeeded.

In the various negotiations which extended from the summer of 1646 to the late autumn of 1648, the outstanding issues continued to be much the same. The main obstacles to agreement with the King were: control over the militia and the other armed forces, the future of the church, the King's right to choose his ministers, and the fate of his leading supporters during the war. Both Parliament and the Army wished to exclude the latter—in varying numbers— from the general pardon and indemnity which it was agreed by all must be part of any true settlement.

These political developments were interrupted by a fresh crisis in 1647, one of the most important of the whole century. This was provoked by a Presbyterian plan to disband part of the Army and ship the rest off to Ireland without settling their grievances. A new element now erupted on to the political scene. There was a revolt among the rank and file in protest against this treatment: 'we are not a mere mercenary army', they claimed, demanding a voice in the political settlement. Their representatives—the Agitators as they were called—were in touch with, and up to a point inspired by, a new political group in London, people known to history as the Levellers. This name, previously applied to anti-enclosure rioters who levelled hedges and fences, was given to them by their enemies. Some of the soldiers' spokesmen were also Leveller political theorists—John Lilburne, a popular hero who had suffered for his opposition to Laud back in 1637, and John Wildman. Other Levellers were civilians; the two intellectuals who played most part in formulating the party's radical and democratic programme were Walwyn and Richard Overton. This revolt of the Army rank and file, partly under Leveller influence, partly because of the soldiers' immediate grievances, forced the generals, particularly Cromwell and his son-in-law Henry Ireton, to act more drastically than they would otherwise have done. Cromwell provided a personal link between the Army and the House of Commons, and it was only the military revolt which compelled him to side decisively with the soldiers.

By accepting some of the Agitators' demands and by securing custody of the King's person, Cromwell and the Independents defeated their opponents. The House of Commons was purged of eleven Presbyterian leaders. Later in the year the Independents also got the better of their previous allies—the Agitators and Levellers, by suppressing their organisation and then adopting more of their policies. In August Ireton produced the 'Heads of Proposals', the first full-scale written constitution ever to be drafted for this country. Charles I would have done well to accept this. It was a plan for a modified constitutional monarchy with a wide measure of religious liberty; sovereignty was to be shared between Crown and Parliament. Members of Parliament were still only to be elected by a minority of the nation, though there was to be a redistribution of seats to correspond with differences in the wealth and population between different counties and the growth of new towns.

Shortly after this, the Levellers produced their programme, the 'Agreement of the People'. This came much nearer to democracy as we know it today. The spokesmen for these two programmes met each other in a series of remarkable debates held at the end of October and beginning of November 1647 in Putney church. The General Council of the Army, which had been formed during the demobilisation crisis in the spring, included all the senior officers and the Agitators as representatives of the rank and file. Ireton and other officers spoke on behalf of the Independents, one or two officers and several of the Agitators for the Levellers. Cromwell was present, but he left most of the arguing to his more intellectual son-in-law. The debate centred on the question whether, as the Independents alleged, the measures of political democracy advocated by the Levellers would lead to economic democracy—that is to greater equality of wealth, even to communism or—as Cromwell seems to have feared—anarchy.

The Levellers stood more or less for household suffrage, not for every adult male having the vote and certainly not for women's suffrage. But even that was a very great advance on the degree of representation that ordinary people had in parliament until the later nineteenth century; indeed it was not to be exceeded until 1918. It was approximately the franchise that came in with the second and third Reform Acts of Disraeli and Gladstone (1867 and 1884). The Levellers also believed that parliament itself, though the sovereign part of the government, should be bound by certain 'fundamental laws', which it could not break. These were to include religious liberty for all protestants, and no military conscription. They also attacked trade monopolies, legal and corporate privileges and wrongful enclosures (the only point of similarity with the name their enemies had given them). They did not, however, attack inequality of wealth as such, let alone the institution of private property.

Some historians have seen in the Leveller movement the natural culmination of the popular, democratic tendencies inherent in protestantism. Certainly some of their leaders, notably John

Lilburne, became Levellers after being radical Puritans. However, Walwyn and others have more in common with the secular humanism of the renaissance, while among their opponents none attacked them with greater bitterness, regarding them as an ab- horrence and an abomination, than the most orthodox Puritan group, the Presbyterians. The truth seems to be that within protestantism, and particularly within the Puritan movement, there was always a tension between two conflicting tendencies, which in the 1640s emerged as an open conflict between opposing forces. In one direction Puritanism led to a narrow rigid system, based on the assumption that the Elect (those chosen by God or through the agency of His Grace for salvation) should rule over the rest of mankind. This might take the form of a carefully graded, and by the later 1640s socially and politically con- servative Presbyterian system, or of a revolutionary élite such as some of the radical groups, like the Millenarians, aspired to constitute. The best known, and indeed the most colourful of these were the sect known as the Fifth Monarchy Men. They believed that the four temporal monarchies of the world had passed away and that the fifth, that of God's servants, was about to begin as an immediate preliminary to the Second Coming of Christ on Earth, that is the 'Millennium'. They were not a peaceful sect, but be- lieved in direct military action to hasten the establishment of the Fifth Monarchy. On the other hand, from the protestant belief in the equality of all believers—anyway of all who were capable of reading the scriptures for themselves—came the ideas of political or at least civic equality, and of opposition to all ideas of social hierarchy and special privileges. Out of this grew the Leveller movement. This can be seen, for example, when at Putney Colonel Thomas Rainborough, one of the few officers of field rank who supported the Agreement of the People, said in defence of its clause on electoral reform: 'The poorest he that is in England hath a life to live, as the greatest he, and therefore . . . every man that is to live under a government ought first by his own consent to put himself under that government; and . . . the poorest man in England is not at all bound . . . to that government he hath not had a voice to put himself under.'

The Levellers were laid more open to the charge of communistic tendencies by the existence of another small group. Known as the Diggers, and led by an ex-textile merchant from Wigan, Gerrard Winstanley, they only emerged into the open in 1649, but were probably already gathering support. They wanted the direct take-over of unused common land, and its cultivation by people collec-tively. This was a step towards common ownership of the means of production. Unlike the Levellers, they were not a serious political force, but their existence gave slightly more credibility to the charge that the Levellers were, as we should nowadays say, crypto-communists and not merely radical democrats, which is what they could more accurately be called. Indeed, the Levellers were not even socialists; neither Lilburne nor any of the other leaders except perhaps Walwyn wrote anything that could be called socialistic, though their creed was nearer to political and social democracy than anything that had been seen before. Altogether the years 1646–9 saw the most serious political challenge from the common people of England since the Peasants' Revolt of 1381.

In the course of getting the better of their rivals on both sides (the Levellers on the left and the Presbyterians on the right) Crom-well, Ireton and the other Independent leaders lost any remaining faith in the King. This was especially true after the Second Civil War which broke out in 1648. Charles made a secret alliance with the Scots, as a result of which they intervened on his side in Eng-land; he promised them a Presbyterian church settlement, at any rate for a term of years, in return for their military help. This was the most discreditable episode of all Charles' many underhand dealings. He had been negotiating this alliance secretly, while at the same time he was treating in public with Parliament and the Army. Charles also tried to escape from the Army's charge. He had previously been handed over to Parliament by the Scots, in return for arrears of pay due to the Scottish army and a promise to honour the 1643 alliance, the Solemn League and Covenant. The Army had taken over his custody in June 1647, as part of their campaign against the Presbyterians in Parliament. Now Charles fled to the Isle of Wight, but he misjudged the local garrison com-mander, a cousin of Cromwell's, who put the King under arrest.

Like so many of his projects, this left Charles in a worse position than he was in before.

The Second Civil War was severe but short. The Scots were defeated, as were those ex-Cavaliers and ex-Parliamentarians (that is Presbyterians) who had risen on the King's behalf in England. The Independents themselves became more radical, some even moving towards republicanism. The Army leaders decided that they must get rid of Charles, 'the man of blood' as they now called him; as a consequence of this, some of them concluded that they should abolish the monarchy. Perhaps because only a very few even of those peers still sitting supported them, they also decided to get rid of the House of Lords.

This change of attitude resulted in the second crisis of these years, in the winter of 1648–9. As in 1647, the Army was provoked by the Presbyterians in Parliament. Back in the winter of 1647–8, Parliament had voted to break off negotiations with the King. Those who normally wavered between the two positions, perhaps some of the Presbyterians themselves, had then joined the Independents in the view that Charles was incorrigible. But the Army's victory in the Second Civil War seems to have swung them back into agreement with those who wanted a civilian settlement at almost any price. This meant a treaty between King and Parliament, as opposed to one imposed by the military. Coming at the very time when the Army leaders had decided that Charles must go, this renewal of negotiations by the parliamentary majority precipitated a direct collision. Since there was a sizeable majority in the Commons who favoured accepting the King's terms and only a small minority who would agree to deal with him more drastically, some of the Army leaders decided to purge the House. This followed on logically from what they had done in the summer of 1647, but this time it was on a much larger scale and had more dramatic results. 'Pride's Purge' of December 1648 (named after the Colonel who took the lead in excluding the Presbyterian M.P.s) made it more difficult to preserve the fiction that Parliament was the only source of legally constituted authority in the country. At this time Cromwell was out of London, still engaged in mopping-up operations after the renewed fighting. But Ireton was

9 'The Patentee'

...nopolists, often called 'pro-...ors', enjoyed their rights by ...ent from the King, hence the name patentee.

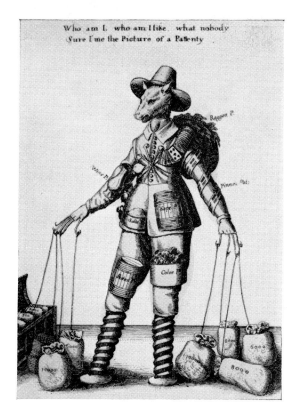

Who am I, who am I like, what nobody
Sure I me the Picture of a Patenty

(SUCKLINGS) Roaring Boyes.

10 The Sucklington Faction, 1641–2. Suckling was a royalist poet, and this political caricature shows what their enemies thought Cavaliers were like when not in action.

11 CHARLES I by Anthony Van Dyck

Note Charles' vacillating expression, brought out in profile. On the warrant for his execution, the first signature is Bradshaw's, President of the Court which tried the King; Cromwell's is third, and Ireton's level with it in the next column. Several of the signatories were executed as traitors in 1660–1.

12 Charles I's death warrant.

one of its guiding spirits; even Fairfax made no move against it. And there is no reason to suppose that Cromwell disapproved, though the idea that he arranged the whole thing as part of a deliberate plan to become a dictator, has been discarded by most historians.

In alliance with the Army, the purged Parliament then proceeded to set up a special High Court for the trial of the King. Meanwhile, soon after this, to make their other flank secure, the Independents began to purge the Army of Levellers, most of whose leaders were under arrest by the spring of 1649. According to Lilburne, when he was waiting to be examined, he heard Cromwell thump the table and say, 'You must break these men or they will break you.' A show-down for control of the Army was bound to come, but the Levellers had been discussing a compromise programme with the Independents only a few weeks before, so they had some cause for feeling betrayed. The ease with which the Levellers were defeated in 1649 is curious, considering their strength in 1647-8. Lilburne retained his personal popularity, especially in London, but only two or three regiments were prepared to defy their officers and resort to mutiny. By 1649 some of the soldiers' practical grievances were less acute, and perhaps only a small minority had ever really supported the wider democratic programme. The generals too, were better prepared than in the first Army revolt; they refused to allow the re-convening of the General Council of the Army, in which Agitators and senior officers had met and debated, if not as equals at least as man to man, at Putney in 1647.

The Trial and Execution of the King

The trial and sentencing to death of Charles I rested on extremely shaky legal foundations, and the King made the most he could of this. Basically it was a political and not a legal act, comparable for example to the Nuremberg trials of German war criminals after the Second World War. It has often been said since that Charles I died a martyr for the Church of England, that it was his unshakable defence of his Anglican principles and his refusal to compromise or surrender these, which led to his judicial murder by

K

the extreme Puritans. This argument is not very convincing. More than once during the tortuous negotiations of 1646–8, Charles had agreed to accept a Presbyterian system for a longish period. His apologists might argue that this was done in bad faith, but if so, it is strange that he did not lie consistently, and so survive to continue his duplicity after 1649. It is also maintained that whatever his previous constitutional leanings had been and whatever he had stood for earlier, Charles finally died a martyr for the laws and liberties of England. In a negative sense there is more truth in this. The people who brought him to trial, in a sense did so illegally. The charge of waging war against his own people was tantamount to treason; but this was an offence against the sovereign, that is himself. There was a certain amount of double-talk here. Moreover those who brought him to trial only represented a small minority whose power rested on military force, that is on the Independent-led Army. Had it been possible to have free elections or a public opinion poll, a majority would undoubtedly have preferred some kind of compromise; that the King should be restored on conditions, not that he should be brought to trial, still less executed. Rising to the occasion, Charles faced his death with more dignity and good sense than he had often shown in his life. Yet for all this, he cannot truly be said to have stood for the laws and liberties of the country. If he had won the Civil War, he would have proceeded in much the same way, bringing his enemies to what would have been called justice and setting up something like an absolute monarchy. Remembering the 1630s, let alone his activities in the mid- and late 1640s, it is impossible to picture Charles as a sincere constitutional ruler.

As Cromwell and his party saw it, the real point of the trial and execution was to prove that kings were accountable to their subjects for what they did. Their secondary purpose was undoubtedly to commit those taking any part in the proceedings to the Independent, republican cause. Once the King had been executed there was a seal of blood set on that cause, which there could be no reversing; this would commit people as nothing else could. On the other hand, they did not simply want to destroy Charles by an act of butchery. Inconvenient as his existence was, and well justified as they were after the Second Civil War in concluding that he was incorrigible, they refused to contemplate having him murdered as earlier kings had been. The trial and execution were deliberately made as solemn as possible, with the greatest semblance to normal judicial proceedings, despite their obvious legal weaknesses. English Kings had often come to a bad, violent end before: two in the fifteenth and two in the fourteenth century. But the two former had been killed in battle or just after, while Edward II and Richard II had been tried and deposed and then killed afterwards. The great difference is that Charles I was executed *as King*; Cromwell is reputed to have said, 'We will cut off his head with the Crown upon it'. Charles Stuart, King of England, was executed, and then the institution of monarchy was abolished.

Although the English Republic only lasted just over eleven years, the King's death and the abolition of the monarchy form the most important single political event of the century. It influenced the whole future development of the country. It symbolised the outcome, not only of the Civil War, but of the much longer and more far-reaching constitutional conflict. Although the settlement of 1649 was not permanent and although monarchy was to be restored and to remain as a part of the government in Britain, the balance of political power was more decisively affected by this than by any other event in our history. It also affected what the English political system stood for in the eyes of foreigners. Charles' fate can be said to presage that of Louis XVI of France and that of the last Tsar of Russia, Nicholas II. To some extent it set the pattern for these great events and for other lesser revolutions from the eighteenth to twentieth centuries; it had a great influence on the Americans in their revolt against another English King, George III, just over 100 years later.

What Cromwell and the others who executed Charles I and introduced the Republic were really saying, or what at any rate has come to be the judgment of posterity on what they did, was: that monarchy might flourish, if and when it was a practical success, but that it was not a divine institution which was untouchable by ordinary mortal men, and that kings were in the last resort accountable for their actions to society just like anybody else.

5 : The Republic
(1649–60)

From the beginning of 1649 to April 1653 the country was ruled as a 'Commonwealth', by a minority of the House of Commons in the Long Parliament. Normally the House consisted of about 60 members; as many as 120 attended some meetings; about 200 (out of over 300 Parliamentarian M.P.s of 1642–8) may have sat at some time during these years. Parliament ruled through an elaborate system of committees, as it had done ever since 1642. Some were parliamentary committees, some were mixed, consisting of M.P.s and others, some were local for counties or even smaller units. At the centre, co-ordinating this structure, was the Council of State, a body to some extent modelled on the old Privy Council, but elected by the Commons. It replaced the previous central executive of the Civil War period—the Committee of Safety, which had become the Committee of Both Kingdoms after the Scottish alliance. There were some army officers and others who were not M.P.s on the Council of State, but most Councillors were also members of the 'Rump', as the purged Parliament came to be known. The small number of generals elected, other than Cromwell who was also an M.P., suggests an anti-military bias among its civilian members.

The proposal to try the King had been too much even for the handful of peers who were all that remained of the House of Lords. Only a minority of peers had stayed at Westminster during the Civil War as parliamentarian supporters; now even the radical minority of these felt unable to go along with the purged Commons. The Lords were accordingly by-passed. Just as Parliament in 1642 had claimed the right to legislate without the King, so now the Commons assumed the sole legislative authority. Not surprisingly, when after the King's execution a Republic was proclaimed, the

House of Lords was abolished along with the monarchy. The peers also lost their legal privileges and immunities, though not their actual titles—for the Independent leaders were themselves mainly gentlemen, and certainly not levellers. Whatever may be the truth about the relative fortunes of the aristocracy and the gentry in the eighty years or so before the Civil War, there can be no doubt about the almost total eclipse of the previous upper class from the middle of the Civil War until the Restoration. The parliamentarian peers had resisted the self-denying ordinance of 1644–5, excluding members of both Houses from civil and military office, because they claimed to be the 'natural' commanders of the country's, in this case in practice Parliament's, armed forces. Their removal from command in the Army and Navy hastened their decline. And the Republic saw their temporary destruction as a separate 'order' at the top of the social and political pyramid. Whether or not the Republic marked a more general shift towards social equality is a more difficult question to which we shall return.

The Achievements of the Commonwealth

Ireland was swiftly reconquered. Cromwell was sent over and won a series of decisive victories; much argument has gone on whether he used unnecessary ruthlessness, in having the garrisons of Drogheda and Wexford massacred after their surrender. According to the laws of war, as they were generally recognised in the seventeenth century, if a garrison refused to surrender after being summoned, they forfeited any right to be treated as prisoners of war; though barbarous, this was the normal practice of the time. It should also be said that many Englishmen, especially strong protestants, regarded the Irish catholics as savages and a menace to the English way of life—perhaps in the way that some Europeans until very recently regarded people living in other continents. The reconquest of Ireland led to much more thorough schemes of colonisation and the expropriation of native Irish landowners over far more of the country, than under the Tudors or early Stuarts. Ireland was more effectively colonised and a larger English ruling class imposed on it; this was reversed to a lesser extent after the Restoration than the land changes in England.

The Scots again intervened, on behalf of Charles I's son and successor, the future Charles II, who had been in exile with the remains of the active Royalist party since 1646. They were again decisively defeated, though with greater difficulty, in 1650–1. To the dismay of many of the old Anglican Cavaliers, Charles II like his father accepted a Presbyterian church settlement and even took the National Covenant, as the price of a military alliance with the Scots. The final defeat of this attempt at the battle of Worcester in 1651, removed for the time being any serious military danger of a Royalist comeback. And as a result of their defeat, a union with England was imposed on the Scots by the English Parliament. It was in the nature of a 'shot-gun marriage', and was never accepted as a permanency by more than a small minority in Scotland.

The Commonwealth also saw further changes in the church. In practice it became rather less Presbyterian than had been planned in the later 1640s. There were elements of Independency about the settlement, but it was also 'Erastian' in that the church was not to be autonomous but subordinate to the state, that is in practice to Parliament itself. The great majority of ordinary parish clergy, probably about two-thirds of the pre-1642 incumbents who were still alive, accepted this Puritan settlement. The remainder had already been purged, or were so now if they refused to accept it. Outside the church, a large number of Puritan sects enjoyed some measure of toleration as a result of the Independent victory; of these, the Baptists were by now the most numerous and firmly established. However some smaller groups, of whom the most important were to be the Quakers, were felt to represent too radical and direct a challenge to the authority of the church or indeed to any formal, institutional religion. They were not tolerated, even by most Independents. Cromwell differed in this respect from his own party; he was more tolerant, readier for example to accept the Quakers, than most of his allies and supporters.

The other principal achievement of these years was a more material one. Vast sales and transfers of landed property had been in progress since the mid-1640s. Church property which had belonged to the bishops and the deans and chapters of cathedrals was confiscated and then sold; most of the lands of the Crown were sold, some being given to the officers and soldiers of the Army instead of a cash settlement of their pay arrears; the estates of many leading individual Royalists were also confiscated and sold. Others had to pay heavy fines in order to get their estates back; these 'Compositions', as they became known, were mainly levied in the later 1640s but they were still in process of collection during the early 1650s. Quite a number of Royalists had to sell parts of their property, others were able to borrow enough money to pay their Composition fines, but many of them got into great economic difficulties as a result. The purchase of church, Crown and Royalist lands, partly by London merchants, lawyers and speculators, partly by the officers of the parliamentary armies, meant that a new landowning class came into existence in these years. At any rate there was a more drastic change in the pattern of landownership than at any time since Henry VIII's dissolution of the monasteries and the consequent sales of monastic property. But, as we shall see, much of this change of ownership under the Republic was to be reversed in 1660.

What kept the supporters of the Commonwealth together in these years? First, they were all committed, by the King's execution and the abolition of the monarchy as well as by the great share-out of property and public offices that had taken place. Secondly, whatever their own divisions, they had to present a common front against their enemies both abroad and at home—the Royalists and their own erstwhile allies, the Presbyterians and the Levellers. There was a limited degree of political and religious unity among the different supporters of the Commonwealth, though beyond what has already been described, it is difficult to say how far this went. They cannot quite be identified with the Independents of the years 1644–8, though they correspond more closely to this group than to any other.

Its Difficulties

The Commonwealth was undermined partly by the completeness of its victories over all these enemies. The dangers from the Royalists, Scots and Irish were all removed by the autumn of 1651. The Republicans could now afford to quarrel among themselves.

A disagreement also developed in foreign policy, over relations between England and the Dutch. Many people had hoped that the setting up of a Puritan Republic would lead to a close alliance or even union with the other strongly Calvinist republic in Europe, the United Provinces of the Netherlands. But it was a kind of love-hate relationship; unless the two countries were closely linked, despite their common political and religious outlook, they were almost bound to be on bad terms, because of their many material disputes. They were colonial rivals in the East Indies, the Caribbean and North America, but rivals too for the carrying trade of Europe itself, with fierce competition in shipping and fisheries. The Navigation Act of 1651 confined the carriage of European imports to British ships or to those of the country from which the goods originated; imports from Asia, Africa and America were to be carried only in British ships. This was a direct challenge to the Dutch as carriers of European goods, and war followed almost directly from it the following year. Technically the English were the aggressors. The war continued for rather over two years, without a decisive victory for either side, though it swung gradually in England's favour; since the Dutch were more dependent on seaborne commerce than the English, they were more vulnerable to blockade and interference with their normal trade. Cromwell and the Army leaders, perhaps because they were more interested in religion than commerce, were unhappy about this conflict, which was really prosecuted by a clique of leading civilians in the Commons in alliance with various business groups in the City of London.

Another factor was the extreme slowness of the Rump to come to any decision about a constitutional settlement. Roughly speaking, there was disagreement whether there should be piecemeal by-elections as in 1645–8 to fill up the many vacant places in the House (by this time many constituencies had no Members still sitting), or whether a new Parliament should be elected; and if so, whether the representative system should be the traditional one, that suggested by Ireton in 1647 or something different again.

The Rump was also very slow with other domestic reforms.

There was a widespread feeling, shared by Cromwell himself, that the legal system was slow and expensive and often unfair, and that it needed drastic reform. Although it set up many committees to consider this, the Rump achieved little. From the autumn of 1651 on, but particularly by the winter of 1652–3, the tension between the military and the civilian supporters of the Commonwealth became acute. The Army leaders came to believe that the civilians wanted to cut down the size of the armed forces and reduce their influence, while the civilians were afraid, rightly as it turned out, of some kind of military coup.

It would be wrong to picture the Rump as a mere gang of self-seekers, mediocre and unconstructive, bent only on plunder. That is the picture given by their enemies—Royalists, Presbyterians and Levellers; it is a caricature, traces of which are still to be found in some modern writings on the period. Undoubtedly some individual politicians and Army officers used their positions to amass large fortunes by dubious means. Sir Arthur Haselrig, one of the surviving Five Members, seems to have built up a kind of 'private empire' in the ex-Bishop of Durham's possessions, and he fell out with the Leveller leader John Lilburne about one particular colliery there. On the other hand another Leveller, Wildman, himself became a successful dealer in confiscated property. Sir Henry Vane, a champion of the more extreme sects and probably a more convinced Republican than Haselrig, was amply pensioned on retiring from the Treasurership of the Navy. Other instances could be cited. Yet most of this was no worse than the normal practice of courtiers and office-holders under the monarchy. One difference is that the Independents (the future Republicans) had mostly come into office within the few years 1645–9, so giving their take-over the appearance of a sudden spoliation. Another difference is that some Republicans at least did have higher standards in such matters. Ireton for example refused grants of money and land when he was Lord Deputy of Ireland, and in general officials were deliberately paid higher salaries in the hope that they would recoup themselves less at the expense of the state and the public. If the Rump got a bad name for corruption, this may partly be because it was being judged more severely than previous régimes.

Moreover, even in domestic reform the Commonwealth can be given some credit. The ending of indefinite imprisonment for petty debts, the use of English in all legal proceedings and a further lowering of the legal maximum rate of interest chargeable on loans (the last such reduction had been achieved in the Parliament of 1624) were progressive steps, though only the third of these was to survive the Restoration. And some at least of the money and resources gained from the bishops and the cathedrals was devoted to founding more schools, especially in areas which had previously been educationally backward, such as Wales.

Its Fall

The practice of sending Puritan missions into Wales, however, caused a dispute which helped to precipitate the downfall of the Rump. The leader of the radical wing of the Army, Thomas Harrison, the patron of the Baptists and of those extreme Puritans, the Millenarians, supported these missions, which were opposed and eventually prohibited by the Independents in Parliament. In general there was a threefold division at this time on religious questions, between Presbyterians, Independents and sectaries, besides this particular issue over the Welsh missions which brought Harrison and the radical Puritans of the Army into collision with the House of Commons.

The crisis came to a head in April 1653 when Cromwell dissolved the Rump. In the immediate sense, this was due to a sudden switch by the parliamentary leaders from a plan for a general election by an agreed date, to which they seemed to have committed themselves, back to one for piecemeal by-elections—with the existing Members keeping their seats. At this time Cromwell's path was an individual, even a lonely one. He took the final decision, but he was under pressure from the more conservative-minded Army officers (his son-in-law Henry Ireton had died in Ireland, and this group was now led by John Lambert, a less able but still gifted administrator and political thinker, and a successful general). On the other side pressure was also exerted by the radical wing of the Army, this time led not by Lilburne and the Levellers, but by Major-General Harrison, spokesman of the Millenarians. This suggests the temporary ascendancy of the restrictive over the democratic tendency within the Puritan movement.

From the dissolution of the Rump in April to the setting up of the Protectorate in December 1653 there was an uneasy interval. The state was still technically a Commonwealth, though no regular parliament was in existence. A representative body of a sort was called, which sat from July to December, sometimes known as the Nominated Parliament. This is really the best name for it, since its members were chosen from the Independent and Baptist congregations, and it was not elected like an ordinary parliament. It is sometimes called the Little Parliament because its membership was smaller; and sometimes derogatively, the Barebones Parliament, after Praise-God Barbon a London tradesman and one of the members for the City, whose nomination was approved by Cromwell personally. This Parliament represented a compromise. It was meant to work out a settlement, not itself to constitute one; it was perhaps nearer to the wishes of Harrison than to those of Lambert, and can be thought of as a kind of party assembly of the Puritan churches. Just as it has been named after Barebones, so it has often been represented as a body of crackpots. In fact the Nominated Parliament undertook a number of perfectly sensible reforms which the Rump had toyed with but never put through. Its fall was due to a split on two issues: whether compulsory tithes should continue to be paid, to maintain the ministers of the state church, and whether law reform should be limited and piecemeal, as the more moderate reformers wanted, or drastic and sweeping, as some of the radicals in the sects (like the Levellers) wanted. The alarm taken by the more conservative elements—such as Lambert—led to a further military coup against the majority in Parliament, deadlock having been reached with the radicals narrowly in the ascendant on these two great questions.

From Cromwell's own speeches to his later parliaments, it appears that he personally had set great store by the Barebones experiment. He had hoped that here at last was an assembly consisting of none but unquestionably godly men who could unite, as the Long Parliament and then the Rump had so conspicuously failed to do, in undertaking the necessary work of reformation in church and state. And it was always more in sorrow than in anger that he spoke of their failure. Yet in a sense this only underlines Cromwell's own fundamental conservatism, or at least the contradiction in his outlook between the desire for reform, for wide toleration (in England extending even to catholics) and for a popular basis of support, and the contrary tendency towards authority, hierarchy and order. This tendency was personified in his own role as the leader of an Army that had become in his and others' eyes the very embodiment of God's purpose on earth. Historians who mourn the Barebones as the tragic climax of the whole Puritan saga perhaps err in making too little of this second, narrowing and authoritarian, element. Those who see it as a mere postscript to the heroic endeavours of the Levellers and Diggers and as doomed to inevitable failure make too little of its potentialities. Likewise they perhaps mistake the nature of Puritanism, again by identifying it too completely with social and political democracy. The truth is that the area of agreement on constitutional and social policy among the various Puritan parties and sects was very small; it was hard to seek in the church too, once the system of Charles I and Archbishop Laud had been well and truly overthrown. Cromwell, however, did not abandon the quest for a Puritan polity and for like-minded men to help him erect it in an orderly, constitutional way.

Cromwell's Protectorate

This was immediately followed by the setting up of the Protectorate. The new government of December 1653 was based on a written constitution, produced by Lambert but modelled on Ireton's Heads of Proposals; this was called the Instrument of Government, under which the country was ruled from then until the next constitutional settlement was attempted in 1657. Cromwell had been the most important single person in the country since 1649; but he was not its actual ruler until the dissolution of the Rump (for example he had opposed the Dutch war), and not the official ruler until the end of the year. Even after that, despite his unique position as Lord Protector and commander-in-chief of the Army, Cromwell's rule was not a complete personal dictatorship, nor was it a mere military despotism. The inauguration of the Protectorate was itself an attempt to give his power a constitutional basis. Cromwell himself certainly did not want to be a despot or a military dictator; his Council provided some check on his personal power, and he tried hard to find a constitutional settlement.

The years 1654–8 saw two serious attempts by the Lord Protector to turn himself into a constitutional ruler, working in partnership with a parliament such as the Instrument provided for. Why did he fail? First, whatever constitution might be implemented, the basis of support for the Protectorate was too narrow. Many of the ex-Rumpers, the Republicans like Vane and Haselrig who had been in control from 1649–53, now turned against Cromwell, seeing a Protectorate as a step back towards monarchy and opposing the rule of a 'single person'. Then there was the division in the Army, between the conservatives and radicals (Harrison was soon purged, after his opposition to the Protectorate became obvious). Thirdly there was the chronic disagreement between the civil and military elements; this became a split within the ranks of the Cromwellians as well as among the Republic's supporters generally, between administrators and what were called 'the swordsmen'. Nor was there any real conciliation of the groups outside the Republican parties, among those who had not supported the Commonwealth; some such, mostly Presbyterians, did come back into public affairs but not enough, while the radical sectaries and the ex-Leveller supporters remained irreconcilable. Lambert's constitution was ingenious, and in many ways sensible. But neither of the Parliaments elected, in 1654 and 1656, would accept it, and both had to be purged before they could safely be allowed to proceed. The first one came to grief more quickly, getting into a series of disputes with the Protector concerning his control of the armed forces, and financial provision for the Army, as well as on the issue of religious liberty; here Cromwell was undoubtedly in advance of opinion in his Parliaments and his own party. After the dissolution of this Parliament in 1655, and following a revival of plots by the Royalists on behalf of the exiled King, Cromwell put the country under eleven Major-Generals, who were to be in charge of internal security and the collection of a new penal tax on Royalists to pay for the militia.

The significance of the Major-Generals has sometimes been exaggerated. Cromwell did not act as a military dictator and subject England and Wales to the rule of eleven petty, regional tyrants. To begin with, they were only to be in command of the militia and responsible for security against further plots and risings; at most they were meant to supervise the other activities of local government. But, as time went on, some of them undoubtedly interfered more than others with the ordinary work of the J.P.s, for example over the licensing of inns and alehouses. In this way, their rule exacerbated existing civil-military tensions, while in the public mind it became associated with repressive Puritanism, with the suppression of traditional sports and pastimes as well as vice and crime. This had great psychological after-effects, though these were deliberately exaggerated by anti-Republican propaganda after the restoration of the monarchy. The lasting dislike of extreme Puritanism and military rule owes something to the activities of the Major-Generals in 1655-7.

The second Protectorate Parliament of 1656-8 saw a swing towards a 'civilianising' of the Cromwellian régime. This process was marked by the end of the rule of the Major-Generals, the offer of the Crown to Cromwell by Parliament and the introduction of a new constitution, the 'Humble Petition and Advice', in which the Army had a more modest place and the Lord Protector was more like the King (as of about 1641) in all but name. Like that of 1654, this House of Commons had to be purged before it began to sit; but it then had a majority for Cromwell not merely as Protector but as King. The Protector refused the Crown, but accepted the rest of the new constitution. His own personal preference, and perhaps his conscience, may have decided him against becoming King, but he was also under very heavy pressure from the Army to refuse, not only from a few individual generals but also from many of the medium- and junior-ranking officers, who were zealous Republicans. Lambert resigned all his offices rather than accept even the Petition and Advice without the kingship, perhaps because it made the Protectorate hereditary and he had himself been hoping to succeed on Cromwell's death. Cromwell may have felt that he would be overthrown by an Army revolt if he accepted the Parliament's offer. But by refusing the Crown he lost his best chance of consolidating the régime on a more traditional footing. His rule was already conservative enough to have alienated many of his one-time radical supporters. Now, by refusing to accept the outward symbol of compromise with the old order, he forfeited all hope of gaining enough support from upholders of tradition, especially members of the peerage and gentry, to make this kind of settlement likely to outlast his own lifetime. It depended too much on Cromwell's personal position and abilities, and his hold over the Army, though it might have lasted if he had accepted the Crown.

The 'Petition and Advice' which Cromwell accepted (less the Kingship) in the summer of 1657 differed in other respects too from the 'Instrument of Government' according to which he had ruled since the winter of 1653–4. Under the Instrument, the Council of State had considerable powers as a check on the Protector, especially when parliament was not sitting; this gave the other generals a legitimate constitutional position which corresponded, in some measure, to their actual power. Under the Petition the Protector's Council had virtually the same powers and duties as the old royal Privy Council; this meant that in the last resort it was a subordinate, advisory body whose executive powers depended on the Protector. Seats in the so-called 'Other House' (the name House of Lords like that of King was still unacceptable) did not compensate for this. Hence when the generals came into collision with Cromwell's successor in 1659 they had to make a direct military threat, because constitutionally Richard Cromwell could overrule them. In other ways the Petition weakened the executive as a whole—Protector, Council and administration—compared with the Instrument, in that all previous laws and customs not repealed by Parliament were declared to be in force. This weakened the government's claims to emergency powers, for example against suspected royalists, and to levy taxes not authorised by Parliament, some of which had already been challenged back in 1654–5. It also called in question the actual electoral system used, under the

Instrument, in calling the Parliaments of 1654 and 1656. Troublesome as these bodies had been, and necessary as it had proved to purge them, the representation of Ireland and Scotland had given the government extra seats, since the M.P.s for these countries were almost all English officials, pro-English 'collaborators' or army officers. Likewise the revised franchise, made deliberately narrower in the counties, may have helped the middling gentry, as opposed to the greater landowners with their dependent tenants and servants, many of whom enjoyed the old forty-shilling freehold franchise. That there were proportionately more county and fewer borough members under the Instrument is another suggestive reminder that, whatever was true under the Rump, the Protectorate was a régime less of the middle-class townsmen than of the gentry or rather, to be more exact, of certain sections among the gentry in alliance with parts of both the rural and the urban middle classes. The proportion of merchants in the House of Commons remained surprisingly constant (no doubt with short-run ups and downs from one parliament to the next) all the way from 1640, through the Protectorate into the next century, at least as far as 1760–1.

The replacement of Instrument by Petition was one reason why Richard Cromwell and his advisers went back to the old franchise and electoral divisions in the winter of 1658–9. They kept only—and this was surely an indefensible compromise—the Irish and Scottish members from the 1653–7 constitution. Paradoxically this meant that the House of Commons of January to April 1659, despite great battles over the recognition of the 'Other House', as well as over the M.P.s from outside England and Wales, was slightly less difficult to handle than those dissolved by Oliver in 1655 and 1658. Again this left the army officers with little alternative but military action when by the spring of 1659 Protector and Parliament together seemed to be threatening the Army's vital interests.

The Protector also quarrelled with his second Parliament over the 'Other House', which was to replace the old House of Lords under the new constitution. More Republicans and Army officers were offended by this, though some military men accepted Crom-

13 OLIVER CROMWELL

This miniature portrait by S. Cooper was probably painted about the time when Oliver turned out the Rump.

4 The House of Commons. his print of the Commons tting can be dated to 1649–53, y the absence of the royal arms om above the Speaker's chair.

15 London before the Fire

This panorama shows old St Paul's top left and London Bridge on the right. Note coal-ships on the left. In the foreground is Southwark, site of most of the theatres (which were closed by the Puritans, 1642–60). The city churches and buildings shown here were largely destroyed in the Fire.

wellian life-peerages. Those M.P.s who had been excluded before were let back into the Commons, and as a result the Republicans again had a majority there. Cromwell then dissolved this Parliament, and ruled by direct military power for the last months of his life.

Cromwell's failure with the two Protectorate Parliaments has recently been ascribed to his inefficient political management. On this view, he failed because he did not grasp the need to build up a properly led and organised government party in the House of Commons—rather like James I's failure to keep enough Privy Councillors there. In fact Cromwell did have a number of able Councillors in the Commons, also several of his military colleagues, some of whom were quite effective spokesmen for the government. However there was a deep military-civilian split among his own supporters, not only between them and the opponents of his régime. Cromwell himself was still isolated from most of his own party on the issue of religious liberty. There are other reasons apart from this question of parliamentary management, to explain his failure to establish a lasting constitutional Protectorate—or monarchy in Britain.

Foreign policy again became an issue in these years. Cromwell had reversed the Rump's policy by making peace with the Netherlands. He then became involved in a war with Spain, initially in the West Indies, later in Europe as well. An expedition sent against San Domingo was an ignominious failure; instead it resulted in the capture of Jamaica—the largest English tropical colony to date. The war was criticised as leading to loss of trade with Spain and to gains for the Dutch, who were neutral at this stage. It was also said to be reducing the power of Spain in Europe and so increasing that of France, now a greater political threat. Cromwell and his Secretary of State, John Thurloe, preferred to have France as an ally, being less dangerous as such than as an enemy and a backer of the Royalist exiles. On the other hand, they can legitimately be criticised for helping to build up the power of France, which in the long run was likely to be more of a threat than either Spain or the Netherlands.

The difficulties in the way of a constitutional settlement arose

L

partly from the Protectorate's revenue system. Although Cromwell's 'Court' was more modest and his administration more efficient than those of his regal predecessors, the size of the armed forces meant that the financial burden on the country was still far heavier than before the Civil War. The land sales and the penal compositions from Royalists had virtually come to an end. Apart from paying people in confiscated Irish land, as a part of the 'settlement' which followed the reconquest, there was little alternative to heavier taxation at home. The Excise, which fell most severely on the poor in their capacity as consumers and on some commercial interests, looked like becoming a permanent part of the system. The Customs duties had been increased, and some merchants resisted this, very much as others had done under Charles I. The 'Assessment', the direct tax on property, fell mainly on landowners and their tenants. Despite its being reduced by over two-thirds between 1654 and 1657, it was still heavier than Ship Money had been in the 1630s. Indeed it was worth more to the government than Ship Money and Wardship combined, and its collection was much more economical; there was nothing like the huge additional amount going into the pockets of middlemen and officials, which had made the burden on the country of revenues like Wardship so much heavier than their apparent value to the Crown would suggest.

Still, the upper and middle classes clearly felt over-taxed, and they were certainly less under-taxed than before the Civil War. No parliament could possibly accept a constitution—be it republican, protectoral, or monarchist—without insisting on control over taxation. Almost certainly they would insist on a large reduction, entailing drastic cuts in the Army, and on a re-distribution of the tax burden, away from the landowners and towards the mass of the people. The only alternative would have been for the government to follow a more radical policy, to make a deliberate bid for popular support and tax the rich more heavily. After his breach with the Levellers and then the Barebones reformers, this alternative was scarcely open to Cromwell.

Turning to trade and the economy of the country, Marxist historians have interpreted the Civil War and the Revolution as a class conflict which established a 'bourgeois' in place of a 'feudal' state. Whatever one's view of this, the middle classes had undoubtedly provided the backbone of the opposition to Charles I during the Civil Wars. So it is well worth considering how commerce and business interests generally fared under the Commonwealth and then the Protectorate. As elsewhere in the century, we have too few reliable figures to give an exact answer. In so far as the quantity and value of exports and imports paying customs duties are a safe guide (the difficulty being whether smuggling and evasion were constant or variable in amount), there was a definite recovery after the years of civil war. The first Anglo-Dutch War comes as near as any in history to being a war waged exclusively for economic motives. Even so, while it suited particular economic interests—notably the East India and Baltic traders—this does not mean that the country as a whole gained in wealth more than it lost; that the Netherlands suffered proportionately more than England is beyond dispute. The brief interval of peace in 1654–5 probably marked a peak of prosperity in the country's foreign trade, whether exceeding the level of the mid-1630s remains more debatable. Cromwell's war with Spain, though undertaken partly at least for colonial and commercial reasons, caused severe losses— in Spanish markets and from enemy privateers. So of course did other wars later in the century, such as that against France in the 1690s. But the dramatic downturn of trade in 1657–9 might be taken to indicate a swing away from mercantile back towards agricultural interests when we couple it with the cuts made in the Assessment, the main tax on landed wealth. A fall in the yield from Customs and Excise (due to wartime trade depression) plus the lowering of the Assessment, to win gentry support in Parliament, meant that Cromwell's increased military and naval spending on the Spanish war could not possibly be met. As under James I and in 1639–40, the gap between revenue and expenditure yawned dangerously wide. Although it had a more efficient tax system and a more honest administration than the early Stuart monarchy, the Protectorate, too, lived from hand to mouth, and by 1658 its position was getting rapidly worse. But on the whole it seems more likely that financial difficulties, made worse by the increasing reluctance of wealthy Londoners to go on lending, were a result of political instability and of fears for the future, rather than that the collapse of the republic in 1659–60 was brought about by a financial crisis.

The situation at the death of Cromwell in 1658, was in some ways alarming for the Republican cause but by no means desperate. The government was in debt, due to its military and naval expenditure and its difficulties in getting taxes voted by parliament, but the financial situation was not hopeless. No permanent constitutional settlement had been reached, although it was possible to call another parliament, on the basis of either the Humble Petition, or the Instrument. The Spanish war was increasingly unpopular, although victories had been won at sea and in Flanders, and control over Jamaica had been consolidated. Plots whether by Royalists, Presbyterians, or one-time Levellers continued but were unlikely to succeed provided the Republicans remained united. There was no reason to expect an immediate collapse. Cromwell's hold over the Army was unshaken to the time of his death, despite his having had to get rid of many of the leaders including Harrison and Lambert. Thanks partly to the naval victories won by Blake, Mountagu and other admirals, England's prestige in Europe stood higher than for many decades. There had also been some improvements at home. The religious situation was slightly more stable, and despite the damage caused by the Spanish war a measure of economic prosperity could be seen. Moreover Cromwell was less of a repressive Puritan than the rulers of the Commonwealth, or than some of his own military colleagues; and in some ways his rule was more enlightened and perhaps more beneficial than that of the Long Parliament or indeed the monarchy before that.

The Fall of the Republic

Why then do we find such a sudden and dramatic collapse between the peaceful succession of Cromwell's eldest son Richard in September 1658, and the return of Charles II in May 1660? One answer lies in the inadequacy of Richard Cromwell. He failed to keep control of the Army, and showed a general lack of political capacity; and there was nobody else. His younger brother Henry, who was in charge in Ireland, was an abler man but less popular; since the death of Ireton in 1651, there was no one who had the necessary political and military capacities to succeed Oliver. Secondly the division between the Army and the civilians now developed into a struggle between those for and against the Lord Protector—Richard Cromwell becoming completely identified with the Protectorate's civilian supporters. In Richard Cromwell's Parliament of early 1659, the Army leaders swung back to an alliance with the anti-Protectorate Republicans, that is their one-time opponents—the supporters of the Rump. To some extent this also marked a split between the conservatives, such as the Members of the 1656–7 Parliament who had offered the Crown to Oliver, together with the civilian officials in the government, and the radicals or out-and-out Republicans, whether military or civilian. These two divisions need to be distinguished, though in 1659 they had the same general effect.

The fall of Richard Cromwell was followed by the restoration of the Rump. It now represented the revived alliance between the Army leaders and the anti-Protectorate Republicans; in some ways this was a return to the situation of 1649–51. In the spring and summer of 1659 stability was still possible; this régime might have lasted at least as long as the Commonwealth had before. It failed to do so because of renewed antagonism between the civil and military elements, which became apparent almost at once and had undermined the restored Rump by the autumn of 1659. There were also serious differences inside the Army. Lambert, now restored to office, was the ablest of the generals, but the others would not accept his predominance, though none had the capacity to keep the Army united and loyal to the government. His prestige rose as a result of successfully suppressing a premature Presbyterian-Royalist rising in Cheshire, but this only precipitated the breach between the Army and the Rump, which the Army leaders had themselves restored in the place of Richard Cromwell and the third Protectorate Parliament. In the autumn the Rump was dissolved a second time and then at the end of the year it was restored a second time. There was general confusion in these months with no effective legal government; the country really did seem to be drifting

towards anarchy, or worse still a series of competing military des-
potisms. The general loss of confidence in the Republic affected
a number of waverers. People who had previously not wanted
to commit themselves openly to the cause of the exiled monarchy
now saw the restoration of the King as inevitable, and that
persuaded them to climb on to the bandwaggon and support his
cause.

In these and the following months the key role was played by
George Monck, Cromwell's commander-in-chief in Scotland.
Monck was an ex-Royalist, but a professional soldier who had
been genuinely loyal to Cromwell and probably to his son, but
was not prepared to accept a military dictatorship under Lambert
or anybody else. Whether he was from his first intervention a
crypto-Royalist is doubtful; the only hope of achieving a temporary settlement he saw was by bringing his own army, better
disciplined and thoroughly purged of political dissidents, down to
England, which he did in the winter of 1659–60. When Monck
arrived in London he found that the Rump was already sitting
again, and he soon decided that the only hope of stability was not
only to support Parliament as against the Army, but to insist that
those M.P.s who had been excluded back in 1648 should be re-
admitted. This meant a return to the House of Commons much as
it had been before the purge conducted by Colonel Pride, with a
moderate Parliamentarian or 'Presbyterian' majority, of monarch-
ists rather than republicans. Whatever Monck's exact intentions,
this inevitably led to the restoration of the monarchy.

Another key figure was Admiral Mountagu, Samuel Pepys'
patron. He brought the fleet back from the Baltic, where it had
been guarding English trade interests, but decided not to oppose
the King's return and co-operated closely with Monck. Like
Monck, he had been a trusted servant of Oliver Cromwell, and
both men continued to support the Republic until after the fall
of Richard Cromwell. Besides them, Roger Boyle, Lord Broghill
(brother of Richard Boyle, the famous chemist), had also played
a big part under the Protectorate, helping first Monck in Scotland,
then Henry Cromwell in Ireland. He had favoured Cromwell's
acceptance of the Crown in 1657, and would have liked to serve a

Cromwellian constitutional monarchy in much the same way as men like Stanhope, Walpole, Carteret and the Pelhams were to serve the Hanoverians in the next century. But the threat of anarchy, with fanatical military dictatorship as the apparent alternative, drove Monck, Mountagu, Broghill and others into royalism. The English republicans were not defeated by the royalists but by themselves. During the winter of 1659–60 smallmindedness, lack of trust and inability to compromise or to settle for less than ideal perfection proclaimed the bankruptcy of republican—and Puritan—statesmanship.

Even at this stage the continued divisions in the ranks of the Republicans, and within the Army itself, made the task of Monck and the restored Long Parliament easier than if there had been united resistance. Monck also acted in close alliance with the City of London; as in 1647–8 their preference was monarchical and Presbyterian, and above all for civilian as against military rule. By the spring of 1660 there was an absence of any practicable alternative policy to that followed by Monck. Furthermore, unlike Cromwell in 1657, when the crucial moment came to choose between constitutional monarchy and military rule, Monck was prepared to see the Army disbanded and a complete return to the traditional forms of civil government. He was also prepared himself to accept a subordinate place in the state, though a very honourable and profitable one as it turned out. This gave him far greater freedom of action than any other military leader of the period. Among the other supporters of the Protectorate, some saw the possibility of making their peace with the restored monarchy and moved over, taking advantage of the opportunity to do this in the last weeks of the Republic. Some perhaps preferred the monarchy to a further spell of Army rule; some were just out to save their necks. Others held out to the last; many wavered and did nothing; some fled abroad.

In the final analysis the fall of the English Republic was due to the lack of support for any one solution of its problems, to its internal divisions, and to the breadth of the external opposition. Even Cromwell himself could never quite decide whether he was a radical or a conservative revolutionary leader, whether he was a military or a constitutional ruler. And certainly nobody else could repeat his success, even for the lifetime of one person. It does not necessarily follow from this that the restoration of Charles II would have happened as and when it did either if Cromwell had lived longer, or if there had been a really able man to succeed him. Partly perhaps the mere passing of time had weakened the Republican cause, with the change of generations. By the end of the Protectorate, men were growing up who could not remember the Eleven Years' Tyranny of Charles I, but who were reacting against Puritanism and military rule as they had known these in the 1640s and 1650s.

The King's Return

A more puzzling historical problem to understand is why Charles II got back unconditionally in the spring of 1660, without having to accept the sort of stringent terms that his father had been faced with in 1648, 1646 or even 1641–2. The first reason for this is the deep division between the Presbyterian (that is monarchist, but not Cavalier or Anglican) majority in the Long Parliament, as it was restored by Monck, and the Republican minority there; they were unable to agree on any particular set of terms to be put to the King before they finally dissolved themselves. Secondly, overlooking the existence of numerous Royalists especially in the upper classes, who had been excluded from public life since the Civil War, the Presbyterians were foolishly over-confident of getting their way. They saw themselves in combination with Monck as the restorers of the monarchy, and believed that they would keep control of the situation after the King got back; this was a disastrous miscalculation.

Besides, Charles II played his hand well. He avoided any rash folly like his alliance with the Scots in 1650–1; he took advice from Edward Hyde, one of the ablest of his father's advisers and a parliamentary reformer of 1640–1. Charles accepted the minimum programme put forward by Monck, as the conditions for his return, and embodied this in a document known, from the place where he was staying in Holland, as the Declaration of Breda. This was an astute move because it put the onus on a newly elected parliament, to settle several of the most contentious problems that would have to be decided when the monarchy was restored. The first of these was the scope and limits of the pardon for what people had done during the Civil Wars and under the Republic. Except for the exclusion of the 'regicides' (that is, those who had actually signed Charles I's death warrant), discretion was to be left to parliament. The second was the religious settlement; there was a strong hint of toleration, but parliament was to decide what should be done about restoring the Church of England and the scope of religious liberty. Third, there was the land question. Again parliament was to decide about the return of church, Crown and private property, and whether the buyers should be compensated. Fourth, there was the urgent practical point of settling the Army's arrears prior to its disbandment. This referred particularly to Monck and his army, but it also affected the other military forces in England. The Long Parliament had put these under Monck's control after some feeble opposition to his southward march by Lambert, who made a second desperate attempt as late as April 1660 to raise a military revolt on behalf of the Republic. So Charles II had very few commitments, just as he had to accept very few conditions for his return.

In the technical, legal sense the position when he came back, was that all Acts of Parliament passed by the two Houses and the King up to February 1642 were valid, unless they were repealed or replaced. But all the so-called Acts, or parliamentary Ordinances passed by the two Houses, the Commons alone, or the Protector and his Council or his Parliaments since then, were invalid, unless specifically re-enacted. This left the constitutional position more or less as it had been in the winter of 1641–2; the Grand Remonstrance however had never had any statutory authority.

As with the fall of the Personal Rule in 1640, the attitude of the common people towards the Republic is something of an enigma. In London the Army seems to have become thoroughly unpopular with all classes by the winter of 1659–60. In the country at large as always there was much apathy. To some, if they thought about it at all, the government meant no more—or anyway fewer—cakes and ale; for all it certainly meant that beer and cider were dearer.

Total taxation was heavier, and proportionately more of it may have fallen on the poorer classes, compared with before the Civil War. Yet in other ways, such as a nearer approach to equality before the law (another Leveller objective partly accepted by their Independent allies, later opponents), life under the Republic may have been more congenial to the non-gentle classes. Such benefits, however, would have been appreciated more by those with some property and some education than by the worst off and the destitute. Even the enforcement of the Elizabethan poor law may have been as effective anyway under the Major-Generals as under the Personal Rule. We can only say negatively that the common people did not raise a finger to defend the Republic or prevent the Restoration; whether they acted in their own best interests in this is a different question.

It is tempting to say, as some historians have done, that Charles II simply took up in 1660 where his father had been in 1641. It can then be argued that the entire interval, the whole twenty-odd years of Civil War and Republic, is a gigantic and unnecessary aberration from the main line of steady, gradual constitutional evolution. But this is a very unhistorical approach. The political situation of 1641 was quite unstable; Charles I was not a man with whom that or any other parliament could ever have worked in trust and harmony. The compromise which did emerge between Crown and Parliament in 1660 and after, could only have been arrived at through some such sequence of events, some test of their relative strengths in the fire of battle. In that sense, what happened between 1640 and 1660 is very much in the main stream of English history, indeed it is crucial to the development of the constitution. Much of what happened in those years—civil conflict, proscriptions, executions—can be called tragic, but not an aberration, or a wasted, unnecessary tragedy.

6 : The Restoration Era

i. The Settlement, 1660-2

Its Terms

To understand what happened in 1660 and the years immediately following, we must always remember that the Restoration was not a simple Royalist victory. It had been due to an alliance of General Monck and other one-time Cromwellians with the ex-Presbyterians or moderate Parliamentarians of the 1640s, together with some of the old Cavaliers. The latter can in turn be divided into those who had been in exile with the young King and those who had stayed at home and made the best of things. This broad alliance was itself the result of the general swing of opinion away from the Puritans, the Army and the Republic in 1659. Thus the events of 1660 were far from marking a straight victory for the Royalist party of 1642, or for the Anglican Church.

The Restoration saw the return of the traditional upper class as well as the monarchy. The House of Lords was also restored; so, a little later, was the right of the bishops to seats in the Lords and of the clergy to hold lay offices, along with the rest of the Anglican hierarchy of church government. Control over local government and the militia came back into the hands of the peerage and the greater gentry in the counties and of the traditional oligarchy of Lord Mayor, Sheriffs and Aldermen in London. By an Act giving power to alter their membership, the independence of town corporations was reduced. The exertion of popular pressure on parliament was made more difficult by an Act to restrict mass petitioning, which had been a marked feature of the 1640s. Most offices of state and junior posts in the King's Household and the rest of the central government went to Royalists, except at the top where there were quite a number of survivors from the Republic, including Monck and his friends, and several Presbyterian leaders; there were some exceptions, too, lower down the administrative ladder. There were long queues for many offices. Pathetic hard-luck stories of what people had done and suffered during and after the Civil Wars accompanied many applications, but there were far more candidates than posts available.

Along with the traditional institutions (apart from the preroga-tive courts abolished in 1641 and the Court of Wards since then), and the traditional kind of men in them, the old administrative methods and attitudes were largely restored. The Republican sys-tem of paying officials bigger salaries, in order to get better value out of them, was continued. But some office-holders had the best of both worlds here, in that the old system of fee and gratuity pay-ments, of life tenure, reversions and the sale of offices came back too. Not until the end of the century (after the Revolution of 1688) was there any further advance towards something more like a modern civil service, for example in naval administration. As an official, Samuel Pepys, whose *Diary* gives a matchless picture of the central government at work in the 1660s, was very much a child of the Republic, in spite of his moral reaction against Puritanism. His attitude reflects both the older and newer ideas—of officials as the King's servants and as the public servants of the state.

Another notable feature of the settlement is that revenge was taken only on relatively few people. Those actually tried and exe-cuted were almost all regicides, plus one or two more who had been particularly involved in the death of Charles I, or in trying to prevent the Restoration; in the case of Cromwell, Ireton and others revenge was taken even on corpses. Shocking as these execu-tions may seem to us, their number was unusually small, compared with the normal standard in sixteenth- and seventeenth-century Europe after the suppression of a rebellion. For, in the eyes of the King and his supporters, that was what the Civil War and the Republic had been.

At the same time, an attempt was made to put the King's finances on a sounder footing than those of his father and grand-father before the revolution. This task fell to the Parliament which was elected in the spring of 1660 to replace the Long Parliament, the Convention as it was called because it was summoned and the Members elected before the King's return. Most Members of the

Convention were not in fact keen that Charles II should have too large a regular, ordinary revenue. They did not want him to be able to act independently of parliament, especially if he intended to pursue an ambitious foreign policy. They hoped to keep a measure of control over him, through ensuring that he was not financially self-sufficient; and, as it turned out, this was a very shrewd move. In a sense this did constitute a limitation, which was imposed on the King, though not a precondition of his being restored. To look at this financial settlement in slightly more detail: the King surrendered his traditional feudal dues (the chief one being Wardship, which had already been taken away by Ordinances passed in the Long Parliament); this takes us back to the Great Contract proposed by Salisbury in 1610. In return, the Excise, the duty on ordinary consumer goods, which had been introduced by Pym in 1643, was now—as far as beer and cider, and soft drinks (tea, coffee, chocolate and sherbet) were concerned—made a permanent part of the revenue system; and half this, reckoned at £100,000 a year, was specifically to be instead of the feudal dues. The effect of these changes was to put a relatively greater burden on the poor and on some business people, and a relatively lighter one on landowners; any idea of a regular tax on landed property or on incomes was rejected, and the King's own spokesmen then demanded the Excise, as the only reliable alternative. Apart from some special once-for-all taxes, voted in 1660–1 to pay off the Army, the Hearth Tax (a duty on the number of fire-places in people's houses) was the only new direct tax in these years; this too, though it excluded the very poorest homes, hit the poor relatively harder than the rich. There was also the income from the restored Crown lands. Much more important, virtually the whole existing Customs revenue was confirmed to the King, either in perpetuity or for his lifetime, and a new schedule of duties (or 'Book of Rates') was introduced at the same time. Despite these measures, the King's revenue did not reach the Convention's peacetime target of £1·2 million a year until well into the 1670s (Cromwell's revenue had been about £1·5 million per annum, though a realistic comparison is difficult because the Republic never had a full financial year without war). This deficiency on his estimated income meant that for the first half of his reign Charles II was in a weaker bargaining position in relation to parliament than he would otherwise have been.

As for the land settlement, many of the new owners lost their property. Crown and church lands were confiscated from their purchasers without compensation, though some of those holding ecclesiastical property got the option of becoming tenants of the restored owners. The land which had been confiscated from some leading individual Royalists—peers and others with political or Court influence—was also restored outright. But in two important respects the land settlement fell short of being a complete restoration. Many sales of Royalists' lands had technically been voluntary, that is ordinary commercial transactions, undertaken in order to pay penal fines and taxes and not due to confiscations. These were not automatically reversed. It was possible for Royalist landowners to take their chance by bringing legal actions to recover their property, but unless they were wealthy and influential enough to get a private Act of Parliament passed, this was a risky and expensive procedure. A number of them did lose some of their land permanently; perhaps more important, a much larger number had got heavily into debt, as a result of borrowing in order to pay the Composition fines. The lasting effects of this indebtedness may have been delayed as late as the 1670s and even beyond, when many middling and lesser ex-Cavalier families were in great economic difficulties, and in some cases had to sell up.

The other major modification was in Ireland. There, more of the one-time Cromwellians kept much of the property they had acquired, because it had not been taken from English Royalists but from Roman Catholic Irish owners. Vast areas had been confiscated after the suppression of the rebellion (or attempted war of independence) in the years 1652–4. In Ireland the conflict had been a three-cornered one between Anglican Cavaliers, Puritan Parliamentarians and the natives; and it was the latter who went to the wall in the settlement which was concluded, to the advantage of both the other groups. It has been estimated that only about one-sixth of the original Irish catholic owners recovered their property, and that this represented only about a fifth of the total acreage which had been taken. A new protestant ascendancy class had thus come into existence in Ireland. These great changes in the Irish social system were more important than those which took place after the Revolution of 1688, and which used to be considered more far-reaching.

By contrast with Ireland, where the Restoration settlement was very much of a partnership between Royalists, Presbyterians and Cromwellians, in Scotland it was altogether more partisan. There, it rested on a much narrower basis, was more aggressively Royalist, and despite the participation of some one-time Presbyterian leaders, saw the reintroduction of an episcopalian church system. This never commanded the support of more than a small minority of the Scottish people, and it rested on the use of troops recruited largely from the Highland clans. A period of repressive minority rule followed which for all but the aristocracy, the bishops and the Highlanders was a change for the worse from the Cromwellian Union, unpopular as that had been.

Religion

In England, the most complicated and controversial question of all was that of religion and the future of the church. We have to remember the ferocious religious conflicts of the mid-century, some of which had been fought out in the Civil War, likewise the bitter divisions which had then arisen among the Puritans. The obstacles to any agreed church settlement and the effects of religion having been a source of conflict are obvious to anyone who studies the period. Although the principle of religious toleration had had eloquent apostles, including Roger Williams one of the founders of the New England colony of Rhode Island, some of the Levellers and the greatest poet of the age, John Milton, it was still not generally accepted. By this time two lines of thought can be distinguished. One possibility was that the more moderate non-Anglicans, mainly Presbyterians (here used in the religious, not the political sense) but possibly also the Independents and Baptists, should be given some kind of minimum toleration for private worship, though not equality of political and civic rights, outside the state church if they could not be accommodated within it. The other alternative was that the church should broaden itself to bring as many of these people as possible back within its fold, as had been the case in the Elizabethan period. The first policy has become known as that of 'Toleration', the second of 'Comprehension'. Opinion among the more enlightened Anglicans tended to veer between these two possibilities from 1660 until 1689. The Anglican Church suffered from its failure to adopt the comprehensive solution in so far as it became the church of a single class in the eighteenth and nineteenth centuries. At the time, however, acceptance of the principle of Toleration and its practical application was even more valuable.

In all these discussions the position of the Presbyterians was crucial. They were the Puritan group, who were least deeply divided from the Low-Church Anglicans; indeed it was only on the question of bishops that they seriously disagreed with each other. The Presbyterian laity had included many parliamentary leaders of the years 1641–8, not all of whom had been 'Root-and-Branch' men in the first place, while many of the Low-Church Anglicans had been against Laud and had supported the early ecclesiastical measures of the Long Parliament. The Presbyterians are often blamed for having over-played their hand in 1660–1, that is for not having accepted bishops and formed a united front with these Low-Church Anglicans. However, though there is some truth in this, the situation was less simple than it implies. The High-Church party among the Anglicans, the one-time Laudians or Arminians, were against any compromise at all with their old Puritan enemies, and opposed both Comprehension and Toleration; they wanted a return to the church system of the 1630s. They failed to restore the church and its leaders to their former role in the state; never again was there to be an ecclesiastical first minister in a position comparable to Laud's in the later 1630s. The church courts were never to be as active again; the Court of High Commission did not reappear at all (except very briefly in a quite different context). But for all this, the High Churchmen succeeded in preventing a more generous settlement. In 1660 they played for time, because of the King's own leanings towards Toleration and their not having a majority in the Convention Parliament. There was a potential

Puritan and ex-Parliamentarian majority in the Convention House of Commons. Indeed, the ex-royalists constituted a distinct minority. The Puritans, however, were divided and demoralised; they had no united leadership, while a recent study has shown that both at the very beginning of the sitting—before the King's return, through the summer, and during the crucial second session in the autumn, the leaders of the royalist minority made effective use of their opportunities. Negatively, they were able to prevent any bills passing the House which would have forced the King to use his veto unless he were to accept a presbyterian church system, or constitutional limitations going beyond those of 1641. More positively, although the revenue provisions proved to be inadequate, the kind of taxes which the Convention voted were more in line with what the King's advisers wanted than with the suggestions of the Court's opponents. In addition to internecine divisions and the demoralisation of defeat, the King's father's and his own one-time enemies also succumbed in considerable numbers to the use of royal patronage. This was not just a matter of disillusioned cynics selling themselves to the highest bidder, or to the restored source of bounty; government had to be carried on, and short of an administration staffed entirely by ex-royalists, the moderate parliamentarians of 1648 and 1659–60 were its natural heirs. None the less, as the history of the next Parliament was to show, the presbyterians in particular, and all moderate puritans up to a point, had missed their last chance of trying to impose a church settlement which could embrace both themselves and their erstwhile Anglican enemies. And this Parliament was dissolved at the end of 1660 when the revenue settlement was completed.

The 1661 elections produced a very different result: a Parliament of extreme Royalist—that is Anglican and Cavalier sympathies, which seemed bent upon revenge and on undoing as much as possible of what had happened in the 1640s and 1650s. The High-Church leaders could now command a majority for a much tougher and more partisan settlement. This policy is traditionally associated with the man who was then the King's chief minister, Edward Hyde, soon to be created Earl of Clarendon. But it was not really his doing; Hyde's own preference would seem to have

M

been for a more moderate solution. The Acts named after him, the 'Clarendon Code', constituted a series of repressive measures, designed not only to narrow the Church of England, to make it more catholic and less protestant, but also to persecute the Puritans outside it and make life intolerable for them. These were not Clarendon's personal handiwork; indeed, the most savage of them, the Second Conventicle Act, was only passed in 1670, some years after his fall. The result, particularly of the Act of Uniformity (1662), was that even the most moderate Presbyterians either had to conform or to get out of the church, much as had happened in 1604 under James I and Bancroft. By the end of 1662 nearly two thousand ministers had lost their livings; this was a far more sweeping change in the personnel of the church than had happened at any one time in the 1640s or 1650s, though the grand total of ministers deprived in those years was probably larger. Those who left the Church of England set up on their own, in some cases forming secret Puritan congregations. Together with the sects which had co-existed with the state church under the Republic, these are the ancestors of the modern Nonconformists, at least of the Presbyterian, Congregationalist, and Baptist churches; the Methodist church stems from an eighteenth-century religious division.

Persecution under the Clarendon Code varied in severity. For much of the 1660s and 1670s it was not quite as bad in practice as would appear in theory. Charles II twice, as well as his brother James II later, tried to initiate a policy of Toleration. Both Kings were doing this primarily in order to help the Roman Catholics in the country, Charles having secret if lukewarm catholic leanings and James being an avowed catholic. But they were also doing it to help the Puritan Nonconformists, if only to win their political support and not because they believed in the principle of Toleration. Persecution was probably at its worst from 1681 to 1685 when, as we shall see, the Crown and the Anglican party in the state were in the closest working alliance; it was not as bad either before or after those years, when this alliance was less firm.

The Anglican–Cavalier reaction of the 1660s was helped by the danger—real or imagined—of a Republican rising, on behalf of what had come to be known as the 'Good Old Cause'. There were one or two very small outbreaks of violence by Fifth-Monarchy fanatics, while more serious plots were strongly suspected. This strengthened the case of those who demanded drastic measures and maintained that any weakness or compromise would only bring back the rule of the 'swordsmen'—Cromwell's soldiery or the more fanatical sectaries. This reaction was undoubtedly helped by the personality of Charles II. Alone among the Stuart kings, he had the common touch; he could get on with ordinary people of all classes. To some extent the Cavalier Parliament and the Church of England came in on his coat-tails, profiting from his personal popularity.

Changes since 1640

One of the greatest differences from the period before the Civil War is that after the Restoration, Puritanism came increasingly to be the religion of a single social class. It became the creed of a substantial section of the middle class, and virtually ceased to be a movement cutting across social divisions, generating energy and piety throughout the nation.

The apparently total defeat of the Puritan and Republican cause should not stop our seeing that Charles II was on a very different footing from his father. Despite his strong personal position he lacked the machinery, even if he had had the will, to re-erect a Tudor type of conciliar or near-absolute monarchy. Non-parliamentary taxation never reappeared on any appreciable scale. Far more than before 1640, Parliament was now accepted as a regular part of the government, even though the King still had a discretionary power as to when it was assembled, adjourned and dissolved. The corollary of this was that in order to manage public affairs with reasonable efficiency and smoothness, the King and his ministers needed to have support in the House of Commons. They had to control both Houses, but more particularly the Commons since they were the masters in revenue and taxation matters. This could be achieved by various means. Influence could be used in elections so as to get supporters of the King returned, especially for the borough seats which were more open to pressure than the county ones; patronage could be used by the distribution of government and Court appointments, contracts, etc. among Members of Parliament; support could be organised through forming a party to advance the King's policies in the Commons. In response to this, those who wanted to oppose the King's policies successfully also had to organise themselves in the same ways. Opposition, however, still tended to be equated with faction, often with something only barely distinguishable from treason. There were 'Court' and 'Country' Members of Parliament in these years, but there was not yet, nor for some time to come, a government party and a 'loyal opposition' waiting to take its place.

In some respects we are still very far from knowing how much lasting effect the Civil War and the Republic had on what followed. For example, the restoration of royal government in 1660 meant the return of the old, pre-war administrative system, whereby public offices under the Crown were treated much like pieces of private property, and their holders recouped themselves largely by fees and gratuities from members of the public and from fellow officials, and from the Crown in perquisites or on a turn-over basis. Yet, at the same time there was a strong element of continuity from the Cromwellian régime (though not from the restored Commonwealth of 1659). At the top Monck, Mountagu and others, further down the administrative ladder Samuel Pepys and other subordinate officials, bridged the great divide of May 1660 between republic and monarchy. Likewise, some of the Long Parliament's and Commonwealth's innovations survived too: notably the payment of higher salaries to the holders of important posts, especially to those responsible for the collection, auditing and spending of large sums. To be cynical, the ministers and civil servants of Charles II had it both ways: they enjoyed both the higher salaries introduced during and after the Civil War, and the gratuities and other perquisites usual before 1642. However, despite the setbacks and scandals of the second Anglo-Dutch war, the standard of efficiency was almost certainly higher than under James and Charles I, while the King's Household in the social and ceremonial sense consumed a distinctly smaller percentage of total royal resources under Charles and James II than it had done under their father and grandfather. England's advance towards imperial power in the eighteenth century, despite the sinecures and corruption of that period, was buttressed by a slightly less inefficient and dishonest system of administration in the government service than were her first gropings in that direction under Elizabeth I. Above all, however much their memory was vilified by Royalist and Anglican preachers and writers, the Republicans had demonstrated that men for the most part not drawn from the hereditary upper class could govern the country with tolerable success: a salutary lesson for any royal family and aristocracy to learn. So here is one great paradox of the Restoration. Charles II, the 'merry monarch', with his numerous mistresses and his flippant, sometimes vicious Court, was also the ruler of a country where some lessons had been learnt, and where, even if this was not made explicit, some mistakes would not be repeated.

Moreover despite the defeat, and indeed submergence, of the Puritans after 1660 their continuing constitutional influence must not be overlooked. Many Puritans conformed and did not join the persecuted sects. This was especially true of the peers, gentry, lawyers and wealthier merchants, who had provided the conservative wing of the movement in the mid-century revolution. And these were precisely the classes with most political influence in both houses of parliament and in local government. Hence the indirect influence of the Puritans is not limited after 1660 to those who were Puritan in the sense of being Nonconformists, subject to religious persecution and civic disabilities. And it may be that the revived political opposition of the 1660s and 1670s, which arose in protest against various aspects of royal policy, owed more than appears on the surface to this influence from the period of the Civil War and the Republic. But it certainly was due also to the growing disillusionment with Charles II and his policies of many who were his most fervent supporters in the halcyon days of 1660–2.

It is important to look at the balance of social as well as political forces after the Restoration. If the Republic had failed partly, perhaps mainly through lack of support from the traditional upper or ruling class in the country, then equally the restored monarchy would not be able to get on without this support. But the restoration of the old balance of class power did not simply represent a return to the situation before the Civil War. For example, many government controls over different aspects of social and economic life had been removed; monopolies had been swept away, except in certain branches of foreign trade, where they were popular with some interests in the City of London. There was a great expansion of overseas trade and colonisation after 1660, with continuity in both men and measures from the Protectorate. There was certainly greater freedom for business enterprise; and compared with the years 1603–40, perhaps even with the Tudor period, commercial interests, especially those of the City, enjoyed more political influence. The Navigation Act of 1651 was not merely re-enacted but extended in scope, restricting exports as well as imports to English ships. Passed by the Convention in 1660 and confirmed in 1661, the Navigation Act became the basis of a comprehensive code to regulate commercial relations between England and her colonies, which was rounded out by subsequent statutes. In these limited, but none the less real ways, the whole upheaval of the years 1640–60 can be thought of as a shift of power and still more of opportunity, towards the business and commercial interests, if not as a 'bourgeois' or capitalist revolution in the rigid, sweeping sense suggested by Marxist historians.

This greater scope for business enterprise also applied to agriculture. The old restraints on sheep-farming and enclosure were dropped; at the same time landowners and their tenants obtained a greater degree of protection for some products, such as home-grown grain, against possible foreign imports. The famous Corn Laws, which were to cause so much trouble in the nineteenth century, really date from the 1660s. They also got protection against Irish cattle exports, a setback for the development of Irish agriculture; further restrictions on Irish and colonial trade and manufactures in English economic interests followed at intervals over the next forty years or so. Until the Union of 1707, Scotland too was excluded from many of the benefits of commercial union and its traders subjected to harassing restraints. Inside England the Poor Law was amended so as to check the free movement of people seeking work.

In these respects there was no clear division of economic interest between the upper and the middle class. Up to a point the same is true of their political interests. To a limited extent, the Restoration does seem to signify a shift in power back from the middle to the upper class. The recovery of political and social predominance by the nobility and gentry is obvious compared with the later 1640s and the 1650s. Yet just as it would be a mistake to represent the Civil War itself as a straight class conflict, neither can the Restoration be seen in this light, though it too had an element of this about it.

ii. The Cavalier Parliament, 1661–78

The New Political System

If we compare the political history of Charles II's reign with that of his father's and grandfather's, there are some strong likenesses as well as several striking differences. To take some of the likenesses, by contrast with 1640–60 one feature is the reappearance of factional politics. Centring on the royal court and on parliament, groups of politicians contested for royal favour and control of government. The difference here is that to a greater extent than before, rivalries within the government were now fought out in parliament rather than the royal court. The politics of the court are once more of some consequence; but contrary to what some books suggest, Charles' private life was only of limited political importance. He refused to be lectured or preached at about his moral conduct. One or two of his many mistresses did have some political influence at various stages of his reign, notably the French lady, whom he created Duchess of Portsmouth, in the 1670s and 1680s; but she was not so much the cause as one of the symptoms of Charles' pro-French foreign policy. More important, there were significant divisions both on foreign and home, especially religious, policy among the King's ministers. In the early years of the reign this was mainly a difference of outlook and temperament between Clarendon and some of the younger men who had grown up during the years of exile.

Despite the attempt in 1660 to settle the revenue question, some constitutional issues reappeared that are very reminiscent of the reigns of James and Charles I. For example, in 1665 and 1667, during a period of war, the House of Commons made the voting of additional taxes conditional; they 'appropriated' these, as it is called, to particular kinds of expenditure. A move had been made in this direction back in 1624 but had not been followed up; now there was a definite step by the Commons towards stricter control over both the raising and spending of public money, since they also advanced their right to audit public accounts. Further, and here there are echoes of the attacks on Buckingham in the 1620s, they also criticised the naval administration, again as a consequence of inefficiency and corruption in time of war. Another dispute arose out of the King's right to keep a parliament in being indefinitely, and to have long intervals between sessions. The Triennial Act of 1641, to which Charles I had reluctantly assented, had been a definite limitation on royal prerogative. An amended Act, less offensive to the King, was passed in 1664, providing that there should be a meeting of parliament at least every three years, but it did not prescribe any machinery for enforcing this if the King were unwilling. As we shall see, this did not prove an effective measure. Another issue, bearing some likeness to those of the 1620s, can be seen in the opposition by this mainly Anglican Parliament to the King's policies of religious toleration for catholics and protestant Nonconformists; this emerged in 1662 and again more seriously in the early 1670s.

After 1660, M.P.s and other people in politics can be described in a way that has no exact equivalent before 1640. This classification is more important in eighteenth-century history, but it helps us to understand what was happening in Charles II's time. First there were the courtiers and officials, the 'King's men'. These did not all form a solid pro-Crown bloc, and should not be thought of as a close-knit political party; but they all had something in common, in having posts in the Court or government, or other close ties with the administration. Secondly there were the country gentlemen, independent in the sense of having no such ties, and most of the merchants in politics. They had no connections with government, and were often critical of it; some of them did not want to be involved with the Court. The first group can for short be called 'the Court', the second 'the Country', in this sense meaning simply those who were not of the Court. The Country provided the political opposition in so far as they were critical of, and even against government policy. Both Court and Country were divided by the religious and political issues inherited from the mid-century. Both included ex-Cavaliers and ex-Roundheads, Anglicans and Puritans, so that neither was a united party, though they did sometimes act unitedly for or against particular policies and individuals. Lastly, in some ways the most interesting through being the most mobile and varied, were the political leaders. They did not necessarily hold office all the time, but had political ambitions; they usually commended themselves to the King by their ability to handle the House of Commons. Indeed by this time politicians needed to have a following in the Commons if they were to get very far. As we shall see, new political leaders emerge in the 1660s and 1670s precisely because of their ability to handle Parliament better than the King's existing ministers.

A feature of these years which has no parallel in the years 1603–40, but is faintly reminiscent of the Long Parliament itself, is provided by the effects of one Parliament being in session on and off from 1661 to 1678. A number of the original Members were men of some age, and many died in the course of the Parliament's existence; others either succeeded to peerages, or were themselves raised to the Lords. By the end of its time only about 200 out of the original 509 were left. The influence both of the Crown and of the various political and family groupings—or 'connections', to use another term which is to anticipate the eighteenth-century political system—was used strenuously in by-elections. So the independence and spontaneity among the new Members chosen in these, to make up the loss of the original ones, was less than it would otherwise have been. Also, because the same Parliament was together for so long, it was more worthwhile using offices, contracts, pensions, even bribes, to build up a party in the Commons; the King's chief minister in the 1670s did this in a more systematic way than any government leader had before. In particular he used a large number of pensions, which in the 1660s had been payable out of the Excise revenue, and put these on to a surer footing, to be paid direct from the Exchequer. Rather unexpectedly therefore, in one sense this Parliament became tamer with age, more corrupt, more open to influence in these ways. On certain issues, more effective criticism of the government tended to come from the House of Lords. By the mid-1670s it was opposition spokesmen there, not in the Commons, who were demanding a general election and a new parliament; some were even calling for parliamentary reform on the lines of the 1640s and 1650s, and were attacking the vested interests of existing M.P.s.

Something has already been said of the renewed friction between Crown and Parliament. In the immediate sense this concerned the raising and spending of money, but it also involved the King's ministers and officials being made accountable to Parliament in matters of foreign policy and religion. We need to look at this rather more in chronological terms.

Clarendon's Ministry

The first years of the restored monarchy saw a coalition government. Monck had a senior position in it, as did other ex-Cromwellians, some of whom had been Parliamentarians in the Civil War, but it was basically the ministry of Clarendon who was Lord Chancellor, the first holder of this office (as opposed to the less dignified post of Lord Keeper of the Great Seal) since the fall of Bacon in 1621. His principal partners were the Duke of Ormonde, once a protégé of Strafford and the leader of the Anglo-Irish Royalists, the Earl of Southampton, the respected but far from dynamic representative of the Cavaliers who had stayed at home through the Commonwealth and Protectorate, and Secretary Nicholas, a professional administrator who had once given loyal service to Buckingham and Charles I but was now elderly and very slow.

Clarendon's predominance was never accepted or assured. On one side were some of the Presbyterians and ex-Cromwellians, of whom the most formidable because the ablest was Anthony Ashley Cooper (as Lord Ashley, Chancellor of the Exchequer 1661–72), whom we shall meet again under his later title, as Earl of Shaftesbury. Monck however was not among them. He took very little part in political manoeuvres, being content to be a Duke, Knight of the Garter, Lord-General, Master of the Horse and (until persuaded to retire in favour of Ormonde) absentee Lord Lieutenant of Ireland; he also received grants of money and land. His wife had Presbyterian leanings and was regarded as a greedy and snobbish woman, and some of the General's relatives were advanced to high positions in church and state. Monck himself saw to the demobilisation of the Army (1660–1), except for his own and one Cavalier regiment—the King's own guards (ancestors of the Coldstream and Grenadier Guards respectively); otherwise he was content to leave politics to the politicians, though his services were available in time of crisis. Monck's position bears some resemblance to that of the Duke of Wellington in the years after the battle of Waterloo; but unlike Wellington, he wisely never aspired to the highest civil offices or attempted to become the King's chief minister.

On Clarendon's other flank, he was harassed by various Royalists who were jealous of his position, especially after the marriage of his daughter to the King's brother and heir apparent, James, Duke of York. These enemies included Buckingham, son of the first Duke, a vicious and unstable character but with versatile talents and some gift for political leadership, marred by his inability to stick to anything for long. Buckingham was the original of Dryden's Zimri in *Absalom and Achitophel*—

> '... who in the course of one revolving moon
> Was chymist, fiddler, statesman and buffoon ...'

Another was the Earl of Bristol, whose father had been prominent in the 1620s and again in 1640–1; he had himself, as Lord Digby, been a brilliant but disastrous Secretary of State to Charles I in 1643–5. He accused Clarendon of treasonable correspondence with Rome—a fantastic charge from a man who was himself a known catholic and one which boomeranged and temporarily strengthened the Chancellor's position. More important were the 'Young Cavaliers' who had grown up since 1640. The ablest of these tended to attach themselves to the Duke of York—hence their baffled rage at James' marriage to Anne Hyde. The leaders of this group were the sons of Charles I's Lord Keeper of 1625–39, William and Henry Coventry, Charles II's ex-Agent in Madrid, Henry Bennet (later created Lord Arlington) and one non-exile, Sir Thomas Clifford, a leading Devonshire Royalist who subsequently became a Roman Catholic.

Clarendon had some allies in the House of Commons, such as Sir Hugh Pollard, another Devon Cavalier, but he found it difficult to adapt himself to changed conditions. Although he had been a reformer in 1640–1, Hyde was a deeply conservative, traditionalist statesman; besides, he had grown up in the morally stricter, more serious days of Charles I. The looser sexual morality, the new style of wit and humour, the fashionable theatre-going and irreligion of the 1660s were all alien to his outlook. This tended to cut him off from the King, and from his own son-in-law, the King's brother.

His conduct of foreign affairs added to Clarendon's unpopularity. Dunkirk, conquered from the Spaniards by Cromwell when he was allied to France (1657–8), was—perhaps sensibly—sold to Louis XIV. As with Calais under the earlier Tudors, a continental bridgehead was likely to involve England in constant wars to little advantage. At the same time, however, the Lord Chancellor was building himself a large and splendid house in Piccadilly, which his enemies were quick to nickname 'Dunkirk House'. The implication of corruption was false. Clarendon accepted gratuities and perquisites like any other statesman of his time, but as far as bribes or foreign pensions went his record is better than that of his successors, including some who encouraged these slanders against him. The net effect of these attacks was to force him into a closer alliance than he would perhaps have wished, with the orthodox Cavalier and Anglican elements in Parliament and the church. To that limited, negative extent, the Acts discriminating against the Nonconformists are justly named 'the Clarendon Code'.

The first important political change spans the years 1664–6, and marks the decline of Clarendon's influence. This roughly coincides with the Second Anglo-Dutch War. Like the first one, this was nearer to being a war undertaken for purely economic considerations, than any other in our history. It was essentially an imperial and commercial conflict, and was initiated by an English surprise attack, before war had been declared, on the Dutch colony of New Amsterdam in North America (now better known as New York). During this war England was struck by two appalling calamities. In 1665 came the last savage outbreak of the bubonic plague, particularly severe in London—the Great Plague described by many writers of the time; next in September 1666 there was the Great Fire of London, which was ascribed by panic-stricken public opinion to the sinister machinations of the Jesuits or other popular enemies. In fact it was almost certainly a sheer accident. A great deal of damage was done, most of the old City of London being burnt to the ground. An opportunity was then presented to re-build central London in a more splendid and spacious way. Among those involved in plans for the rebuilding was Christopher Wren, greatest of English architects, but then relatively young and little known. Not surprisingly, his grandiose and rather hasty scheme for reconstructing the whole western part of the City was rejected, though he was able to display his great talents at least in the re-building of St Paul's cathedral and the smaller City churches. However, despite the limiting effects of commercial greed and public apathy, new standards were enforced for houses and streets, which resulted in an undoubted improvement on the old, largely medieval London.

The Dutch War was evenly contested, in a series of hard-fought, sanguinary battles. As in the war of 1652–4, the conflict was exclusively naval except in America and the Far East. The major battles were all fought in the narrow seas—off the English and Dutch coasts. Despite their indecisiveness, these campaigns, together with Blake's operations against Spain in the 1650s, point the way towards the naval warfare of the eighteenth century. But whereas by then Britain was the foremost sea-power in the world, at this time the Netherlands were more dependent on overseas trade and shipping, and were a generally more maritime country. The Dutch admirals might well have agreed with the British naval C. in C. of the First World War who said, 'I do not know who can win the war, but I know that I am the only person who can lose it in an afternoon'. Considering their greater vulnerability and England's superior resources, the Dutch did well to avoid defeat. On the English side, counsels were often divided; as Lord Admiral, the Duke of York was courageous but lacked the qualities of a great commander. Also too many ships were in the charge of courtly 'gentleman captains', instead of trained seamen, while even among the professionals most of the Admirals in these wars were Army officers who had only taken to the sea later in their careers. Blake and Monck are both examples of this. All in all, the future greatness of the British Navy owed more than is often realised to its severe apprenticeship in these conflicts.

By 1666–7 the English were desperately short of money, and therefore laid up their battle fleet. The Dutch took advantage of this, sailed up the Medway, and did a good deal of damage to the English ships there. But it was not so much the actual loss inflicted as the public disgrace resulting from this attack which was— rather unfairly—blamed on Clarendon. As the chief minister he was made a general scapegoat for the government's unpopularity and the failure to carry this war through to a successful conclusion. In 1667 a fierce attack was launched against him; in its violent and almost hysterical character, it was comparable to that on Buckingham in the 1620s or Strafford in 1640–1. It had a twofold aspect: firstly there was the campaign led by his rivals within the government, especially Bennet, who was now Secretary of State, and William Coventry, an able if unscrupulous administrator—the leaders of the war party. They wanted to get rid of Clarendon and take over the government; they were temporarily in alliance with Buckingham, and they tried to persuade the King and York to dismiss Clarendon. In a sense they engineered his dismissal from within the government, but they did not want to destroy him. Then there was the 'Country' opposition, the people who were critical of government policy as a whole, above all the conduct of the war; some of them no doubt believed that Clarendon had made a vast personal profit out of the sale of Dunkirk. This opposition was worked on by Buckingham and a number of discontented minor politicians, who hoped to rise in the government as a result of Clarendon's overthrow. Some of them wanted more sweeping changes and not just to push him out but to destroy him;

it was they who instigated his impeachment and would have gone on to an attainder.

Clarendon was no longer firmly supported by Charles, who had grown tired of him and perhaps felt that he had to be made a scapegoat. It is indeed tragic that this now ageing man to whom the Stuart cause owed so much, had to go into exile a second time to avoid imprisonment, if not death. The only good that came of it was that in his second exile (his first having been during the years 1646–60) Clarendon was able to complete his *History*, as well as his own *Life*—the most important historical works by any Englishman in the seventeenth century, and the former among the greatest produced in any age.

The Cabal

The removal of Clarendon led to a new political alignment, and the ministry known as the 'Cabal'. This word originally simply meant a small inner clique, a secret if not clandestine political grouping. It is wrong to think that the Cabal of 1667–72 was a united ministry. It is so named after the initial letters of its members' names. Lauderdale, an ex-Presbyterian, was not very much involved in English or foreign affairs; he ran Scotland for the King with brutal efficiency. Buckingham, the son of James and Charles I's favourite, was incapable of any consistent policy; he followed the political whims of the moment, but could sometimes pick on issues which would give him a following, especially stirring up the opposition of the Country against the Court. Ashley was in some ways the most interesting member of this group. He had gone into opposition to Cromwell in the mid-1650s and had made his terms with the restored monarchy very successfully; he was promoted to be Lord Chancellor briefly at the end of the Cabal period. Ashley was strongly anti-Dutch, very concerned to advance English colonial and commercial interests. Up to a point this interest was shared by the King and his brother York; like them, only for different reasons, Ashley was even ready for a military alliance with France against the Dutch. Another element of continuity with Republican policy can be seen there. The other two members of the Cabal were straight Cavalier types; Clifford already with catholic leanings, and the more cynical Arlington. Alone of the five, they came to be involved in the King's own secret pro-Roman Catholic, as well as his more open pro-French projects. It has been well said of the Cabal, that its members had little in common except that all were opportunists and none was an Anglican.

The King's pro-French, pro-catholic policies at home and abroad, were embodied in the two Treaties of Dover (1670). The pro-catholic part however, which only two of the five ministers knew about, was in the first, or 'Secret' Treaty only. In this Charles II undertook to restore the Roman Catholic religion in England as soon as circumstances were favourable; Louis XIV undertook to provide money and other support. The second, or 'public' Treaty was a military alliance against the Netherlands, which was also contained in the first Treaty; in this the whole Cabal was involved.

Some apologists for Charles have suggested that he was all but forced to adopt this foreign policy by the meanness and general irresponsibility of Parliament. Some have gone on to argue that he managed to take the French King's money without becoming a mere 'satellite', and that in any case the Dutch were still England's more serious rivals, so that his policy was in the national interest. There is little evidence that these were Charles' motives. His preferences were much more personal: he admired his great cousin's absolutist rule, he preferred the catholic faith ('the only religion fit for a gentleman', is probably an apocryphal remark but sums up his attitude well), and he shared Louis' dislike of middle-class Calvinist republicans. Nor, while Parliament may not have voted enough money for the Dutch Wars (in the sense of as much as the government would have liked to be able to spend), did they get good value for what was voted. Indeed the after-effects of the Second Dutch War and the preparations for the next one, combined with general extravagance, involved something very near to national bankruptcy. In January 1672, with the so-called 'Stop of the Exchequer', all payments to royal creditors were suspended for a year. Those hardest hit were the London goldsmiths and other financiers—forerunners of modern bankers. Only after the Revo-

16 London burning. The Great Fire devastated most of the area shown in Plate 15 (opposite page 153) and a great deal more besides. Only the presence of mind of the King, the Duke of York, and Monck, in ordering the clearance of buildings in its path, stopped the Fire from spreading even further.

17 The Four Days' Battle by A. Storck. This was the longest and one of the hardest fought actions in the Dutch Wars. Before the development of an agreed system of signals, the main feature of fleet actions was confusion.

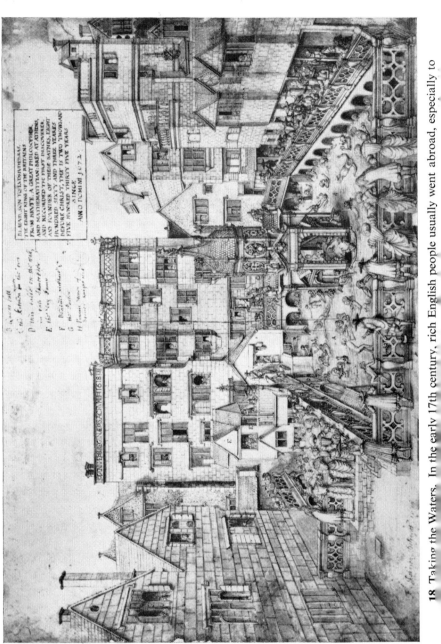

18 Taking the Waters. In the early 17th century, rich English people usually went abroad, especially to

lution of 1688–9 were the problems of public finance to be tackled in such a way that England could, as under the Commonwealth and Cromwell's Protectorate, use her economic resources to wage successful war and enlarge her overseas empire. With Charles II, as with his father and grandfather, it was a vicious circle. The Commons mistrusted royal policy, and therefore kept the King in short supply; he made as if to follow a more acceptable policy, but with ill success; this in turn increased their suspicions—of mismanagement if no worse—and made them more reluctant to see more money go down the drain. As under James and Charles I, a foreign policy more in line with the Commons' wishes and backed by more efficient administration would have found a more liberal response. However, ministers were still essentially the King's servants, appointed and removed by him. In practice they were answerable to Parliament (if only by impeachment), but there was still no accepted convention that they were collectively 'responsible' to it in the modern sense.

The opposite extreme, the view that Charles II deliberately sold his country to France, squandering his subjects' hard-earned money on his mistresses and other courtly extravagances, is equally untenable. The most that can be said of him is that he was two-faced, in that his public statements did not correspond with his true feelings. As head of the government, Charles' worst fault was laziness, or at least lack of steady application to business. The same was true of his brother, though James took his pleasures more heavily, and spiced his dissipations with religious zeal rather than a sense of humour.

Both treaties of Dover bore fruit in 1672. The King renewed his policy of attempted religious toleration, by issuing a Declaration of Indulgence to allow public worship in licensed chapels to Nonconformists and private worship in their homes to Roman Catholics; this was Toleration by use of the prerogative rather than by legislation. At the same time the Third Anglo-Dutch War was begun. This was generated less by spontaneous commercial and colonial rivalry between the two countries, and was more a part of royal diplomacy and religious policy. England, or at least the King went to war more for pro-French than for anti-Dutch

N

reasons, though there were still people, including Shaftesbury at this date, who thought that England should go on fighting the Dutch until they had been decisively defeated and ruined economically. This time the Dutch were on the defensive at sea, as well as being invaded by the French overland. Poor co-operation between the allied fleets, plus their own skill and courage, saved the Dutch from disaster; again the major battles were indecisive, but at least the allies failed to gain control of the Dutch coast and so destroy the Netherlands by blockade. During the course of this war there was an important swing of opinion. By contrast with the Second Dutch War there was criticism not just of its conduct but of the war itself and the whole policy of alliance with the French against the Dutch. These feelings were inseparable from hostility towards the King's religious policy as embodied in the Declaration of Indulgence.

The Crisis of 1673–4

This revulsion against royal policy led to the first major crisis of the reign, a far more serious and significant upheaval than the overthrow of Clarendon. There was a real explosion in Parliament, among the Anglican and Cavalier rank and file, against the King's foreign and religious policies. The Cabal disintegrated in the face of this. Its members had never been united; indeed though a useful nickname for them, the five did not comprise a team of ministers with enough in common to stick together when a storm blew up. Shaftesbury and Buckingham went over to the opposition; as a known catholic, Clifford was forced to leave public life; Arlington faded into obscurity with a senior post in the Household; only Lauderdale went grimly on. This was not in fact a victory for the back-benchers, the Country party proper, but a take-over by a new group of political leaders who had until then been in the second rank of the government as junior ministers and administrators. The most important of them was Thomas Osborne, a Yorkshire squire who became Lord Treasurer; then there were Heneage Finch, from a distinguished legal family, the other Coventry, brother of the man who led the attack on Clarendon, and Edward Seymour from the south-west, a strong Cavalier area. These men who already had some experience of government, now pushed out the Cabal and took over at the top.

To a considerable extent Charles gave way to this revolt. He abandoned his previous religious policy, revoking the Declaration of Indulgence; in return for this, he managed to obtain further supplies for the Dutch War which he tried to continue. But he found that the war was increasingly unpopular; the new ministry had no desire to go on with it, and peace was soon made. If not completely neutral England became at least non-belligerent, remaining on the touch-line until peace was made between Louis XIV and the Dutch in 1678. So the King had given up his main schemes in foreign affairs and religion, in the face of this revolt by his one-time fervent supporters in the Cavalier Parliament.

Danby and the Opposition

The years 1674-8 saw the political ascendancy of Osborne. He had several titles at different stages of his career, but is best known as the Earl of Danby. His rule coincided with a considerable expansion of overseas trade, as a result of which the Customs and Excise revenues rose sharply. In combination with Danby's careful management of royal revenue and expenditure, and some secret financial help from France (the amount of extra money that Charles II received from Louis XIV should not be exaggerated), this gave the King a much wider financial margin. It enabled him to act more flexibly than ever before, in that he was not dependent on the House of Commons, unless he became involved in a major war or some comparable expenditure.

Danby used patronage and it must be said bribery as well, to build up a much more solid Crown–Cavalier–Anglican alliance in parliament and the country than had been attempted before. To some extent this was a revival of Clarendon's policy, certainly by contrast with the period of the Cabal; but more up-to-date, sophisticated methods were used, and it was more successful. For a time Danby did manage to reconcile the rather grumpy, disillusioned rank and file of the old Royalist party to the Crown's policy with far more success than had been achieved under Clarendon, let alone the Cabal.

During these years almost all the other political leaders moved into opposition. In the case of some this was restrained and not very effective. Yet another leader of the Yorkshire landowning class, George Savile Lord Halifax, and the anti-Clarendonian of the 1660s, William Coventry, led a moderate opposition. In the case of the two ex-members of the Cabal, Shaftesbury and Buckingham, it was radical opposition to the King's ministers and their policies. These two were out to destroy Danby and what he stood for, not just to criticise his administration. In particular Danby wanted to give members of the established church a permanent monopoly of every branch of political and public life. Under the Test Act (1673), itself a product of that wave of feeling on which Danby had risen to power, only communicant Anglicans could hold any civil or military office under the Crown. This had forced the resignations of Lord Treasurer Clifford and—more startling—of the Lord Admiral, James Duke of York. Danby wished to extend this 'Test', which was anti-Nonconformist as well as anti-catholic, to peers and M.P.s, so that parliament too should be 100 per cent. Anglican. The opposition were able to muster enough support to defeat this, but the old issues of the 1630s and 1640s, of Anglican *versus* Puritan, were again brought to the fore.

This can also be related to a significant difference in the whole political pattern. In the 1660s and early 1670s the terms Court and Country can be used to describe Members of Parliament more or less according to whether or not they had government connections. By the later 1670s Court and Country come much nearer to being the names of two embryonic political parties; they begin to correspond to government and opposition respectively. In these years the opposition itself began to organise and to use patronage, parliamentary management, and systematic electioneering. Another new development in these years is the appearance of clubs and coffee houses in London, as centres of political management and intrigue. Effective opposition came to be increasingly under Shaftesbury's leadership. He was tougher, cleverer and more persistent than any of the other opposition leaders. Unlike Buckingham he had a programme; indeed, he was the only person who did, except Coventry, whose criticism was essentially moderate, as might be expected since his own brother (Henry) was at this time one of the Secretaries of State. At least one historian has, however, suggested that the ridicule thrown on the government by the wit and sarcasm of Buckingham, was at first more damaging to it than the plans and organisation of Shaftesbury.

On the surface the years of Danby's supremacy, especially from 1675 to 1677, show a certain stability in the country. It might appear that the alliance between the Crown and the Anglican–Cavalier party, which had come into existence again under his leadership, could have gone on indefinitely. There was opposition, it is true, to the King's manipulations of Parliament, especially the long prorogations between sessions, and to the same Parliament being kept for so long, and there was a ground-swell of opposition to the King's known or suspected pro-French and pro-catholic leanings. On the surface this opposition does not seem to have been strong enough to have overthrown the government alliance. And we need to look more closely at what was happening in these years, to understand the background to the crisis that was shortly to burst upon England, the most acute of Charles II's reign, dwarfing those which we have already looked at.

There was considerable opposition by ex-Roundheads, Puritans and others to Danby's attempt to give the Anglicans and Cavaliers a complete monopoly of public life. Here Charles had given way, even at the price of his brother's enforced retirement from office. With regard to foreign affairs the situation was a little more complicated. Danby as the chief minister was held responsible, very much as Clarendon had been before, for a policy that he did not approve, or even support; he took the blame for Charles' pro-French policy. Although as Lord Treasurer Danby was prepared to accept French money and was indeed personally responsible for receiving this from Louis XIV and overseeing the use made of it, he was himself anti-French. He thought that England should follow a pro-Dutch policy; in fact he favoured another marriage alliance with the House of Orange—that of James' elder daughter Mary to the young William III, the Stadtholder who had led the heroic national opposition in the Netherlands to the French invasion of 1672. England was now non-belligerent. Danby would have liked to switch alliances, but he was not able to persuade the King, and as the price of remaining in office he rather unwillingly and grudgingly executed a pro-French policy, and accepted French money. Danby did not receive a personal pension from Louis, though paradoxically some of the opposition leaders in these years did. This harks back to the so-called Spanish pensions of James I's reign. It was a usage of the period, to be found in the foreign relations of other European countries; there is nothing uniquely shocking about it. But it does make one pause, to find in the midst of all these patriotic fulminations against French influence at Court and so on, that some of those concerned, not Shaftesbury himself but several of his allies, were themselves on the French King's pay-roll.

There was also growing opposition on the part of the Country to the King's maintenance of a standing army in time of peace. This is often said to have been one of the most important differences between England and the Continent and the main reason why the Tudor and early Stuart monarchs did not erect a system of absolute government. However, though the monarchy was less absolute in England after 1660 than before 1640, there was a standing army. As we have seen, it began with only two regiments—Monck's and the King's—but by the 1670s there were several thousand men in arms. For different reasons, both the ex-Cavaliers and the ex-Parliamentarians in the Commons and in the country generally were very much against this. The Cavaliers opposed it because of their memories of Cromwell and the Major-Generals and the whole period of military rule, which had seen the eclipse of their class; the Parliamentarians did so because they saw in it a sinister device for erecting a despotism on the French model. To some extent both were wrong. Its chief significance was as a development of military organisation in the period. If England was to play even a modest part on the European political scene, it was inevitable that there should be a small peacetime standing army which could be rapidly expanded in wartime; England's growing overseas, colonial commitments also required it. But the Commons had good reasons for discontent, not least because Danby himself behaved in a rather two-faced way. He got money voted for disbanding part of the Army, and instead used this to keep up and even enlarge it; he also got money for a campaign against France and then renewed the alliance with her.

The Succession Problem (see Table 2, page 192)

The most important aspect of opposition was a vague but widespread fear of the King's half known but widely suspected religious designs. The full contents of the Secret Treaty of Dover did not become known until much later, or Charles II would probably have lost his throne. But he had made two serious attempts to gain toleration for Nonconformists and catholics. Although in fact he had learnt his lesson in 1673, it was suspected that Charles still harboured designs for a general pro-catholic policy.

During the 1670s anti-catholic feeling became increasingly focused on the question of the succession to the throne. Charles II had several illegitimate but no legitimate children, and the ordinary rules of hereditary succession pointed to his being succeeded when he died by his brother James Duke of York, by this time an open, admitted Roman Catholic, with a catholic second wife. Although James had two daughters by his first wife, who had been brought up as protestants, a son by his second marriage might well be brought up as a catholic and would have precedence over these daughters. By now it was virtually certain that Charles would not have a legitimate child by his wife, the Portuguese Princess Catherine. In order to avoid the succession of a catholic king, the opposition suggested several different lines of policy, none of which proved possible for them and the King to agree on, but all of which became political issues of varying importance.

One plan was that Charles II should follow the precedent of his predecessor Henry VIII, divorce and re-marry, in order to try to get a male protestant heir. Although he had been persistently and repeatedly unfaithful to his wife, Charles rejected this idea indignantly. It may be a pointer to his own secret catholic leanings, that he apparently felt divorce was worse than adultery on however monumental a scale. Another was that special statutory limitations should be put on a catholic king, with the understanding that these would only be temporary; James might in fact be king on the assumption that he would not be succeeded by another catholic.

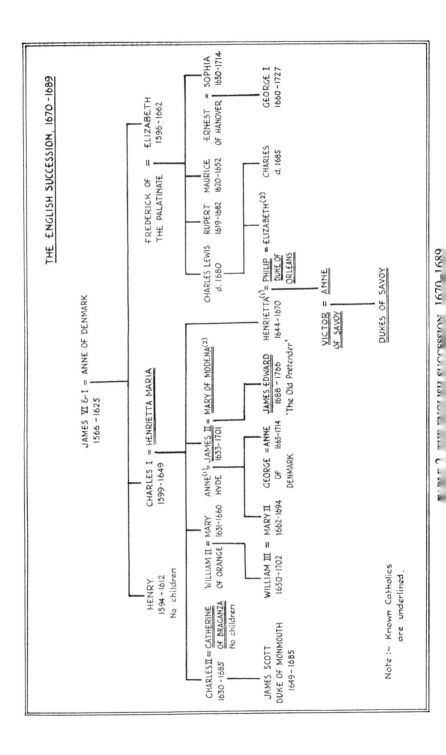

THE ENGLISH SUCCESSION, 1670-1689

JAMES VI & I = ANNE OF DENMARK
1566-1625

HENRY
1594-1612
No children

CHARLES I = HENRIETTA MARIA
1599-1649

FREDERICK OF = ELIZABETH
THE PALATINATE   1596-1662

CHARLES LEWIS   RUPERT   MAURICE
d.1680   1619-1682 1620-1652

ERNEST = SOPHIA
OF HANOVER 1630-1714

CHARLES
d.1685

GEORGE I
1660-1727

CHARLES II = CATHERINE
1630-1685   OF BRAGANZA
             No children

WILLIAM II = MARY
OF ORANGE   1631-1660

ANNE(1) = JAMES II = MARY OF MODENA(2)
HYDE   1633-1701

HENRIETTA(1) = PHILIP = ELIZABETH(2)
1644-1670   DUKE OF
              ORLEANS

VICTOR = ANNE
OF SAVOY

DUKES OF SAVOY

JAMES SCOTT
DUKE OF MONMOUTH
1649-1685

WILLIAM III = MARY II
1650-1702   1662-1694

GEORGE = ANNE
OF   1665-1714
DENMARK

JAMES EDWARD
1688-1766
'The Old Pretender'

Note :- Known Catholics
are underlined.

Temporary limits to the Crown's control over the Church of England were one obvious point in any such programme. That was a policy which Charles, under pressure, at least said he was prepared to discuss, but no agreement could be reached. In any case, some historians believe that he was insincere about this, and only made such offers to gain a tactical advantage. Another rather disingenuous plan, and one to which some of Shaftesbury's party committed themselves, was that the King's eldest and favourite illegitimate son, James Duke of Monmouth, should be declared legitimate and so become the lawful heir. It is reasonably certain that Charles had not in fact married Monmouth's mother Lucy Walter, but a great deal was made of the fact that he might have contracted a secret marriage with her, when he was a very young man in exile, and the evidence was said to exist in a certain 'Black Box' which the King would not allow to be opened. Others simply said that Monmouth should be legitimised by Act of Parliament. Charles II was not prepared to consider by-passing his brother in this way, although he was fond of Monmouth and very indulgent towards him. Nor did he have any illusions about his brother; he is said once to have remarked with joking seriousness, 'they will never kill me to make Jamie King'. Another possibility was that James should be by-passed, in favour not of Monmouth but of his own elder daughter the Princess Mary. This became a more serious political question when in 1677, as a result of Danby's diplomacy, she was married to her cousin the young William of Orange, but William was unwilling to be made a tool of the opposition to his uncles and his own father-in-law. And those who were agreed in wanting to exclude James from the succession failed to agree on whom they should have instead.

All these alternatives were being actively canvassed by the late 1670s. These years saw an outburst of political pamphleteering unlike anything since the Interregnum; the press censorship which had been re-imposed in 1662 lapsed in 1679. It might be expected that Danby and his supporters would have wished to exclude James, or at least to limit his powers if he did succeed. After all, if it was proper to exclude catholics from all subordinate offices in the state, as had been done in 1673, it was scarcely logical to allow one in the highest office of all. And it may be that some of the more realistic members of this party would have preferred at least some special limitations on James' powers. But most of those who had voted for the Test Act, even for the second Test, the 1675 Bill, were simply ostrichlike over the Succession question, while hoping like Mr Micawber in *David Copperfield*, that 'something would turn up'. A few may have been corrupted by office or Court favour. More, however, were such devotees of royal prerogative, including the principles of hereditary succession and of non-resistance to a legitimate sovereign, that even their religious bigotry was subordinated to these considerations.

These various tensions set the stage for the crisis which followed, even though it was precipitated by other, more dramatic, if less reputable developments.

7 : Crisis, Reaction and Revolution (1678–89)

The Popish Plot and the Exclusion Parliaments

THE crisis which had been building up for some time came to a head as a result of two almost simultaneous developments in 1678–9. The man who had been the English envoy in Paris moved over into the opposition because of disappointed political ambitions, and revealed the facts about Danby and the receipt of the French subsidies. Louis XIV was not himself sorry to see this come to light. It was a complicated situation; Louis almost certainly wanted the fall of Danby brought about, because he knew that although Danby was the instrument of Charles' pro-French policy, he did not himself support it, and Louis was afraid of Danby's pro-Dutch sympathies. So, although this might open the way to a much more anti-French policy, Louis even encouraged the revelations. These brought a tremendous storm of attack. All the accumulated suspicions about getting money voted to disband the army boiled up, with violent disapproval at the King and his minister having been secretly receiving money from France when they were supposed to be non-belligerent, and had indeed been concluding the marriage alliance with the Netherlands.

Still more important for its effect on public opinion, was an extraordinary episode, which has become known to history as the Popish Plot. This consisted of a series of 'revelations' made by a man who had had a remarkably disreputable career as a priest in two different religions, having been defrocked by both of them, a certain Titus Oates—one of the great pathological liars of history. Oates, and various other professional informers who soon gathered about him, like bluebottles round rotting meat, came to make a thriving trade out of accusations against the catholics in the country. Oates' revelations did, partly by coincidence, include one or two elements of half-truth, for example that the Duke of York's ex-secretary, now his wife's, had been involved in extraordinarily foolish discussions of a treasonable nature about reintroducing catholicism into England. But Oates went far beyond this, and claimed to have proof of a vast underground catholic conspiracy, to kill or otherwise get rid of the King, and to install James as his successor; arbitrary rule was to be brought in at the same time and leading protestants massacred. The exact details varied even according to Oates, let alone according to his coadjutors. Sometimes the unfortunate Queen was a party to the plan to assassinate her husband; sometimes the whole royal family was to be swept away. Sometimes it was just the Jesuits; sometimes it was the English native catholics as well, who were involved.

Such a farrago was only credible because of widespread suspicion of catholic designs. It was also true that in seventeenth-century Europe catholicism was, up to a point, identifiable with absolute monarchy—in the great empires of Spain and France, and with religious persecution aimed at the elimination of heresy. At this very time a re-catholicising policy was under way in France, which only reached its climax in 1685 with the revocation of the Edict of Nantes and the forcible reconversion of the Huguenots (with flight overseas as the only alternative). By contrast protestantism was identifiable with constitutional (that is, parliamentary or republican) rule, at least in England and the Netherlands.

All this had helped to produce an atmosphere in which many people were ready to swallow the stories produced by Oates and his crew. Almost the only person who was initially sceptical was the very man whose life was supposed to be in the greatest peril—the King. But Charles was not prepared to exert himself sufficiently; he went away to Newmarket to attend the races at an early stage in the excitement, and a chance of nipping the whole thing in the bud by showing that Oates was a liar on an epic scale was lost. Some of the King's Council themselves had a vested interest in spreading belief in the Plot, to try to get rid of Danby and York; while even Danby at first hoped to turn it to his own advantage. Other Councillors were too timorous, or themselves not confident enough to expose Oates. On the other side, it is a fascinating psychological problem whether Shaftesbury was really taken in, or saw through it all but realised that fate had handed him a fistful of trumps which he could not bring himself to abstain from using.

The Plot was given greater credibility by a mystery which has never been solved to this day; it is one of the very few unsolved murder stories of real political importance. A London magistrate, Sir Edmund Berry Godfrey, before whom Oates had made some of his most sensational depositions, leaving with him a written testament of his charges, after being missing for several days was found dead on the outskirts of London. Historians, lawyers and criminologists have argued a great deal as to whether Godfrey in fact committed suicide, or was murdered; and if he was murdered whether or not it was in the circumstances in which his body was found. Assuming he was killed, it may have been by the alleged catholic conspirators, as was believed at the time, by other catholics, desperate with fear at what Oates' depositions might lead to—a more plausible hypothesis, by the agents of Oates himself or even of Shaftesbury, in order to plant the crime on the catholics and so give greater plausibility to Oates' other charges, or by desperadoes with no political motive—this is most unlikely, since Godfrey's watch and money were not taken. Suicide (he is known to have been a melancholy, perhaps unstable person) followed by the faking of the scene to look like murder, is another possible explanation. Whatever the truth, which will never now be known, a wave of panic swept through London and to a lesser extent the whole country; no balanced appraisal of Oates' statements or Godfrey's death could be hoped for. From then on a feverish atmosphere developed which lasted for the next two or three years.

In the winter of 1678–9 these two crises came together, to produce an intense campaign against the catholics, against the King's pro-French policy, and at the same time against Danby. His predominance had originally been founded on an Anglican–Cavalier alliance which was very far from being pro-catholic or necessarily pro-French. But Danby had become increasingly cut off from many of his own followers, despite his having built up a party by the distribution of pensions, bribes and offices, and he now found himself isolated. The main body of government backbenchers began to desert him; they did not all swing right over to the opposition, or join in the attack on James Duke of York, but a good many did so. So there were two parallel lines of attack in the last months of the Cavalier Parliament and in the next one that followed it, against the catholics and against Danby. A 'Second Test Act' (1678), excluding catholics—and in theory Dissenters as well—from both Houses of Parliament, had been passed at the very end of the Cavalier Parliament under the influence of the Plot; this was the measure that Shaftesbury and his allies had opposed, and managed to defeat when it was proposed by Danby a few years before.

The militant opposition led by Shaftesbury went on from a general anti-catholic policy, to campaign for the exclusion of York from the succession. Hence the name sometimes given to this period—the Exclusion Crisis. It was only at this stage, with the attempt to exclude his brother from the throne, that the King seems to have felt himself to be directly involved. Charles II had two interests at stake: first that the full extent of his own secret dealings with Louis XIV should be kept dark. The cat was out of the bag as far as French financial help was concerned, but Charles' agreement with his cousin, the French King back in 1670 about re-catholicising England in return for military and financial help, would have been a far more serious revelation, and Charles might easily not have survived it. He was also interested in preserving monarchical prerogative intact, at least as it had come to him in 1660. Although in many respects he was not a man of principle, far from it in his own private life, he seems to have felt that hereditary succession to the throne was something that he had an obligation to preserve. So he now began to exert himself negatively to stop the truth coming out about the Secret Treaty of Dover, and positively to prevent his brother being excluded.

The government, however, was far from presenting a united front. The King, York and Danby each had his own interests: Danby to save his skin, York both to preserve his succession and forward the cause of his religion, and the King as explained. In particular, though they were both under heavy attack from Parliament, Danby and York were very suspicious of each other, the one still standing for an Anglican policy, the other as the patron of the catholic cause. The opposition was equally divided, in what they wanted and the means they were ready to use. This was soon shown when Charles reconstructed his government, and several of the opposition leaders including Shaftesbury, were brought into a new and smaller Privy Council. (Danby had by then been put in the Tower, really in order to save him from the Commons' wrath.) At the same time the King cast about for new men to replace those he had lost. He found them in a new Court group, including one of Clarendon's sons, Laurence Hyde later Earl of Rochester, Godolphin an able Cornish financier, and Spencer Earl of Sunderland, who developed into a competent foreign minister and skilled political manager but was perhaps the most unprincipled of all political leaders in an age not notable for scruple or consistency in politicians. But the time for these men to take command of the situation had not yet come; meanwhile Charles had to ride out the storm, and even to bear with having Shaftesbury and some of his Exclusionist allies in the government, though they no more enjoyed the King's confidence there than they had in opposition.

Charles' opponents were agreed in little more than wanting to get rid of Danby. Some were prepared to come to terms with the King over York's position, if Charles would agree to special limitations on a catholic successor. It was at this stage that Charles II proved himself superior to his father in political skill. He was far more successful at sensing the potential disunity in the opposition, and at playing off the rival groups against one another by exploiting the ambitions of the individual leaders and the differences of policy between them. He offered a number of important restrictions on York's power, and at one stage in the crisis sent his brother into temporary banishment. These limitations, on royal control of the church, the armed forces and choice of ministers were to be for James' lifetime only and not permanent. Shaftesbury and the opposition might have been well advised to accept this offer, at least to negotiate on this basis, if only to test the King's sincerity. Several of those who had been keenest to get rid of Danby and to do something about York's succession, were won over and therefore opposed Shaftesbury's policy of outright Exclusion. Among them was the latter's relative by marriage, Halifax, a man of great political abilities especially as a debater and pamphleteer.

As in 1640, there were two general elections in 1679, both of which returned anti-Court majorities, the second an even larger one than the first. But there the similarity with 1640 ends. The first Parliament sat for some months in 1679; the second was prorogued before it met, and did not in fact sit until the autumn of 1680.

The Origin of Parties

In these two Parliaments a new and important political division appears, based on the Exclusion issue. In the second Exclusion Parliament the parties concerned acquired the names by which they were long to be known. Those who supported Shaftesbury and wanted to get rid of James were at first called Exclusionists; then, because the meeting of this Parliament was put off, they organised a large number of public petitions that the King should allow it to assemble, so they were called Petitioners. Whereupon the supporters of the Court, who were prepared to accept the King's solution and approved of his postponing the Parliament, produced rival manifestoes 'abhorring' this encroachment on royal prerogative, and so became known as Abhorrers. These two movements and the political parties which developed out of them, might have been known for the next two hundred years or more as Petitioners and Abhorrers—rather awkward and obscure names. But they were also given derisive nicknames by their opponents. The Petitioners, that is Shaftesbury and his allies, were named after the Presbyterian guerrilla fighters in the south-west of Scotland, who were still resisting the repressive policy of Lauderdale and the Crown there—Whiggamores, usually shortened to Whigs. There was in fact a small-scale rebellion by the irreconcilable Covenanters in the south-west of Scotland, which was defeated by a royal army in the summer of 1679. Ironically the commander of this force was the King's son, James Duke of Monmouth, on whom the hopes of the English 'Whigs' were coming to be pinned. On the other side, the Abhorrers, that is the pro-Crown, pro-James party, were nicknamed Tories, after the Irish catholic guerrillas who were still

The harvesting methods shown here were to change little until the coming of mechanisation in the last 100 years.

19 Horsepower and Manpower.

In wet weather the roads were so bad that packhorses were the best overland goods transport. Heavy, unsprung waggons were only usable on most roads in good weather.

20 CHARLES II by
E. Lutterell

21 The Committee. This 1680 cartoon, a Court or Tory counter-attack, satirizes those who had taken advantage of the Popish Plot, as Puritans and republicans who were trying to bring back the 'bad old days' of 1640–60 while pretending to protect the King and the Church.

operating in the interior, among the bogs and hills of Ireland. It was these two rather more picturesque names, Whigs and Tories, as opposed to the drier but originally more descriptive Petitioners and Abhorrers, which stuck.

To suppose that everyone who took any part in politics during these years was either Whig or Tory would be to over-simplify the situation. Some of the most important individuals and groups cannot be classified under either of these headings. For instance Halifax, the leader of the moderate opposition, was not a Tory or a courtier; yet he helped the King to defeat the second Exclusion Bill of 1680 in the House of Lords, after it had passed the Commons with ease. In his own political testament Halifax described himself as a 'Trimmer', by which he meant to suggest that there was a balance of political power which a middle party, or more precisely middle-men should trim between, in order to keep the state on an even keel. Others who opposed the King and were uneasy about James' succession were not Whigs, at least not in the sense of being Shaftesburyite Exclusionists. But for the time being the party division is a more important way of classifying M.P.s and other people in politics than that between Court and Country, or 'Ins' (office-holders) and 'Outs' (non-office-holders), although these divisions still existed. Political parties had emerged, but they were not accepted as a normal, still less a desirable part of the constitution; in particular, the notion of an opposition party was still equated with factious behaviour, with something only just removed from treasonable conspiracy.

It is worth trying to sum up the differences between the parties in their early years. The Whigs were the more anti-catholic of the two, more so than they were pro-Nonconformist, though especially in London and some other towns they drew quite a lot of their support from these 'Dissenters' as they had come to be known by their Anglican opponents. Even more important was the continuity with those Parliamentarians and Puritans of the mid-century or their successors who had conformed after 1660 and were now technically Anglican in religion. The Whigs also stood for further limitations on royal prerogative, and on executive power in general. They were against a standing army; some of them

O

were in favour of parliamentary reform, notably more frequent elections and regular sessions. Much of this, however, was the programme of the 'Country', of those in opposition, rather than being specifically 'Whig'. Later, when the Whigs were in office, much of it was discarded by them and taken over by the Tories who were by then in opposition.

The Tories were the great upholders of the Church of England and of the royal prerogative. They were in no way pro-catholic; like the Cavaliers of the Clarendon and Danby periods they stood for an Anglican monopoly of public life. In this negative way they were as anti-catholic as the Whigs, but they did not make political capital out of anti-catholicism, as Shaftesbury and the Whigs tried to do out of the Popish Plot. With the memories of 1642–60 ever in their minds they, and particularly their clerical allies—the High Churchmen—developed a theory of 'Non-Resistance', according to which rebellion against the legitimate ruler was never justified; in effect this was a negative version of the earlier 'Divine Right' of Kings. The question was what would happen if the two principles of Anglican supremacy and Non-Resistance came into collision. As we shall see, this happened in the next reign, and it forced the Tories to make an agonising reappraisal.

Each side had its extremist wing. At Whig meetings in their well-known London centre, the Green Ribbon Club, the faces of old Republicans from the 1650s reappeared. This was used by their opponents to discredit them; just as the pro-catholic, absolutist leaning of the extreme anti-Exclusionist fringe provided a good target for the Whigs, so their own Republican fringe made them more vulnerable to accusations that they were trying to undermine the whole Restoration Settlement along with the position of the monarchy. Some historians have suggested that the Whigs had only minority support among the aristocracy and gentry and depended on the backing of the commercial middle class. There is some truth in that, but on the other hand the leadership and most of the parliamentary membership of the Whig party consisted of peers and gentry as much as did that of the Tories. Shaftesbury was just as conscious of his aristocratic position as any Court or Tory leader.

Charles II's Victory

Charles II defeated the Whigs partly as the result of a swing of opinion against them, partly as a result of his own superior handling of the situation. Looking at the crisis of the years 1679–81, on the surface it seems as if the country was back on the verge of civil war, with Shaftesbury and his supporters on the one side, James and his on the other prepared to organise armed resistance rather than allow the other to triumph by peaceful means. Charles was seriously ill in 1679; if he had died then or at any time in these years, there would almost certainly have been fighting which might have led to civil war.

However, although the King had taken a stand to preserve the prerogative, he was determined in his own famous phrase, 'not to go on his travels again'. Charles wanted to die in his bed, as he was to succeed in doing. Also, except for a few Republicans, the opposition were not prepared to use force. Shaftesbury knew he was not Pym, and that the situation was not like that of 1641 or 1642; people had not reached the stage of disillusionment with Charles II that they had with his father, and there would have been little support for a policy of armed resistance to the Crown. After his political defeat in 1681–2, Shaftesbury allowed himself to become involved in a political conspiracy. Perhaps even then his extremist followers concealed from him what was being planned, but certainly in 1679–80, threats of resistance were bluff. Opinion among all social classes was against anybody who seemed to be threatening a revival of civil war. There was great opposition to the danger of royal absolutism and popery on the one hand, and to that of Puritan or republican rule on the other. Both alike seemed to threaten the country with military despotism. There was a strong middle-of-the-road feeling which wanted to avoid both these alternatives, and the renewal of civil war. This rather inarticulate, but important body of opinion was critical of Charles and Danby in 1679, still very suspicious of the King in his defence of York in 1680, but beginning to swing back in favour of Charles by the winter of 1680–1. The King took advantage of this swing to win such opinion over to his side in the early 1680s.

This can be seen in the third and last Exclusion Parliament, which the King summoned to Oxford a Tory, rather than London a Whig, stronghold. Charles again offered to discuss 'limitations' on a catholic successor; the Whig majority in the Commons again refused, and after only a week the King dissolved Parliament. This was the moment of choice for Shaftesbury and his supporters. Would they resist the dissolution, and by so doing take a decisive step towards armed resistance and revolution? The King had posted regiments round Oxford, and there is no doubt that he would have met any illegal action with armed force. As it was, the Whigs were allowed to disperse unmolested, though proceedings were begun against Shaftesbury later in the year. Charles is sometimes said to have dissolved the Oxford Parliament so summarily because he had just negotiated a fresh agreement with Louis XIV, and so was sure of enough money without parliament. In fact it was probably the psychological feeling of independence and the absence of any external threat, rather than the actual amount of money received or promised, which gave Charles the self-confidence to act as he did.

The more puzzling question is why he summoned this Parliament at all when he was not compelled to by financial necessity. The First Exclusion Parliament had been virtually forced on the King by the general tumult of the Plot and the attack on Danby; it would have been more dangerous not to call one. The Second seems to represent an error of judgment by the King and his advisers, who hoped it would be more tractable than its predecessor. The lengthy prorogations show Charles' unwillingness to meet it, once the results were known. Even in the Third, there may have been a slight miscalculation. Opinion had already begun to swing towards the Court; but the Whigs had built up an efficient electoral machine, and the results were scarcely less favourable to them than before. However, once he had got this Parliament on his hands, Charles showed great political skill. Another difference was that in 1679 and even 1680, the Exclusionists had been trying to prevent James succeeding without going beyond that. By 1681 most of them were committed to Monmouth as an alternative successor. Despite his popularity with ordinary people in some parts of the country, Monmouth's illegitimacy was still a barrier with the upper classes; here Shaftesbury made a serious error of judgment, which Charles was quick to exploit. The King now had the support of many more than the narrow range of courtiers, or Tories in the party sense. The situation was comparable to that in the autumn of 1641 when middle-of-the-road opinion had been swinging back towards Charles I. There are two differences. Charles II did not do anything foolish like Charles I's attempt on the Five Members, to dissipate this moderate sympathy; secondly his financial position was better, so he could afford to dissolve the Third Exclusion Parliament. There was another way in which Charles II took advantage of the swing of public opinion. During the period of Exclusionist or Whig predominance, the kind of men who had been in public life during the Republic and perhaps in the Convention but had not played much part during the years of the Cavalier Parliament, began to reappear at the local level as well as in parliament. The early 1680s saw a reaction against this. There was a widespread reassertion by the peerage and older-established gentry of their influence in local government and parliamentary elections. A campaign was begun against the Whigs and those who had manufactured and taken advantage of the Popish Plot. This is sometimes called the 'Tory Reaction', though it could perhaps better be called a gentry or Royalist reaction, because it was wider than the Tory party of these years. It included a purge of dissident intellectuals in the universities, and an attack on the independence of the boroughs. In spite of the measures taken at the Restoration, many towns had been Whig centres; their charters were now called in, and their control over their own affairs as well as their ability to return anti-Court candidates to Parliament reduced. The bitterness of Tory politics in the 1680s may still have owed something to the economic difficulties which many Cavalier families had fallen into during the Interregnum. Jealousy of commercial wealth and of financiers with government connections (such as military contractors), was to be a recurrent theme in 'Country', especially opposition Tory politics in the generation that followed the Revolution of 1688. Macaulay's portrayal of the typical Tory squire and Anglican parson, in chapter III of his

History, may have a touch of caricature in its exaggeration of their poverty and uncouthness; but there can be little doubt about their general political and social attitude.

Again by contrast with his father in 1641, Charles II was able to regain control of London. The crucial point here was when he managed to get two of his supporters elected as Sheriffs in 1682. Since the Sheriffs were responsible for the selection of jurymen, it would now be possible to get London juries to find for the Crown in political cases against the opposition, which had been impossible in the years 1679–81—hence the dismissal of the Crown's charges against Shaftesbury. The attack on the City's charter which followed was not resisted with the determination that would have greeted a similar action by Charles I, because a Court or Tory counter-revolution was already under way inside the City. There was a class element in this too. It suggests that the Whigs were a slightly more 'popular' party, and that the King had more support from the Aldermen and the other wealthy merchants and financiers of London, as well as from the peers and gentry in the countryside.

In the last years of his reign, when Charles II appears to have beaten Parliament and the Whigs and to have consolidated the position of the monarchy, he is sometimes said to have erected a 'second Stuart despotism'. This suggestion needs critical consideration. Charles did in fact break one statute, the modified Triennial Act of 1664, when another parliament became due in March 1684. He did not, however, attempt to reintroduce any of the instruments of arbitrary rule. He did not appreciably enlarge the standing army or make any further political use of it; he did nothing more to advance his pro-catholic designs, which he would surely have tried to do if he was really in the process of erecting a despotism. Certainly he did not attempt to raise taxes without parliamentary consent on any scale; he did not need to do so as long as he pursued a neutral policy in Europe. Indeed he did not even renew his active alliance with Louis XIV. So the so-called 'second Stuart despotism' was a rather tame affair. In fact it was a negative, rather than a positive achievement. Charles had preserved his own position and his brother's right to succeed him. But there is no reason to suppose that he wanted to go on indefinitely without a parliament. He probably intended to take advantage of his purge of the borough charters, and of Shaftesbury and the Whigs being discredited by the extremist fringe of their party. Had Charles held elections he would have got a much more sympathetic parliament, more like the Cavalier Parliament in its early years, but he died before deciding to do so.

The second Stuart despotism of 1681–8 was also felt in England's North American colonies. This was partly economic. The New England colonists were believed to have been flouting the Navigation Acts and other trade laws whenever it suited them. It was also constitutional. The New England colonies in particular enjoyed a wide measure of self-government under the ultimate suzerainty of the Crown; the other colonies either wished to emulate this (as did New York some years after its capture from the Dutch when it was granted to James as his own feudal estate), or else had analogous privileges exercised through Lords Proprietors, like Maryland or the Carolinas (held by a court syndicate formed in the 1660s). Even in a 'crown colony', such as Virginia, which was not governed either under a proprietary grant or by a chartered company, the popular, or constitutional, element in government seemed excessive alike to tidy-minded bureaucrats and to Divine Right theorists. So in the 1680s two campaigns, for mercantile enforcement and political conformity, led to the calling in of colonial charters and the setting up of a new, less self-governing unit, the Dominion of New England. No doubt the lines of division in America were different from those in England, but 1688–9 saw more or less parallel revolutions on both sides of the atlantic. Some features of later Stuart colonial policy survived the Revolution: dislike of proprietary grants, and of those who infringed too shamelessly the main provisions of the Navigation and trade laws. But not until the 1760s–1770s can anything so systematic be seen in the way of an attempt to reorganise and tighten up imperial control, and then—in vastly changed circumstances—with what could only be disastrous results for Britain. In the 1680s as in the 1630s, if there had not been revolution at home, there might well have been a separatist breakaway in North America. As it was, 1689 perhaps marks the last point at which we can sense a feeling of transatlantic community between Englishmen on both sides of the ocean, which was gradually to be replaced by an increasingly awkward relationship between Englishmen and Americans.

The reasons which persuaded people to leave the British Isles for America and the West Indies after the Restoration have less directly to do with the constitutional problem at home than those involved in the 'great migration' of the 1630s. Renewed persecution of Puritan dissenters after 1662, and the spur of distress and the hope of economic betterment again operated. Nor was it quite so hazardous and unfamiliar an undertaking as it had been in the days of the earliest settlers in Virginia, New Plymouth, Massachusetts or Barbados. The last and greatest proprietary grant, of Pennsylvania, was followed by a deliberate appeal on the part of its founder, the Quaker William Penn, to all sorts and conditions of men; it was in the 1680s that the non-British element in European emigration to North America began to be appreciable. Just as England had gained from the coming of Huguenot and other continental refugees, so did America; but in the long run their presence may have helped to weaken the American sense of community with the home country.

James II's Policies

The extent of Charles II's victory largely explains the ease of James' succession in February 1685. And the new King's first asset was his peaceful succession, since the Whigs and others who had wanted to exclude him from the throne had been thoroughly beaten in the years 1681–3. James was also helped in the first months of his reign by two small-scale risings against him. One was led by his nephew and one-time rival Monmouth, who landed and tried to raise a rebellion in the south-west of England. Monmouth got a certain amount of popular support, but very little indeed from the gentry or even the solid middle classes in that part of the country; the rest of England made no move to come to his aid. Monmouth's rebellion has sometimes been called the last kick of the Good Old Cause. There was indeed an air of Puritan and even democratic enthusiasm about the support he received. At the same time there was another rising by the Presbyterians in the west of

Scotland, led by the Marquis of Argyll, son of the man who had been the mainstay of the aristocratic Presbyterian opposition to Charles I; this too was fairly easily suppressed. Despite the problems which arose from his being a catholic monarch, in the early months of his reign James enjoyed a wide range of loyal support from previous Trimmers and non-party men as well as from courtiers and Tories. The religious situation was a very open one; nobody quite knew what would happen. Some catholics obviously had high hopes, though the more sensible of them were worried lest the King should spoil their case by trying to get too much for them too quickly, and so arouse resentment and renewed hostility. Some Dissenters also hoped for something from a non-Anglican King.

In the first general election held since the winter of 1680–1 the measures that had been taken in the intervening years produced a much more pliant Parliament. The House of Commons of 1685 was as favourable to the Crown and its policies as any since the early 1660s. One sign of this is that it voted James a larger regular, peacetime revenue than any king had ever had before; it granted him supplies in excess of those that his brother had been enjoying at the end of his reign.

In view of his apparent popularity, the quietness of the country, the easy suppression of the two rebellions and the support of Parliament, it is extraordinary how quickly James brought about his own downfall, together with that of the cause for which he stood. Although he was not particularly scrupulous in his own political or moral behaviour, James was a sincerely religious man. He was determined not just to be a catholic king in a protestant country and to obtain limited concessions for his co-religionists, but to restore the Church of England to the catholic religion, that is to re-catholicise the country. Both his cousin Louis XIV and even the Pope at different stages, as well as many English catholics, took alarm at this policy, seeing that it would be likely to do more harm than good. James might have pursued even this policy, in a more circumspect manner, for longer than he did. As a result of the way he went about it, the situation changed rapidly from the last months of 1685 on.

Certain aspects of James' policies are important, without going into a detailed chronological account of his reign. The first is the increased brutality and repressiveness of government. The so-called 'Bloody Assize' in the south-west after the suppression of Monmouth's rising caused a popular revulsion. Although it was no more bloodthirsty than the aftermath of unsuccessful rebellions in other countries, the severity was considered excessive by many people who had in no way supported Monmouth. Linked with this was the very flagrant way in which the judges were again being used to serve the government's political ends. The notorious Judge Jeffreys (not withstanding recent attempts to rehabilitate him), as Chief Justice and then Lord Chancellor, did not even observe a pretence of impartiality where the Crown's interests were involved.

Turning to the executive side of the government, the King started with a coalition ministry inherited from his brother. He soon began to replace the middle-of-the-road men, even the moderate Tories, by his catholic friends and supporters, and by such careerists or adventurers as were prepared to go along with him. Halifax disappears from high office, and Sunderland, a member of the new Court group, becomes increasingly prominent. Even he had some qualifications for office, which is more than can be said for most of those whom James brought in. The 'Ins', the office-holders in the Court party, rapidly became identified with a very narrow circle. Soon Sunderland was the principal politician still at the top who had been active before 1685; by 1688 the only such one. Soon not only the Trimmers but the Anglican and High Tory leaders either dropped out of their own accord, or were pushed out of the government. The King's two brothers-in-law (through his first wife), Rochester and the second Earl of Clarendon, were in high office at the beginning of the reign but out by 1687.

Although James offered a policy of religious equality and toleration, he won the support of only very few Dissenters. Rather surprisingly one of these was the famous Quaker founder of Pennsylvania, William Penn, who may have been taken in by James' professed belief in toleration. But for the most part the protestant Nonconformists saw through him; they realised that he was simply using them to get concessions for his own co-religionists, and that when they had served his turn he would throw them over. James' real aim, they correctly saw, was not religious equality or toleration, but to restore the Roman religion in England and to overthrow the protestant settlement as it had existed since 1559 and again from 1662. Little cause as they had to love it, most Dissenters refused to co-operate in James' campaign to destroy the Anglican Church.

Another development of these years was only incidentally due to James. The removal of Monmouth from the scene—his execution after the failure of the rebellion—meant that if people wanted a rival claimant to the throne as an alternative to James, they would automatically look to William of Orange. As well as being the husband of James' elder daughter Mary, the heir-apparent to the throne, William was also James' nephew, being descended via his mother from Charles I. He was now the obvious protestant candidate for the throne (see Table 2, page 192).

The diminishing support for James by 1687-8 is sometimes ascribed entirely to his religious policy. His attempt to re-catholicise England involved attacking the church hierarchy, the universities and some individual colleges, and reintroducing a Court of High Commission under a different name. This alienated many lay members of the Church of England as well as the clergy, and it goes a long way to explain the revolution that followed, but it is not the whole story. As always in the seventeenth century, religion, politics and social relations are very closely intertwined. There was a social as well as an ideological basis for the swing away from James by the upper class. Fear of military rule again became intense. Whereas before it had more often been associated with Puritan–Republican dictatorship, now it became part and parcel of the fear of catholic despotism. James began to pack the Army with catholic officers, which was illegal and involved using his prerogative powers of dispensing with, and even suspending the Test Act, since such men should not have been holding military any more than civil offices under the Crown. James also undertook a further remodelling of local government; many borough charters were again called in, and the membership of corporations altered. This time, it was not being done to serve Anglican–Tory interests as in 1681-5, but to install catholics, Dissenters or indeed anyone who seemed prepared to collaborate in the King's designs. At the same time in the counties, since many landowners refused to co-operate in his religious policy, James removed a number from their offices as Lords Lieutenant, Deputy-Lieutenants, J.P.s, and so on. Some of the new people he put in their places were catholics, others Nonconformists, but again they tended to be people of more obscure social origins than those who were removed.

So the King's policy involved a threat to the predominance of the upper class, as well as to the established church. The two were in fact becoming synonymous. And James' campaign against chartered corporations (such as Magdalen College, Oxford), was seen as an attack on religion, liberty and property. Meanwhile, after 1685 the King kept his Parliament prorogued and then dissolved it without another meeting. His assault on rights and privileges was felt by many to herald a renewed attack on parliament itself, since the position it had reached by 1685 was obviously incompatible with James' designs.

His Overthrow

The last year or so of James' reign is characterised by the increasing futility of his efforts. It was partly just a matter of numbers. There simply were not enough catholics in England and Wales to support such a policy. The more open and forceful that his re-catholicising plans became, the less support he got. The other development was a personal one. James' second wife, the catholic Queen became pregnant, and a son was born to her in the early summer of 1688. This put a very different complexion on the future. Until then the heir-apparent had been the protestant Princess Mary, whose husband was the protestant champion William of Orange. Now the heir-apparent was this infant, who would undoubtedly be brought up as a catholic. This opened out the possibility not just of having to put up with a catholic monarch for the rest of James' lifetime (he was by then over fifty) but of an unending succession of catholic kings, in fact of a Popish dynasty for the indefinite future.

By this time James had come into a head-on collision with the Church of England. Historians disagree whether or not he technically infringed the 1641 Act abolishing the Court of High Commission, by setting up his 'Ecclesiastical Commission'. The real point is that he used this new commission not as an Anglican weapon against Puritans, like the old High Commission had been, but as an instrument of his re-catholicising policy. He tried to force the bishops and parsons, the clergy of the Church of England as a whole, to support his policy of Indulgence, that is of religious toleration by use of the prerogative. Ultimately he tried to force them to read his second Declaration of Indulgence from their pulpits. This resulted in another of the great constitutional law cases of the century, perhaps the most famous of the later Stuart period, that of 'the Seven Bishops'. The Archbishop of Canterbury and six other Bishops petitioned the King against this use of the dispensing power, and against his compelling them to publicise his Declaration, which they held to be illegal. James had them charged with seditious libel. This was technically for petitioning against his dispensing power, not for opposing his policy of toleration; but the real issue was obvious. The Seven Bishops' trial was actually pending at the time of the birth of James' son; the Judges of King's Bench were themselves evenly divided, and eventually the jury found in favour of the Bishops. This was the first really major law case to go against the executive under either monarchy or republic. In a sense it marks the emancipation of the judiciary. At the acquittal of the Bishops there were scenes of tumultuous enthusiasm in London, which should have warned James that the writing was on the wall.

It was the collision with the church, together with the birth of the Prince, which precipitated the next act in the drama. Opposition had already been building up. A number of eminent Whigs and others had gone into exile and were gathered at William's Court, but the Prince of Orange held his hand, and refused to commit himself openly against his uncle. Now, a small group of leading men, Tories as well as Whigs, decided to invite William over, to put things to rights. The invitation genuinely cut across party lines; it is both interesting and surprising to see who did and did not sign the famous letter to William. Danby did; not that he had ever particularly loved James, but at any rate he had always been loyal to the

Crown, and he was certainly a Tory. Halifax the Trimmer did not; whether this was due to lack of courage, that he preferred to bide his time and see which way the cat jumped, or whether he felt the invitation was trimming too far the other way, is not clear. Compton, the Tory Bishop of London, was another important signatory, and there were two or three influential Whig peers.

In the summer and autumn of 1688 William went ahead with his preparations. He was ready to come over; he probably wanted to become King of England, but above all he wanted to bring England into the great alliance which he was building up against Louis XIV and the power and pretensions of France in Europe. The French King's position in these months is extremely important in order to understand the ease with which James was overthrown. Louis might, after all, have been expected to come to the aid of his cousin who was following a policy broadly similar to that agreed on by Charles II in the Secret Treaty of Dover, or at least to do what he could if James got in a tight spot. But although Louis XIV's own religious policy had become more rigid and brutal with the Revocation of the Edict of Nantes, and the dragonnades against the Huguenots, he also saw things in their wider European context. He realised the weakness of catholicism in England and the strength of the opposition to it, and he did not approve of James' policy. Furthermore, he was deeply preoccupied with developments on the Continent. He was trying to push his influence eastward into Germany via the Palatinate, and was interested in the disputed succession to the bishopric of Cologne. He also had his eye on the future of the Spanish Empire. Charles II, the last Habsburg King of Spain, was an invalid and almost an imbecile, and had no direct heirs. Although it did not happen till 1700 his death was expected at any time, and Louis was desperately anxious to have his full power available so that he could stake the maximum claim. He was also afraid that if he made any move either towards England to help James, or direct against the Netherlands, he would simply push the two countries into each other's arms, and that a firm Anglo-Dutch alliance would come into existence. Whereas he hoped that if he did not do anything but simply kept aloof in this situation where William was known to be making preparations to invade, then England and the Netherlands would come to blows and more or less neutralise each other's power. It was on the basis of this not unreasonable, but as it turned out disastrously mistaken calculation, that Louis took a fateful decision in September 1688. He moved his main striking forces away from the Dutch frontier, wheeled them in an eastward direction, and began further offensive operations on the middle Rhine. This meant that William was freed from any fear of an immediate landward attack by France.

Those who had invited William over and others who hoped that he would come, were far from clear what they wished him to do. Some of them just wanted William to persuade, or if necessary compel, his uncle to change his religious policy and behave more reasonably. Others felt that James might have to go, but that some sort of Regency should be set up for the infant Prince. Others did not want to see James' son as King but were ready to see Mary as Queen. There was doubt and uncertainty as to what would happen, whether James would be replaced as King, whether there would be actual fighting. The only person who does not seem to have been confused was William. He made his military and naval preparations very carefully; whether or not he intended from the first to become King, he was certainly determined to be the master of the situation and not to be dependent on other people's help. To ensure this, he took an army of 15,000 men with him. The English navy might have given serious trouble, but partly owing to negligence or deliberate sabotage by the Admiral, partly to James' over-confidence, the fleet was caught in the Thames estuary by an east wind, and could not get out. Known to history as 'the protestant wind', it blew William's forces down the Channel, while the English ships were pent up inshore. So despite having about equal naval strength, James was unable to stop William landing. This was the first successful foreign invasion of the country since 1066. William had scarcely landed when it became clear that this was a very different affair from the Monmouth fiasco of three years before. Some people hesitated, but very quickly a great deal of support rallied to William, and James was abandoned even by his own closest military and political advisers, including the second-in-command of his army, John Churchill the future Duke of Marlborough. James' younger daughter, the Princess Anne, deserted her father and fled from London in the company of Bishop Compton to join Danby at York. The King had scarcely a friend left. It was still unclear what was going to happen next. Being unable to oppose William, who was marching on London, and unwilling to become in effect his prisoner, James prepared to flee the country.

Meanwhile William's purpose was still unclear. Was it to restore the position before 1685, that is to restore the Tory–Anglican supremacy of the last years of Charles II; or to go back to something more like the situation before the Popish Plot crisis, even before the Danby era; or to bring about some more drastic change? Everybody: catholics, Tories, Trimmers, Whigs, Republicans, had their own ideas of what they wanted. As always in a revolutionary situation, it was easier for people to be united against what they did not want, than in favour of what they did.

This confusion in 1688 is reflected in the settlement that followed, in 1689. The constitutional developments after 1689 are treated more fully in the next volume of this series. Before saying a little about this settlement, it is necessary to emphasise how remarkable it was that James was removed without another civil war. There was an element of farce, or tragi-comedy about it, because he fled once and was recaptured and brought back. But William was intelligent enough to see that James should be allowed, indeed encouraged to go; he was not going to repeat the mistake made over James' father in 1649. On the other hand, he did not want to have James around, so his second and successful flight—as a political refugee—to France, was extremely welcome to William.

The mass of the people did not come out in James' favour. As with Charles I in the 1640s, a myth has been propagated by one or two writers that the common people supported the Stuart Kings, and that the whole constitutional movement was a selfish conspiracy on the part of the rich. Again as with James' father, the common people showed themselves singularly unaware of this at the time. Nor had James won any real support from the largely middle-class Nonconformists, certainly not to the extent of their being prepared to rally in arms to his cause. Many of them were too deeply involved with the Whig party, others too suspicious that the King was just making use of them. Nor were many of the English catholics prepared to do much for James. They were frightened that their situation would get worse again, and that they would once more suffer penal disabilities as a result of his policy, and the last thing that they wanted to do was to come out in the open to defend him. James might have made a fight of it with his army, if it had not been for the disloyalty of his commanders and the uncertain attitude of the rank and file. A number of the catholic officers would have been prepared to fight but the generals and the soldiers were both thoroughly unreliable. And the Army was in effect taken over by William, or rather it put itself under his command.

The Revolution Settlement

As in 1660, the constitutional future of the country was settled in 1689 by the calling of a Convention Parliament, one not summoned by a reigning monarch. Unlike that of 1660, this Parliament was called under royal, namely William's auspices. He was the obvious person, ready to step in, and the situation was different from that preceding the recall of Charles II.

The various solutions that were proposed and the actual settlement alike reflect the attitudes of the various groups who helped to bring about the Revolution. In some cases they had only helped negatively, by not rallying to support their lawful King, James II. That was particularly true of the Tories who had had to choose finally between loyalty to their church and loyalty to their King. As has been suggested, they had chosen their own material interests as well as their church; as it happened, their choice was what most people would now agree was best for the country.

The conflict between Whig and Tory, which reappeared in 1689, went deeper than differences of political programme—or even of religious sympathies. It involved a fundamental difference in the way they thought about politics, about the problems of government and society. The true Tory believed that government by kings was instituted by God, that resistance to royal authority was a religious as well as a political offence, and that rebellion against a legitimate monarch was one of the most terrible of sins, comparable to

P

Satan's rebellion against God. By contrast, the thorough-going Whig believed that government was a human contrivance, to serve human ends, that legally constituted authority should normally be obeyed, but that a government which was destroying its subjects' rights thereby ceased to serve the purpose for which it had been set up—and so might properly in the last resort be overthrown. This did not, in practice, mean that no Tory ever resisted, let alone never opposed the Crown; nor that every Whig acted as if there was an inherent right of revolution in the people. But it did mean that they approached practical politics from quite different theoretical starting points.

It is hard to see the Revolution of 1688–9 other than as a victory for the Whig view of government. Yet it was only made possible by Tory disillusionment with James II; the Revolution itself and the Settlement which followed it both had as much of Tory practice as of Whig theory about them.

The legitimist view, favoured by the High Tories, was that James was still King. They argued that although he had fled the country the throne was not vacant, and that William, or preferably William and Mary jointly, should act as Regents. This could be so until James' restoration had been negotiated on suitable terms, if he would give up his religious policy and come back pledged to uphold the Anglican Church, or else William and Mary should be Regents on behalf of James' infant son. This proposal was a non-starter except in High-Tory, Anglican circles where the doctrine of Non-Resistance was still taken seriously, but it did have the effect of causing a split in the Church of England. A number of High-Church clergy continued to maintain that James was still the legitimate King. They did not oppose the Revolution or enter into conspiracies against William, but they refused to agree that he or anyone else could become King, as long as James (or his son) was alive. Because they subsequently refused to take the oath of allegiance to William and Mary this group became known as 'Non-jurors'; they formed a small breakaway sect, which soon dwindled in numbers but included some of the most distinguished church leaders of the time.

The second solution suggested was that associated with moderate Tory opinion; in effect it was Danby's plan. He argued that Mary was already Queen, since James had vacated the throne himself and also removed his son from the country, and that as the next heir Mary had automatically succeeded. One difficulty here arose over the infant Prince, born the previous June. Many Whigs, and some other people, committed themselves to the very doubtful, not to say untenable argument that this baby had not really been born to James' Queen at all, but had been smuggled into the palace in a warming-pan. On this view the so-called Prince was in fact a catholic pretender, and so Mary was in any case the legitimate heir. This was a discreditable piece of propaganda, comparable to the story of Lucy Walter (Monmouth's mother) and the 'Black Box'. Danby did not commit himself to it, but his policy seemed to rest on some such assumption. Otherwise it was hard to see how Mary could be said to be Queen, since any son had preference over any daughter in the line of succession. Danby and his allies wished William to be made Prince Consort. This solution had a majority in the House of Lords in the Convention, though not in the Commons. The difficulty was that William would not play. He refused to be a Prince Consort or a Regent, insisting that he must be at least co-equal with his wife. William threatened to wash his hands of the whole business and go home again; this caused great alarm as to what might follow—such as the possibility of James' return.

The moderate Whig solution was then adopted. This was to argue that the throne had been vacated by James' flight, and that William and Mary should be declared King and Queen jointly and in their own right, but that the throne should be offered to them by Parliament. At this stage Halifax made a very important suggestion. He had never been a Whig, but he now suggested that by contrast with what had happened in 1660, certain pre-conditions should be insisted on, and that William and Mary should have to accept these before they became King and Queen. Naturally this plan was favoured by the Whigs, who wanted to establish the principle that the proper relations between a monarch and his or her subjects (that is, those who had the vote and were represented in Parliament), were contractual. It was also supported by the moderate Tories, and its acceptance led to the composition of the document first called the Declaration of Rights; with small changes this became the Bill and then the Act of Rights, when it was passed through Parliament. The Declaration sets out some of the main grievances against James' government, and lists the reforms that Parliament was going to insist on. William and Mary became King and Queen only after agreeing to it.

Two other alternatives were also advanced in 1689. The view of the more extreme but still monarchical Whigs was that William alone should become King, not by any hereditary right, but simply as a result of a contract between him and Parliament. This was unacceptable, not only to the legitimist High Tories but also to Danby and the moderate Tories, even to most of the Trimmers and non-party men. Finally there was the view of the few surviving Republicans, the very last evidence of any political flicker from the Good Old Cause. One or two ex-Republicans did reappear briefly on the political scene. They would have preferred the monarchy to be abolished, as they hoped it had been in 1649; but there was no real possibility of this, either in parliamentary circles or in the country at large. It was not a serious alternative.

The offer of the Crown to William and Mary on conditions was a defeat for the Tories, and a victory for the Whigs and those who agreed with them on this issue without being supporters of the Whig party. But this does not mean that the overthrow of James II in 1688 was a 'Whig Revolution'; later, in the eighteenth century it was to be claimed, even appropriated by the Whigs as *their* revolution. However this was not true. If it had been, the revolution would not have been so successful or so nearly bloodless. Also the Settlement would have been much less of a compromise. The Tories had suffered a terrible disillusionment; the whole Court party of the early and mid-1680s had been based on the assumption of an indissoluble Tory–Anglican alliance with the Crown, and this had simply disintegrated. But this does not mean that Tory–Anglican influences were in complete eclipse. The balance of forces in the Convention Parliament, particularly the re-emergence of Danby, meant that in other respects the Settlement was as much a victory for the Tories as for the Whigs.

Some of its other aspects were also of great and lasting importance. The Settlement marked the restoration of upper-class supremacy, very much as in 1660. Control of local government and the militia was recovered by the peers and gentry—and the ruling oligarchies in the towns. The corporate privileges of colleges and other institutions were restored. Even James had seen the need to abandon these aspects of his policy when he heard news of William's preparations, and he had started to go into reverse gear in the early autumn of 1688, but by then it was too late. It had been in part a religious revolution, against a catholic king ruling a protestant country, and Roman Catholics were now excluded from succession to the throne. This was a parliamentary limitation. Such action had been taken by Parliament before, as early as the reign of Henry VIII, but then it had been done entirely on the royal initiative; in 1689 the situation was utterly different. Parliament also insisted on a change in the Coronation Oath, to be taken by the new sovereigns; they had to swear to uphold the 'protestant reformed religion', which had not been in the text of the previous oath.

It was generally agreed that the Dissenters' loyalty, the fact that so few of them had swallowed James' ground-bait, ought to be rewarded. By this time the view that persecution was not an effective means of achieving religious unity had come to be more widely accepted. The debate was renewed between those Anglicans who wanted a comprehensive solution, to widen the church so as to re-admit at least some Nonconformists, and those who preferred to leave it as it was but extend some degree of toleration to those outside. William was himself a Calvinist. He was not a man to put religion before principles of state, but in faith he was certainly nearer to his Presbyterian, or even Congregationalist, than to his High Anglican subjects, and he favoured practical toleration. However the churchmen's failure to agree on how far they would go, and the split within their own ranks caused by the Non-jurors, led to the final failure of comprehension; the Church of England would never again include all the protestants in the country. The alternative policy is embodied in the Toleration Act of 1689. This did not extend equality of political and civic rights but a minimum measure of freedom for actual religious worship to Trinitarian protestants. Catholics were still deliberately excluded and so were Unitarians and non-Christians; Quakers too were excluded, until some time later special provision was made for them to affirm instead of taking the oaths of Allegiance and Supremacy. In practice the penal laws against catholics were not enforced again, except in times of national emergency, such as once or twice during the French wars when invasion seemed imminent and again after the Highland rebellion of 1715. There was no more persecution in England and Wales simply on grounds of religious differences, though severe civic disabilities remained.

The principle of religious co-existence had won an important, if limited and belated victory. The Toleration Act was a triumph, even if a modest one for liberal, progressive principles. It did not say that the adherents of all religious faiths should be equal, that people in England could follow any religion they liked or none, but it was a recognition that different religions could at least co-exist within the framework of a single political unit or state without disrupting it. That was a very great advance. It was coming to be accepted elsewhere in Europe; it already had been to some extent in the Netherlands, but on the other hand France under Louis XIV was moving in the opposite direction towards the enforcement of greater religious uniformity.

Returning to the more strictly constitutional side, the Act of Rights also dealt with some of the prerogative powers that the Convention felt Charles and James had misused. The royal right to suspend legislation was abolished, and the right to dispense with it in particular cases so narrowly restricted as virtually to be taken away. In the revised Coronation Oath the new sovereigns also had to swear to observe parliamentary statutes, another innovation. James' ecclesiastical commission, which he had used to impose his will on the church, was declared illegal. The illegality of any non-parliamentary taxation was reaffirmed; here James had been infringing various statutes by the autumn of 1688, because his Parliament had voted some of his supplies for three years which had by then expired. But unlike the position earlier in the century, this was not a major issue; that battle had really been won by 1660. The Declaration also condemned the keeping up of a peacetime standing army as contrary to law. There it was on shaky ground, since no previous statute can be found to this effect, and even William before the end of his reign was breaking this part of the Act. But the legal basis of military discipline was unclear, and this resulted in the passing of an annual Mutiny Act; in this way parliament kept some control over the Army. Moreover because the country became involved in a major European war, the new King came to be completely dependent on parliament for extra taxes, to sustain the military effort.

There was to be a much tougher struggle with William concerning his prerogative of deciding on the frequency and duration of parliaments. The 1664 Triennial Act had proved useless. There was a general feeling that something more effective should be put into force, but William just as much as Charles and James II was very reluctant to give way here. Only after some years—though we may anticipate, since it is really a postscript to the settlement of 1689—was a Triennial Act passed (1694), providing not only that a parliament should meet, but that there should be a general election for a new one every three years. This was a reaction against the long Cavalier Parliament of 1661–78 as well as against Charles II's rule without one from 1681 to 1685. The frequency and length of the sessions were not specified further; in practice the financial necessity of the Crown having to work much more closely with parliament, meant that from 1689 on there was a meeting every year. Ten months near the end of William's reign is the longest interval between sessions since 1689.

The greater length, frequency and regularity of parliamentary sittings, marks its assumption of the central place in the government of the country. This did not only apply to legislation and taxation. Parliament played an increasingly positive role through the emergence of a ministerial group which came to be known as the Cabinet, and gradually replaced the old Privy Council as the real executive body. These ministers carried on the business of government and were answerable to the majority in the Commons. This, more than the specific legislation passed in 1689 or later, signifies the real nature of the revolution that had taken place during the century.

Other institutions of government had also changed since before the Civil War. The Treasury had grown into a regular department of state, not wholly replacing the old Exchequer, but largely superseding it in the management of finance and with direct control over the much enlarged staffs of the main revenues—Customs, Excise and other taxes. From 1667 on, the Treasury was more often in charge of a Board of Commissioners than of a single Lord Treasurer; from 1714 it has invariably been so. The Admiralty and Navy Offices too had grown more elaborate, not unreasonably in view of the Navy's expansion in size and the scope of its operations. Apart from James' terms of office (1660–73 as Duke of York, and 1685–8 as King), it had also been presided over by a board, the Lords Commissioners of the Admiralty. The new standing army involved additional changes. The royal Household, by contrast, had undergone a further decline in importance, due partly to the greater prominence of Parliament as a political forum, partly to the establishment of additional offices and departments outside it (for example in military administration). The disappearance of the 'conciliar', or prerogative courts since 1641 meant that the legal side of government was relatively less prominent than it had been before. Probably the Council (and later the Cabinet) had less power over J.P.s and other local officials than the Tudor or early Stuart Council had done; but this was a matter of practice rather than legislation and is hard to prove. Greater colonial commitments and more concern to see laws about colonial trade properly observed, led to a series of experiments. The Lords of Trade and Plantations (1675), though only provisional like their predecessors since 1660, marked a step towards the creation of a regular department—the Board of Trade and Plantations—which was to follow the Revolution, in 1696.

Turning to the position of ministers in the system of government, the Secretaries of State were still the key men, in charge of home security and the execution of foreign policy. Arlington's career illustrates this well. He replaced Clarendon's ally, the elderly Sir Edward Nicholas, in 1662 and himself retired rather than risk the outcome of an impeachment twelve years later. Other Secretaries of the reigns of Charles and James II were little more than efficient senior executives; the main exception is Sunderland (Secretary 1679–81, then dismissed after joining the Exclusionists in the 1680 Parliament, and Secretary again 1683–8). No Secretary of this period came anywhere near the Cecils (William, later Lord Burghley and Robert, later Earl of Salisbury) or Walsingham (another Elizabethan) in importance, but Sunderland played a larger part in policy-making than any other. There was still no rule or convention which great office should be held by the King's first minister. Clarendon was Lord Chancellor, Danby Lord Treasurer, Halifax Lord Privy Seal, Rochester Lord President of the Council and then Lord Treasurer. Indeed the very idea of a first or 'Prime' Minister, like that of collective ministerial responsibility, had not yet been accepted. A first minister was still regarded as tantamount to a favourite, and because ministers were still held individually responsible he was particularly vulnerable to attack.

Later in William's reign royal finances were further reorganised. By this time the King was almost entirely dependent on Parliament for supplies; on the spending side a new division was now made between civil administration, including the royal household, and naval and military or other extra expenses. A fixed sum yearly, known as the Civil List, was voted (1697) for the King to carry on the government and to maintain his household. These two kinds of expenditure were not finally separated until the end of the eighteenth century. But putting the King's government on to a fixed amount meant that the sovereign was ceasing to be a divine arcana of state, personally identical with the government, and was becoming the top official of the realm and the ceremonial Head of State. It was a step in a longer, more complicated process whereby the King or Queen as a person was separated from the Crown as a political institution. The monarch's private and public capacities were gradually becoming more distinct in people's minds. This is a very important idea, because until it was generally accepted there could not be a non-political, non-party monarchy such as has developed in Britain during the last 150 years or so. This process may have been accelerated a little in the mid-seventeenth century by the idea people had of 'the State' or 'the Commonwealth', by which they meant the public service in the years of the Republic; this idea was not wholly extinguished at the Restoration although its re-publican overtones were. But this change was far from happening all at once in 1689. William III was still the effective ruler of the country, even if his powers were more narrowly limited than those of his predecessors had been. For his reign at least, the monarch still ruled as well as reigned.

Much of the later part of the Revolution Settlement, embodied in the measures passed after 1689, was carried out against William's wishes by a new 'Country' party, composed largely of Tories, rather than by the makers of the Revolution itself. This shows how much of the Whig programme of the 1670s and 1680s had in fact been an opposition, Country policy rather than anything peculiar to Shaftesbury and his party. It does not mean that the Tories had all become Whigs; it simply means that Country Tories, being out of office and in opposition, had more in common with Country, opposition Whigs than with the permanent Court, office-holding element among the Tories. The same was true on the Whig side too; the Country wanted to limit the power of the executive, which still meant that of the Crown and the Court.

To understand its full significance, we must look briefly at the Revolution in the rest of the British Isles. In Ireland it was alto-gether less peaceful and unanimous. There was a serious attempt at a Roman Catholic counter-revolution in 1689, a last desperate attempt by the native Irish at a war of liberation to throw off Eng-lish rule. Many of the Irish rose, as they had in 1641, against the English and Scottish settler population and against protestant dom-ination. Even James saw the danger, but his supporters got out of hand, and gained temporary control of a large part of the country. After fierce fighting they were defeated by William, and there was an even more thoroughgoing and ruthless restoration of English power than there had been in the 1650s and 1660s. The Anglo-Scottish protestant ascendancy was clamped even more securely on Ireland, so much so that it was now to last until the early twentieth century. Much severer measures of civic and legal discrimina-tion against catholics were passed, though the worst of these were not imposed immediately after the war but later, during the reigns of Anne and the early Hanoverians. William, like James in the preceding counter-revolution, was carried further than he would himself have wanted to go, by his own supporters. By the time the Irish were defeated England and France were locked in a great European war, and it was more plausible than it had been earlier to say that unless Ireland was firmly under English control, it would be used as a base for cutting England's sea routes, even for invasion by the French.

In Scotland the Revolution took a very different course, but again it was more violent than in England. 1689 marked a complete reversal of 1660. The Scottish Parliament achieved greater independence than ever before. The Presbyterian Church, the Kirk, was restored to its former predominance in Scottish national life; episcopacy was finally abolished. Its adherents were largely supporters of James and later his son, Jacobites as they came to be called; there was no split within the episcopalian front as there was in England, no equivalent to the Seven Bishops' case. Jacobitism was particularly strong in parts of the Highlands. The Revolution and its aftermath were really a victory for the Lowland Presbyterian Scots over the Highland clansmen. This victory was marked by dubious dealings, and the settlement of some old and very bitter scores; the massacre of Glencoe against the clan Macdonald was the most infamous of these. There was a case, however, not for treachery and murder but for suppressing finally the semi-independent clan system with its chronic outcrop of armed violence. Its suppression can be justified on the same grounds as the campaign against the retaining of private armies, conducted in England by the Yorkists and early Tudors. Only in this way, moreover, could the protestant succession be guaranteed in Scotland as well as in England, and the way cleared for the successful Union of the two countries which was to be achieved during the next reign, in 1707.

Conclusion

Iᴛ is sometimes said that the successive political changes of the seventeenth century represented the defeat of absolute monarchy but in the positive sense were simply designed to make England a safe and happy place for the landowning classes, and to a lesser extent for the rich men in the City of London. On this view, the peaceful revolution of 1640–1, the Restoration Settlement of 1660–2 and the so-called 'Glorious Revolution' of 1688–9 were victories for oligarchy against monarchy. The mass of the people were not consulted, and their interests were not so directly involved. There is an element of truth in this. The growth of parliamentary government and the victory of Parliament over the Crown in the constitutional struggle, did not necessarily mean that the democratic rights of ordinary people or the freedom of individual Englishmen were being advanced.

There were, however, some respects in which individual rights improved during the later seventeenth century. After 1670 no jury could be penalised for giving a wrong decision, by being proceeded against at law; until then, if jurors were felt to have found the wrong verdict in law cases, especially ones where the interests of the Crown were involved, they were not safe from prosecution. An Act in 1677 introduced new and slightly improved criteria for considering the validity of evidence in some types of case, and for the regulation of contracts. The famous Habeas Corpus Act of 1679, almost the only positive achievement of the first Exclusion Parliament, put on a statutory basis what had previously only been a legal practice of the courts; it was now made more effective against the Crown, and people could no longer at all easily be held in prison indefinitely for political reasons without being brought to trial. But it was only after 1689, under Holt who became Chief Justice in that year, one of the greatest and most progressive common lawyers since Coke, that a more modern attitude appears to -

wards prisoners, and modern ideas about contractual relationships began to be accepted by the courts. Soon after the Revolution, the 'Licensing' Act for the regular censorship of the press, renewed in James II's reign, finally lapsed. Freedom of expression was still very circumscribed by the laws of seditious libel, which were interpreted in a much more sweeping way than they have come to be since; none the less after 1694–5 there was no censorship of books, pamphlets or newspapers before publication. An amended Treason law in William's reign meant that there had to be two witnesses for the prosecution in cases of treason, and accused persons were given elementary rights which they had not had earlier. To a greater extent than before, actions in which people were charged with treason became legal rather than political in character. There was now more chance of people charged with treason being found Not Guilty and acquitted, which had hardly been the case under the Tudors and only to a very limited degree under the early Stuarts or the Republic. This was symbolised by the fact that the Judges were at last made independent of the Crown; this was not made law until 1701 and did not take full effect until 1714. Under James II the bench had been packed as never before, and there was a general reaction against the conduct and attitude of men like Jeffreys. So the Judges gaining security of tenure and salary can be seen as a postscript to the Revolution. In matters of public order there was not much of a victory for the populace. Decisions as to when law and order were being infringed were put into the hands of local magistrates to an even greater extent than they had been since 1660. There again the operative statute comes a good deal later— the Riot Act (1715). There was also a limited degree of religious toleration, which for protestants was in practice extended by their taking the Anglican communion at irregular intervals and so qualifying to hold public office for example in local government, despite the Test Act.

As against this, individual freedom and people's legal rights were still very narrowly limited by modern standards. Privy Councillors could still have people arrested and kept in prison at their own discretion; general search warrants were still legal until the later eighteenth century; any political criticism of the government could be construed as seditious libel, so that there was in practice still something like a censorship. Although there was a movement in favour of greater economic freedom, signalised by further parliamentary attacks on trading monopolies and privileges during the 1690s, Parliament itself could still make such grants. For instance the charter and monopoly rights of the East India Company were renewed and even extended in the early eighteenth century. Another point not to be overlooked, is that the privileges of Parliament itself could conflict with the rights of the individual. The legislature could and sometimes did encroach on the rights of the electors, limiting improperly who they could vote for. In the first years of the eighteenth century there were to be two cases in which the right to vote for a candidate of the electors' choice was at issue; the House of Commons behaved high-handedly and came into collision with the law courts and with the House of Lords. Furthermore, despite the Toleration Act and the practice of 'Occasional Conformity', religious equality was still a long way off. In fact it was not to be achieved until the nineteenth century.

In combination with continued social and economic developments, some of these changes pointed the way to better things. Among these was the rapid growth of overseas trade, due especially to increased English imports from other continents and larger re-exports to Europe. This has led some historians to speak of a 'commercial revolution' in the later Stuart period. Although agriculture and the landed interest were still preponderant, by the 1690s they no longer dwarfed commerce and shipping as they had done in the 1600s or even the 1630s. But these commercial and financial advances did not lead to rapid industrial growth. Although an attempt to discover the reasons why the Industrial Revolution did not begin its real acceleration until the later eighteenth century would take us far beyond the chronological limits of this book, it is interesting to wonder which prerequisites for the industrial 'take-off', as some economists describe it, were present in England after 1760, but still absent after 1688. Insufficient consumer demand, too sluggish a rate of population growth and excessive direction of investment into trade and finance, as opposed to internal communications and industrial plant, are among the answers which economists might give.

This was also a period of fundamental scientific advance. The reign of Charles II saw the foundation of the Royal Society, and the achievements of the greatest of all English scientists—Isaac Newton, who incidentally was employed in the government as head of the Mint, in charge of coinage, during William's reign. As with other changes during the century, historians remain in wide disagreement about the effect of the civil wars and the republic on scientific progress. Some see the Royal Society as a natural successor to the various scientific groups which had flourished in the 1640s and 1650s, and regard Puritanism as having favoured scientific just as it did economic advance; others find as many Royalist and Anglican as Puritan or Parliamentarian scientists and as much scientific activity before 1640 and after 1660 as between those dates; a few indeed would even go so far as to argue the opposite, that the Civil War and interregnum delayed scientific and other intellectual achievement, which throve best in a more relaxed, if occasionally dilettante, atmosphere. By the end of the century, when both science and business enterprise were more respectable than they had once been, in no longer being open to suspicion of moral or theological unsoundness, the English whigs and low-church protestants certainly claimed an association between their own faith, free government (by which they meant parliamentary monarchy), scientific advance and economic progress. But contemporaries can be wrong, especially about what has been happening just before their own time. So such evidence is not conclusive, though it tells us something very important about these late-seventeenth-century whigs and low-churchmen that they should have wanted to identify themselves and their beliefs with science and business enterprise. The student of history better than anyone else should know that nothing succeeds like success; even more, nothing fails like failure. Perhaps it was the very achievements of these new influences, culminating in the technological and industrial revolutions which began a century or so later, which won them new supporters. During the years we have been concerned with here the picture is not so clear. On balance, as the evidence now stands, those historians who deny any positive connection between puritanism, capitalism and science seem to be straining the facts to fit their theories more than those who affirm that some such connection did exist. That the victory of Protestantism and constitutional government favoured further economic and technical advance seems hardly to be in doubt. But the lesson of communist Russia in our own time should remind us that dictatorship and censorship of free ideas are not always and necessarily inimical to advances in wealth or in natural knowledge and its application.

In philosophy, too, the span of time covered by this book saw the careers of several great thinkers. Again the connection with the political conflict is far from clearcut. Francis Bacon is often hailed as one of the prophets of modern science; although his actual ideas about philosophical and scientific methods have had relatively little influence, he was undoubtedly revolutionary in his insistence that science could and should be used not only to extend continuously our knowledge of the natural world but also to improve our material conditions. And Bacon not merely served James I but would have liked a stronger, more nearly absolute, monarchy than that king or his successor was able to achieve. Thomas Hobbes was the first great materialist thinker in modern European history. Hobbes denied the charge of atheism, and we may accept this, although the penalties to which those openly expressing doubt, let alone disbelief in the truths of Christian revelation were then liable, means that men's true beliefs are sometimes hard to know. The premises and conclusions of Hobbes' thought owe much to the mechanistic science of Galileo, something to the Greek-influenced nominalist philosophers of the later Middle Ages and virtually nothing to Christian revelation or even to Christian moral and political principles. In politics Hobbes argued for absolutism because he could not conceive of a mixed or balanced government; it was absolutism or anarchy, and preferably absolute monarchy. Since his greatest work, the *Leviathan*, appeared in 1651 shortly before Hobbes returned from the Royalist exile circle in Paris to live in England under the Commonwealth, he was denounced for urging acceptance of any *de facto* absolute government, in fact for bowing down before the idol of power. This plus his suspected atheism and his unquestionably violent anticlericalism made Hobbes anathema in Royalist, Anglican circles, though Charles II to his credit defended him from serious attack after 1660. Yet Hobbes' obvious contempt for constitutional government, and his preference for an absolute king over an absolute parliament, made his ideas equally unacceptable to Parliamentarians and then Whigs. Only when later legal and political theorists came to believe in the idea of indivisible sovereignty, that in any society not in a condition of anarchy there must be a sovereign power, as a matter of logical necessity, were Hobbes' ideas resurrected. He is the classic example of a very great speculative theorist having next to no practical influence, except to stir up a host of second-rate men to denounce him bell, book and candle. Very different is the case of John Locke, an Oxford don, who was a client and friend of Shaftesbury. Locke wrote his defence of limited parliamentary government, and of subjects' ultimate right to overthrow a government which was invading their vital interests, during the time of the Exclusion Crisis; but for both political and personal reasons he did not publish it until just after the revolution of 1688. As a result, until the dating of the original text was established recently, it used to be assumed that he had written a justification after the event for the Whig view of, and part in, the events of 1688-9. In fact, his *Two Treatises of Government* represents whiggery on the defensive, and express not a rather absurd fear of an imaginary tyrant but a very understandable alarm at the victorious and revengeful Stuarts in the early 1680s. Unlike the case with Hobbes, there is no particular logical connection between Locke's political theories and his treatment, in his other writings, of human nature and of more strictly philosophical problems. Again, unlike Hobbes, Locke had great practical influence both in eighteenth-century England and outside his own country on the Frenchmen of the Enlightenment, and so indirectly on the French revolutionaries, and more directly on the eighteenth-century Americans and so on the War of Independence and the subsequent system under which the United States came to be governed. The secularisation of political theory, its greater detachment from religion, is one of the most fundamental changes in the course of the century.

Q

Another great change concerns the place of religion in the life of the country. There is no accurate way of measuring whether England was a less religious country in 1689 than in 1603 or 1640, that is whether people were less sincere in their beliefs and less devout in their religious observances. Still, there is a sense in which this clearly was coming to be so. Religious issues—fear of Popery, jealousy of Anglican and Dissenter, hostility to radical sects—were still present, and indeed sometimes potent in politics after 1688–9. But the whole religious basis of the national life was no longer in question. For better or worse, the threefold division had become permanent: the established Church of England embracing at least nominally the great majority, the sizeable minority in the protestant Nonconformist churches, and the now small minority of Roman Catholics. Nor was there any question of the church as an institution, or of churchmen as individuals playing the same part in public affairs as in the days of Bancroft or Laud. To this extent, whatever the degree of individual piety or sincerity, politics and the nation's life generally had become less clerical and more secular by the latter end of the century.

Taking all this into account, the late seventeenth century can fairly be called a more modern age than the times of James and Charles I. This is also borne out by some aspects of everyday life. People's attitudes and behaviour had become slightly less violent and brutal. Gentlemen no longer carried swords as a matter of course, but more often canes or walking sticks. Not only in politics but in social habits, though the age was still shockingly coarse and brutal by modern standards, some progress can be seen; it was slightly more civilised than the age of the Elizabethans or the early Stuarts. But above all the constitutional changes, the victory of Parliament over the Crown, make the end of the seventeenth century decisively different from the beginning, and mark off developments in England from those in most other European countries. There is a sense in which this victory, admittedly won by and for the upper and middle, the propertied classes, and not the majority of the population, was still in the long run a victory for the English people as a whole. As we have seen, there is no evidence whatever that the common people supported the Stuart kings rather than Parliament. And they were right not to do so. Despite the earlier defeat of the Levellers, the creation of parliamentary government had opened up an avenue towards democracy. If victory had gone to the kings and a system of absolute monarchy had been established, any prospect of gradual advance towards democracy would have been closed; this could only have been achieved through violent, bloody, convulsive revolutions such as have taken place in most countries of continental Europe at some time during the last century or two. Whatever their faults and limitations, the forces represented in the seventeenth-century House of Commons stood for ordered progress and the possibility of peaceful reform, as can easily be appreciated if we compare the history of Britain with that of many other countries from the eighteenth century to the present day.

CHART OF COMPARATIVE DATES

Year	General and Political	Foreign and Colonial	Religious, Social and Economic	Thought, Science and the Arts
1603	d. Elizabeth I Accession of James I (1566–1625) Robert Cecil and the Howards in favour	End of the Irish War	Plague	James I's *True Law of Free Monarchies*
1604	James' 1st Parliament: 1st session — Shirley's case; Goodwin v. Fortescue; Apology of the Commons Trial and imprisonment of Sir Walter Ralegh (1552–1618)	Peace with Spain	Hampton Court Conference d. Whitgift Richard Bancroft (1544–1610) Archbishop Church '*Canons*' Trade expansion begins	W. Shakespeare (1564–1616), *Hamlet*; 1st production of *Othello*
1605	Gunpowder Plot			Francis Bacon (1561–1626), *Advancement of Learning* Ben Jonson (1572–1637), *Volpone* (his finest plays were produced 1605–15)
1606	2nd Session of Parliament Bate's case (Impositions)	Flight of Irish resistance leaders	Disputes over Prohibitions Anti-enclosure riots in Mid-lands	
1607	3rd Session of Parliament	Virginia founded		
1608	Cecil created an Earl and Lord Treasurer New Impositions Case of Colville (the *post-nati*)			*King Lear* John Webster (c. 1580–1625), *The White Devil*, 1st production Shakespeare's *Sonnets*
1609	4th and 5th Sessions of Parliament: Great Contract; Impositions	Spanish–Dutch truce		
1610		Assassination of Henry IV Plantation of Ulster begun	d. Bancroft	
1611	Parliament dissolved Decline of Salisbury's influence		George Abbot (1562–1633) Archbishop	Authorised Version of the Bible *The Tempest*; Shakespeare retires to Stratford

1612	d. Salisbury Predominance of Robert Carr (1580s–1645) d. Prince Henry (b. 1594)	East India Co. rent Surat		
1613		Marriage of Princess Elizabeth (1596-1662) and Frederick of Palatinate Sarmiento (Gondomar) Spanish Ambassador in London		John Napier of Merchistoun (1550-1617) discovers logarithms
1614	'Addled Parliament' Suffolk Lord Treasurer		Alderman Cockayne's scheme	William Harvey (1578-1657) discovers circulation of the blood
1615	Rise of George Villiers (1592–1628) Fall of Carr		Cloth trade dislocated	
1616	Dismissal of Chief Justice Coke (1552–1634)			
1617		Ralegh's last voyage	Articles of Perth (Scottish Church Settlement) Merchant Adventurers' charter restored; trade recovers	
1618	Fall of the Howards Supremacy of Villiers (Buckingham)	Bohemian revolt		
1619		Frederick of the Palatinate accepts crown of Bohemia First representative assembly in America (Virginia)		Inigo Jones (1573–1652) begins the banqueting house in Whitehall
1620		Battle of White Mountain Invasion of Upper Palatinate 'Pilgrim Fathers' settle New Plymouth	Slump in cloth trade	Bacon's *Novum Organum*
1621	James' 3rd Parliament: Fall of Bacon; attack on monopolists L. Cranfield (1575–1645) Lord Treasurer Commons' Protestation	Spanish–Dutch war resumed	Bad conditions; general distress (1621-3)	1st visit to England of Anthony van Dyck (1599–1641) Robert Burton, *Anatomy of Melancholy*

Year	General and Political	Foreign and Colonial	Religious, Social and Economic	Thought, Science and the Arts
1622		Occupation of Lower Palatinate		
1623		Massacre of Amboyna; Charles and Buckingham's trip to Madrid		1st collected edition of Shakespeare's Plays
1624	James' last Parliament: impeachment of Cranfield; Monopolies Act	Virginia becomes a Crown Colony; War with Spain; Louis XIII of age; Richelieu first minister; French marriage treaty; 1st English colony in West Indies	Trade improves; Legal maximum rate of interest lowered from 10 to 8%	
1625	d. James I; Accession of Charles I (1599–1649); Charles' 1st Parliament	Cadiz expedition; Barbados colonised	Plague; Scottish Act of Revocation; 1st attacks on Arminians	
1626	Charles' 2nd Parliament: impeachment of Buckingham attempted; Forced loan	War with France		
1627	Darnel's or Five Knights' case (Habeas Corpus)	Isle of Rhé expedition	Archbishop Abbot suspended	
1628	Charles' 3rd Parliament: 5 subsidies; Petition of Right; attack on Buckingham; Richard Weston (1577–1635) Lord Treasurer; Assassination of Buckingham; Thomas Wentworth (1593–1641) enters government	Fall of La Rochelle	Commons attack Arminians; William Laud (1573–1645) created Bishop of London	
1629	2nd Session of Parliament: Eliot's Three Resolutions	Peace of Susa with France; Edict of Restitution; Gustavus enters 30 Years' War; Massachusetts Bay Co. founded	Renewed slump in cloth trade; Bad harvest	

1630	b. of Prince (the future Charles II)	1st victories of Gustavus; Peace of Madrid with Spain; Guinea Co. (trade to West Africa)	Bad harvest; Large-scale emigration to New England begins	
1631	Collection of Knighthood fines		Vigorous enforcement of Poor Law	Van Dyck settles in England
1632	Wentworth appointed Lord Deputy	Gustavus killed in battle; Foundation of Maryland		
1633	Charles visits Scotland; Wentworth goes to Ireland		Economic conditions improve; Laud Archbishop	Philip Massinger (1583–1640), *New Way to pay Old Debts*; George Herbert (1593–1633), *Poems*; John Donne (1573–1631), *Poems*
1634	1st writ for collection of Ship Money			
1635	d. Weston; Treasury in Commission; Ship Money extended to inland countries	France declares war on Spain		
1636	Bishop Juxon, Lord Treasurer			
1637	Hampden's case (Ship Money)		Prosecution of Puritan pamphleteers; Scottish Prayer Book; National Covenant	
1638	Verdict in Hampden's case	Japan closed to Europeans; Battle of the Downs; Fort St George (Madras) founded		
1639	1st 'Bishops' War'			
1640	Short Parliament; 2nd 'Bishops' War'; Council of Peers; Long Parliament meets: impeachment of Strafford and Laud	Portuguese revolt from Spain; Catalan revolt	New *Canons* for the Church of England; 'Root-and-Branch' petition	Censorship breaks down
1641	Triennial Act; Trial, attainder and execution of Strafford	Marriage of Princess Mary and William Prince of Orange	Abolition of High Commission; 'Root-and-Branch' Bill	

Year	General and Political	Foreign and Colonial	Religious, Social and Economic	Thought, Science and the Arts
1641	Abolition of prerogative courts and non-parliamentary taxation Charles' trip to Scotland 2nd session of Parliament begins Irish Rebellion Grand Remonstrance 1st Militia Bill			
1642	Attempt on Five Members King leaves London Militia Ordinance Military preparations Sept. Battle of Edgehill (d.) Battle of Turnham Green (p.)	d. Richelieu Mazarin 1st minister	Impeachment of 12 Bishops Bishops excluded from House of Lords Dislocation of trade	Sir Thomas Browne (1605–82), *Religio Medici* Ordinance closing London theatres
1643	Oxford negotiations Royalist victories in west and north; capture of Bristol d. Hampden Relief of Gloucester (p.) 1st Battle of Newbury (d.) Excise; Weekly Pay Alliance with Scots d. Pym	Battle of Rocroi d. Louis XIII; Regency	Westminster Assembly of Divines Solemn League and Covenant	Long Parliament imposes censorship
1644	Royalist 'parliament' called at Oxford Committee of Both Kingdoms Battle of Marston Moor (p.) Battle of Lostwithiel (r.) 2nd Battle of Newbury (d.)	Revolution in China; Manchu dynasty established	Presbyterian v. Independent split appears Excise extended to food and other necessities	Roger Williams (1604–83), *The Bloudy Tenent of Persecution* John Milton (1608–76), *Areopagitica*
1645	Uxbridge negotiations New Model Army; Fairfax (1612–71) C-in-C. Self-Denying Ordinance Battle of Naseby (p.) Battle of Langport (p.)		'Compositions' with Royalists begun	Gresham College scientific group formed

(*Note: d.* = drawn or indecisive battle, *p.* = Parliamentarian victory, *r.* = Royalist victory)

1646	King's surrender to Scots End of 1st Civil War Newcastle negotiations		Sales of confiscated lands begun; Courts of Wards abolished Episcopacy abolished; Presbyterian Church set up George Fox (1624–91) begins his ministry	Edward Hyde (1609–74) begins his *History* (1st published 1702–4) First Leveller writings
1647	Scots hand the King over to Parliament Demobilisation crisis Army seize the King Split in Parliament Army enters London Purge of 11 'Presbyterian' leaders Independents negotiate with King Putney Debates Mutinies in Army suppressed King escapes to I.o.W.			*Heads of Proposals* *The Case of the Army* *The Agreement of the People*
1648	Negotiations broken off King's treaty with Scots 2nd Civil War Battle of Preston Negotiations resumed Pride's Purge	1st 'Fronde' Peace of Westphalia		John Wilkins (1614–72) forms scientific group in Oxford
1649	Trial and execution of the King Abolition of monarchy and House of Lords Commonwealth proclaimed Levellers suppressed	Re-conquest of Ireland begun	Diggers attempt communal farming Sale of Crown lands begun	Gerrard Winstanley (?1609–1660s), *New Law of Righteousness* Stricter censorship of the press
1650	War with Scots; Oliver Cromwell (1599–1658) succeeds Fairfax as Lord-General Battle of Dunbar	d. William II of Orange; supremacy of the de Witts	Church settlement becomes more Independent, less Presbyterian (1650s) Laws against moral offences and cruel sports	Andrew Marvell (1621–78), *Horatian Ode* (poems 1st published 1776) Samuel Cooper (1609–72), miniature painter, active 1650s

Year	General and Political	Foreign and Colonial	Religious, Social and Economic	Thought, Science and the Arts
1651	Charles II's attempted invasion Battle of Worcester	Parliamentary control over colonies	Navigation Act Economic conditions begin to improve. Rate of interest cut from 8 to 6%	Thomas Hobbes (1588–1679), *Leviathan*
1652		1st Anglo-Dutch war		
1653	Dissolution of the Rump 'Barebones Parliament' 'Instrument of Government' Protectorate set up	Settlement of Ireland begun	Land sales and compositions virtually ended	Winstanley's *Law of Freedom* Isaak Walton (1593–1683), *The Compleat Angler*
1654	1st Protectorate Parliament	Peace with the Dutch Expedition sent to West Indies		
1655	Royalist 'rising' The Major-Generals	Occupation of Jamaica War with Spain	Readmission of the Jews to England Suppression of ale-houses	
1656	2nd Protectorate Parliament			James Harrington (1611–77), *Oceana*
1657	Humble Petition and Advice Cromwell refuses the Crown	Anglo-French Alliance	Trade depressed by Spanish War	William Davenant (1606–68), *Siege of Rhodes* (1st English opera)
1658	2nd Session of Parliament d. Cromwell	Battle of the Dunes Capture of Dunkirk		
1659	Parliament of Richard Cromwell (1626–1712) Rump restored End of Protectorate Booth's rising Rump re-dissolved Threat of civil war Rump re-restored	War in Baltic Treaty of Pyrenees (France and Spain)		Revival of political speculation
1660	Monck's march south Return of 'secluded Members' Dissolution of Long Parliament Declaration of Breda Election of Convention			Samuel Pepys (1633–1703) begins his Diary

	Constitutional / Political	Foreign affairs & war	Religious / Social	Cultural / Scientific
1660	Restoration of monarchy and House of Lords; Return of Charles II; Execution of Regicides; Revenue settlement; Convention Parliament dissolved		Bishops, etc. restored; Navigation Act; Corn Law; King's Declaration on Religion	Theatres reopened
1661	Election of 'Cavalier Parliament'; Act against petitioning; Corporation Act	Portuguese marriage alliance; peace with Spain; Personal Rule of Louis XIV	Savoy Conference	Peter Lely (1618–80) Court painter; Robert Boyle (1627–91), *The Sceptical Chymist*; Thomas Fuller (1608–61), *Worthies of England*; 'Boyle's Law'; Foundation of the Royal Society; Licensing Act (censorship)
1662	Militia Act; Henry Bennet, later Lord Arlington (1618–85) Secretary of State	Sale of Dunkirk	Uniformity Act; revised Prayer Book; 1st Declaration of Indulgence; Amendment of Poor Law	
1663		Grant of Carolina	Declaration of Indulgence withdrawn; Staple Act; revised Corn Law	
1664	Triennial Act	Occupation of New York	Conventicle Act	
1665	Appropriation of supply by Parliament	2nd Anglo-Dutch War; Battle of Lowestoft; Foundation of the Carolinas; Bombay occupied	5-Mile Act; Plague	Robert Hooke (1635–1703) work on combustion; Isaac Newton (1642–1727), work on calculus, light and gravitation
1666		Four Days Battle; War v. France; Dutch in Medway; War of Devolution	Fire of London	Christopher Wren (1632–1723) plan for rebuilding London; Milton's *Paradise Lost*; John Flamsteed (1646–1719) work on equation of time
1667	Treasury in commission; Parliamentary audit of accounts; Fall of Clarendon; his impeachment and 2nd exile; Predominance of Arlington and Buckingham (1628–87)	Peace of Breda		
1668	William Coventry (1627–86) goes into opposition	Triple Alliance (England, Netherlands and Sweden); Peace of Aix-la-Chapelle		

Year	General and Political	Foreign and Colonial	Religious, Social and Economic	Thought, Science and the Arts
1669	Decline of Buckingham's influence			
	Rise of Clifford (1630–73)			
1670		Secret Treaty of Dover	2nd Conventicle Act; persecution worsens	John Ray (1627–1705), *Catalogue of Plants*
		Treaty of Dover	Additional Corn Law	
		Hudson's Bay Co. founded	New Game Law	
1671				
1672	Stop of the Exchequer	French invasion of Netherlands	2nd Declaration of Indulgence	William Wycherly (1640–?1716), *The Country Wife*, 1st production
	Shaftesbury (1621–83) Lord Chancellor; Clifford, Lord Treasurer	3rd Anglo-Dutch War		
		Battle of Solebay	Plantation Duty Act	
		Fall of de Witts; William III (1650–1702) in power		
		Royal African Co. founded		
1673	Break-up of the 'Cabal'	Battle of the Texel	Declaration of Indulgence withdrawn; persecution resumed	Wren begins rebuilding St Paul's
	Danby (1631–1712) Lord Treasurer	War attacked in Parliament	1st Test Act	
1674	Finch (1621–82) Lord Keeper	Treaty of Westminster		
	Arlington resigns			
	Danby chief minister			
1675		Lords of Trade and Plantations appointed	Parliamentary Test Bill	Flamsteed 1st Astronomer Royal; Greenwich observatory opened
			Trade expansion begins	Wren resumes work on revised design for St Paul's
1676		Renewed treaty with France		
1677	Shaftesbury and Buckingham imprisoned	Marriage of Princess Mary (1662–94) and William of Orange		
1678	'Popish Plot'	Anglo-Dutch Treaty	2nd Test Act	Esmond Halley (1656–1742), *Catalogue of Southern Stars*
	Murder of Sir E. B. Godfrey	Peace of Nijmuegen	Trials and executions of catholics begin (also 1679–80)	John Bunyan (1628–88), *Pilgrim's Progress*
	Revelation of French subsidies			
	Danby impeached			
1679	Dissolution of Cavalier Parliament		Censorship lapses	

1679	James sent abroad 1st Exclusion Parliament: Danby attainted; Habeas Corpus Act; Exclusion Bill Shaftesbury Lord President of the Council Battle of Bothwell Brig Charles' illness; James returns Elections for 2nd Exclusion Parliament Parliament prorogued Shaftesbury and Monmouth (1649–85) dismissed from office		'Halley's 'comet' Sir Robert Filmer (d. 1653), *Patriarcha*
1680	James sent to Scotland Petitioning campaign, for meeting of Parliament Counter-campaign abhorring this	Louis XIV's 're-unions' (annexations), 1680–3	
1681	2nd Exclusion Parliament: Exclusion Bill; attainder of catholic peers 3rd Exclusion or 'Oxford' Parliament: Exclusion Bill Shaftesbury imprisoned; jury dismiss case		Persecution of Nonconformists intensified John Dryden (1631–1700), *Absalom and Achitophel*
1682	Return of James Tory Sheriffs of London Attack on charters begun Shaftesbury in exile Halifax (1633–95) leading minister	William Penn (1644–1718), charter for Pennsylvania Attack begun on charters on New England colonies	
1683	Rye House Plot Sunderland (1640–1702) restored as Secretary of State Execution of leading Whigs	Turks besiege Vienna	

Year	General and Political	Foreign and Colonial	Religious, Social and Economic	Thought, Science and the Arts
1684	Laurence Hyde Earl of Rochester (1641–1711), chief minister	Truce of Ratisbon (between Louis XIV and his enemies)		
1685	d. Charles II			
	Accession of James II (1633–1701)	'Dominion' of New England set up		Censorship re-imposed
	James' Parliament			
	Argyll rising; Monmouth rising			
	Battle of Sedgemoor; Bloody Assize			
	2nd session of Parliament; dismissal of Halifax	Revocation of Edict of Nantes	Parliament refuse to modify Tests	
1686	Case of Godden v. Hales (dispensing power)	Calcutta founded	Religious persecution halted Ecclesiastical Commission set up	Newton's *Principia*
1687	Fall of the Hydes	Mission from William to sound English opposition	James' 1st Declaration of Indulgence	
	Dissolution of Parliament		Attack on the Universities	
	Questions put to Lords Lieutenant and J.P.s			
1688	Trial of 7 Bishops (right of petitioning; seditious libel)	Cologne succession crisis	2nd Declaration of Indulgence	
	Birth of Prince (James Edward)			
	Acquittal of Bishops			
	Invitation to William	Louis XIV invades Palatinate; siege of Philippsburg	Charters restored; religious policy reversed	
	Concessions by James			
	William lands at Torbay			
	Flight of James	Revolutions in N. American colonies		
	Dec.–Feb. Interregnum			
1689	Convention Parliament	James invades Ireland	Toleration Act	John Locke (1632–1704), *Letter on Toleration* (2 *Treatises on Civil Govt.*, 1690)
	Declaration of Rights	War v. France (League of Augsburg)		
	William and Mary, King and Queen			
	Revolution in Scotland			
	Mutiny Act			
	Act of Rights			

Suggestions for Further Reading

Note: Any list like this, however long, is bound to be a selection, and a highly personal one at that. To make a further selection within such a list is doubly dangerous; the asterisk (*) should be taken to indicate those books which the present author believes he would have found most exciting at the age of about 18, *not* those which he considers the best by some imaginary standard of absolute historical excellence.

1. Contemporary Sources

E. Hyde, Earl of Clarendon, *History of the Rebellion* (best edn. by W. D. Macray, Oxford, 1888, 6 vols.; note also selections ed. G. Huehns, Oxford World's Classics).

E. Ludlow, *Memoirs* (ed. C. H. Firth, Oxford, 1894, 2 vols.).

G. Burnet, *History of my/or his/own time* (for Charles II's reign, use edn. by O. Airy, Oxford, 1897, 2 vols.; otherwise any of the many eighteenth or nineteenth-century editions).

S. Pepys, *Diary* (best edn. by H. B. Wheatley; will be replaced by R. C. Latham).

T. Hobbes, *Leviathan* (Everyman).

J. Locke, *Two Treatises of Government* (best edn. by P. Laslett, Cambridge).

Among other contemporary works and writers, in approximately chronological order, note especially: Shakespeare; Ben Jonson; The Holy Bible—the Authorised Version; John Donne; George Herbert; Sir Thomas Browne; John Milton; George Fox; John Bunyan; I. Walton, *Lives*; John Dryden; George Wycherly; John Aubrey's *Brief Lives*.

For selections from the poetry and drama, the Oxford World's Classics series may be recommended; see also the *Pelican Book of English Prose*, vols. 1 and 2.

2. Collections of Documents and other Extracts

A. Browning (ed.), *English Historical Documents*, VIII, *1660–1714* (series ed. D. C. Douglas, Eyre & Spottiswoode; the vol. covering the previous period, 1603–60, has not yet appeared).

W. C. Costin & J. S. Watson (eds.), *The Law and Working of the Constitution*, I, *1660–1783* (Black).

S. R. Gardiner (ed.), *Constitutional Documents of the Puritan Revolution, 1625–60* (Oxford).

J. P. Kenyon (ed.), *The Stuart Constitution, 1603–1688* (Cambridge).

G. Prothero, (ed.), *Select Statutes and other documents, 1558–1625* (Oxford).

J. R. Tanner (ed.), *Constitutional Documents of the reign of James I* (Cambridge).

*A. S. P. Woodhouse (ed.), *Puritanism and Liberty* (Dent).

3. Secondary Authorities

i. *General Histories*

*T. B. Macaulay, *History of England* (Everyman 3 vols. or other edns.).

S. R. Gardiner, *History of England from the Accession of James I to the Outbreak of the Civil War* (Longmans, 10 vols.).

S. R. Gardiner, *History of the Great Civil War, 1642–49* (Longmans).

S. R. Gardiner, *History of the Commonwealth and Protectorate, 1649–56* (Longmans).

C. H. Firth, *Last Years of the Protectorate, 1656–58* (Longmans).

G. Davies, *The Restoration of Charles II, 1658–60* (Oxford).

D. Ogg, *England under Charles II* (Oxford, 2 vols.).

D. Ogg, *England under James II and William III* (Oxford).

G. N. Clark, *The Later Stuarts* (Oxford History of England).

*C. Hill, *The Century of Revolution, 1603–1714* (Nelson History of England).

J. C. Beckett, *The Making of Modern Ireland 1603–1923* (Faber).

G. Donaldson, *Scotland: James V to James VII* (Edinburgh History of Scotland, Oliver & Boyd).

ii. *Political and General*

M. Ashley, *The Greatness of Oliver Cromwell* (Hodder, and Collier).

R. Ashton, *The Crown and the Money Market, 1603–40* (Oxford).

*T. Aston (ed.), *Crisis in Europe 1560–1660* (Routledge & Kegan Paul).

G. E. Aylmer, *The King's Servants: the civil service of Charles I, 1625–1642* (Routledge & Kegan Paul).

H. E. Bell & R. L. Ollard (eds.), *Historical Essays 1600–1750, presented to David Ogg* (Black).

H. N. Brailsford, *The Levellers and the English Revolution* (Cresset).

A. Browning, *Thomas Osborne, Earl of Danby*, vol. I (Sidgwick & Jackson).

D. Brunton & D. H. Pennington, *Members of the Long Parliament* (Allen & Unwin).

A. Bryant, *Samuel Pepys* (Cambridge, 3 vols.).

G. N. Clark, *The Seventeenth Century* (Oxford).

K. Feiling, *History of the Tory Party, 1640–1714* (Oxford).

C. H. Firth, *Cromwell's Army* (Methuen).

C. H. Firth, *Oliver Cromwell* (Oxford World's Classics, or Putnam).

*J. H. Hexter, *Re-appraisals in History* (Longmans).

C. Hill, *Puritanism and Revolution* (Secker & Warburg).

J. R. Jones, *The First Whigs: the politics of the Exclusion Crisis, 1678–83* (Oxford).

J. R. Jones, *Britain and Europe in the Seventeenth Century* (Arnold).

H. F. Kearney, *Strafford in Ireland* (Manchester).

J. P. Kenyon, *Robert Spencer, Earl of Sunderland* (Longmans).

D. Mathew, *The Jacobean Age* (Longmans).

D. Mathew, *The Age of Charles I* (Eyre & Spottiswoode).

D. Mathew, *Scotland under Charles I* (Eyre & Spottiswoode).

J. E. Neale, *The Elizabethan House of Commons* (Cape).

J. E. Neale, *Essays in Elizabethan History* (Cape), esp. 'The Elizabethan Political Scene'.

W. Notestein, *The Winning of the Initiative by the House of Commons* (Oxford).

V. Pearl, *London and the Puritan Revolution, 1625–43* (Oxford).

I. Roots, *The Great Rebellion 1642–1660* (Batsford).

R. H. Tawney, *Business & Politics under James I: Lionel Cranfield as merchant and minister* (Cambridge).

H. R. Trevor-Roper, *Historical Essays* (Macmillan).

*H. R. Trevor-Roper, *Religion, the Reformation and Social Change* (Macmillan).

C. V. Wedgwood, *The King's Peace, 1637–41* (Collins).

C. V. Wedgwood, *The King's War, 1641–7* (Collins).

C. V. Wedgwood, *The Trial of Charles I* (Collins).

C. V. Wedgwood, *Strafford: a revaluation* (Cape; 1960, *not* 1935 edn.).

D. H. Willson, *James VI & I* (Cape).

B. H. G. Wormald, *Clarendon: politics, history & religion, 1640–60* (Cambridge).

L. B. Wright, *The Atlantic Frontier* (U.S. edn.) or *The Colonial Civilisation of North America* (Eyre & Spottiswoode).

If you have access to it in a reference library, *The Dictionary of National Biography* is an immense storehouse of material; many of the mid-seventeenth-century 'lives' in it are by Firth.

iii. *Political Theory and Constitutional Practice*

J. Bromley & E. H. Kossman (eds.). *Britain & the Netherlands*, I (Chatto & Windus), J. P. Cooper, 'Differences between English & Continental governments in the early 17th century'.

J. W. Gough, *Fundamental Law in English History* (Oxford).

M. Judson, *The Crisis of the Constitution (1603–45)* (Rutgers).

R

C. B. Macpherson, *The Political Theory of Possessive Individualism: Hobbes to Locke* (Oxford).

P. Zagorin, *Political Thought in the English Revolution* (Routledge & Kegan Paul).

iv. Social and Economic

M. Campbell, *The English Yeoman* (Merlin).

E. M. Carus-Wilson (ed.), *Essays in Economic History*, vols. I & II (Arnold).

G. Clapham, *Concise economic history of England, to 1750* (Cambridge).

G. N. Clark, *The Wealth of England 1496–1760* (HUL).

R. Davis, *The Rise of the English Shipping Industry in the 17th and 18th centuries* (Macmillan).

M. Finch, *Five Northamptonshire Families* (Oxford).

F. J. Fisher (ed.), *Essays in the economic and social history of Tudor and Stuart England, in honour of R. H. Tawney* (Cambridge).

C. Hill, *Society and Puritanism* (Secker & Warburg).

W. G. Hoskins, *Provincial England* (Macmillan).

W. K. Jordan, *Philanthropy in England, 1480–1660* (Allen & Unwin).

J. U. Nef, *Industry and Government in France and England, 1540–1640* (Cornell).

W. Notestein, *The English People on the eve of Colonisation* (Hamish Hamilton).

G. D. Ramsay, *English Overseas Trade during the centuries of emergence* (Macmillan).

L. Stone, *The Crisis of the Aristocracy, 1558–1641* (Oxford).

B. Supple, *Commercial Crisis and Change, 1600–42* (Cambridge).

*R. H. Tawney, *Religion and the rise of Capitalism* (Pelican or Dent).

C. H. Wilson, *England's Apprenticeship 1603–1763* (Longmans).

C. H. Wilson, *Profit and Power: the Anglo-Dutch Wars* (Longmans).

v. Religious

R. S. Bosher, *The Making of the Restoration Settlement 1649–1662* (Dacre Press, 1961, & Black, 1965).

G. R. Cragg, *Puritanism under the Great Persecution* (Cambridge).

W. Haller, *Rise of Puritanism* (Columbia).

W. Haller, *Liberty and Reformation in the Puritan Revolution* (Columbia).

C. Hill, *Economic Problems of the Church* (Oxford).

W. A. Shaw, *The English Church during the Civil War and under the Commonwealth* (Longmans, 2 vols.).

N. Sykes, *From Sheldon to Secker* (Cambridge).

H. R. Trevor-Roper, *Archbishop Laud, 1573–1645* (Macmillan).

vi. *Cultural* (*Thought, Literature and the Arts*)

D. Bush, *English Literature in the Earlier Seventeenth Century* (Oxford).

A. R. Hall, *The Scientific Revolution, 1500–1800* (Longmans).

C. Hill, *Intellectual Origins of the English Revolution* (Oxford).

E. Mercer, *Oxford History of English Art, 1553–1625* (Oxford).

O. Millar & M. Whinney, *Oxford History of English Art, 1625–1714* (Oxford).

*B. Russell, *A History of Western Philosophy* (Allen & Unwin), Book III, Pt. 1.

P. A. Scholes (ed.), *The Oxford Companion to Music* (Oxford).

J. Summerson, *History of Architecture in Britain, 1500–1830* (Pelican).

E. K. Waterhouse, *History of Painting in Britain, 1500–1800* (Pelican).

J. W. N. Watkins, *Hobbes's System of Ideas* (Hutchinson).

M. Whinney, *History of Sculpture in Britain, 1530–1830* (Pelican).

B. Willey, *The Seventeenth-century Background* (Chatto & Windus).

INDEX